VOL 1

100 CONTEMPORARY
WOOD
BUILDINGS

721.
044
8
JOD

IMPRINT

PROJECT MANAGEMENT
Florian Kobler and
Inga Hallsson, Berlin

COLLABORATION
Harriet Graham, Turin

DESIGN
Sense/Net Art Direction,
Andy Disl and Birgit Eichwede,
Cologne, www.sense-net.net

PRODUCTION
Ute Wachendorf, Cologne

GERMAN TRANSLATION
Caroline Behlen, Berlin; Christiane
Court, Frankfurt; Karin Haag, Vienna;
Kristina Brigitta Köper, Berlin; Nora
von Mühlendahl, Ludwigsburg; Gregor
Runge, Berlin; Holger Wölfle, Berlin

FRENCH TRANSLATION
Jacques Bosser, Montesquiou;
Claire Debard, Freiburg;
Yves Minssart, Saint-Avertin;
Blandine Pélissier, Paris

**EACH AND EVERY TASCHEN BOOK
PLANTS A SEED!**
TASCHEN is a carbon neutral publisher.
Each year, we offset our annual carbon
emissions with carbon credits at the
Instituto Terra, a reforestation program
in Minas Gerais, Brazil, founded by Lélia
and Sebastião Salgado. To find out more
about this ecological partnership, please
check: www.taschen.com/zerocarbon
Inspiration: unlimited.
Carbon footprint: zero.

PRINTED IN CHINA
ISBN 978–3–8365–4281–4

Philip Jodidio

100 CONTEMPORARY
WOOD
BUILDINGS

100 Zeitgenössische Holzbauten
100 Bâtiments contemporains en bois

VOL 1

TASCHEN

CONTENTS VOLUME I

CREDITS

CONTENTS VOLUME II

INTRODUCTION

WE SHOULD BE WOOD AND WERE NOT MADE TO WOO

Within these plantations of God, a decorum and sanctity reign, a perennial festival is dressed, and the guest sees not how he should tire of them in a thousand years. In the woods, we return to reason and faith. There I feel that nothing can befall me in life,—no disgrace, no calamity, (leaving me my eyes,) which nature cannot repair. Standing on the bare ground,—my head bathed by the blithe air, and uplifted into infinite space,—all mean egotism vanishes. I become a transparent eye-ball; I am nothing; I see all; the currents of the Universal Being circulate through me; I am part or particle of God.

Ralph Waldo Emerson, *Nature*, 1836

Wood is, first of all, the forest, the "plantations of God." It is in the moonlit woods that the characters of Shakespeare's *A Midsummer Night's Dream* play out their transformative comedy, where life itself is likened to the substance of a tree. It is Helena who says: "We cannot fight for love, as men may do; We should be wood and were not made to woo" (*A Midsummer Night's Dream*, act 2, scene 1), as though wood might also be the symbol of hardness or lack of passion. As always with Shakespeare, such a simple statement contains many layers of meaning, as it seems clear that neither men nor women are made of wood. Metaphorically, or in reality, wood can be seen as an expression of nature, a "part or particle of God."

It is again in the forest that architecture itself, in disguises ranging from the simple column to the temple and the cathedral, finds much of its inspiration. A canopy of branches, or stacked trunks to provide shelter from the storm, wood is a quintessential element of the earliest built habitations, most of which returned to the earth in time, crumbling and leaving hardly any trace. Architecture in wood is often reputed to be ephemeral. Indeed, depending on such factors as climate and maintenance, wooden structures may not last very long. But if properly treated, wood can stand a thousand years even as the earth shakes and the generations pass. Trees live, depending on the species, longer than any other organism on earth. A Great Basin bristlecone pine, aptly named "Methuselah" (White Mountains, California), is estimated to be more than 4800 years old. Pando, a quaking aspen clonal tree colony located in Utah, sends up shoots from a single massive root system thought to be 80 000 years old—a tree far older than human civilization. Trees, both figuratively and literally, are at the origin of built form—shelter and inspiration, the stuff of the earth.

Stories abound of the rape of the forests carried out in Indonesia and elsewhere, and few would defend such practices as having anything to do with an ecological approach to building, yet wood, properly managed and harvested, is living a new life in the 21st century as a material of predilection in architecture. Because a managed forest can be renewed, wood that is not transported over too great a distance is surely one of the most ecologically sound building materials available.

Because its use has been so widespread over time, and by no means only in inventive architecture, wood carries with it something of a reputation. Why have a wooden house when concrete and aluminum seem so much more modern and solid? This book is about an entirely new generation of buildings, surely inspired in part by traditions, but also by the green building vogue. As strict modernism or the even more arid minimalism slip out of fashion, so, too, have many architects and clients sought the warmth that wood conveys, its natural feeling. Being an "old" building material, wood can nonetheless be fashioned using the most contemporary CNC (computer numerical control) milling techniques, making complex forms or unique pieces economically feasible. Then, too, many architects represented in this volume use wood for specific purposes and areas of their buildings. A building may be clad in wood but built of concrete or steel. The point of this book is to give an overview of what is being done in different styles and techniques, from as many locations as possible. By no means exhaustive, *100 Contemporary Wood Buildings* focuses on the 21st century, and indeed mainly on work of the past five years—proof that wood is back as a contemporary construction material.

WOOD IS ALIVE

What a curious change the buildings in wood in this book express. Modern architecture used to be fashioned with steel and concrete, rolling its inevitable grid over the earth as though hills and streams were only waiting to be leveled. In all fairness, there is still a great deal of steamrolling going on. It is not that the recent past has disappeared so entirely in contemporary designs, it is just that other avenues are being explored. One of the most significant and pertinent of these is the use of wood for buildings great and small. Of course "solid" materials such as steel and stone do in principle speak a language of durability in time, but stone long ago gave way to veneers and thinner cladding—the solidity was really only an illusion. Few modern buildings, no matter what their material appearance, are made to last. Their glass and aluminum find their way to the junk heap as quickly as any building made of wood. Once the illusion of permanence in contemporary architecture dissolves, which it has by and large already, clients and architects were ready to see things differently. Finite resources and a growing pressure to include ecologically responsible elements in any design have clearly brought wood back into fashion. Wood wears with time, but so does any material. Some countries, such as Japan, have never really abandoned their time-honored use of wood in construction. This is partially because light construction can, if well conceived, resist earthquakes better than many more "sturdy" buildings. Then too, as Tadao Ando has said, "in Japan… the temple is made of wood. The divine spirit inside the building is eternal, so the enclosure doesn't have to be." To take just one example, the five-story wooden pagoda built in 951 at Daigo-ji, a Buddhist temple, is the oldest building in Kyoto.

BACK TO THE FUTURE

Suggesting that wood is a renewable resource of course implies the careful harvesting and maintenance of forests. Organizations such as the USGBC (United States Green Building Council) have established standards (LEED or Leadership in Energy and Environmental Design) that can serve to certify lumber for environmentally sustainable construction. In this case, the USGBC works with the Forest Stewardship Council (FSC). FSC "is an independent, non-governmental, not-for-profit organization established to promote the responsible management of the world's forests. Established in 1993 as a response to concerns over global deforestation, FSC is widely regarded as one of the most important initiatives of the last decade to promote responsible forest management worldwide." By August 2013, 181 million hectares of forest in 80 countries have been certified to FSC's "Principles and Criteria—the highest standards of forest management which are environmentally appropriate, socially beneficial and economically viable."[1]

For all of its other positive qualities, it has also been shown in numerous studies that wood products, if harvested sustainably and used correctly, should have a positive impact on global warming. In a review of scientific literature published on the subject of wood products and greenhouse gas emissions in 2010 by FPInnovations, a Canadian non-profit forest research center, it was concluded that "by quantifying the range of GHG (greenhouse gas) benefits of wood substitution, this meta-analysis provides a clear climate rationale for using wood products in place of non-wood materials, provided that forests are sustainably managed and that wood residues are used responsibly. An effective overall strategy to mitigate climate change and transition to a carbon-neutral economy should therefore include the sustainable management of forest land for the continuing production and efficient use of wood products."[2] Though some measure of caution may be required with respect to a report published by an organization with ties to the forestry industry, the fact remains that it is reasonable to conclude that wood construction is a better bet for the future of the planet than products like steel.

THE PARADOX OF THE POTTED PLANT

For its many advantages, the industrial system of construction so essential to the rise of modernism has covered the world with buildings that are "rational" but, fundamentally, deeply cold. Only a few masters of modernity like Ludwig Mies van der Rohe in his Seagram Building on Park Avenue in New York City managed to bring the grid alive, to make steel and glass sing in a truly classical way. Others have coated their buildings in granite and marble, steel and glass, leaving users or inhabitants no choice but to make their bit of the grid as "cozy" as possible. How often do architects curse tenants who fill their lobbies and offices with potted plants? What if the reason for this is something other than the bad taste of the client? What if it has to do with something deeper and more "human" than the masters of the grid suspect? The Golden Ratio still exists, but neither the body nor the mind are fundamentally made for a world that has only straight lines, or Euclidean certainties. Even if Shakespeare used it as a metaphor for lack of passion, wood is alive; it is warm, it is inviting to the touch, and even to the sense of smell.

Surprisingly enough, wood is also well adapted to the brave new world of digital design and CNC milling—wood can do anything, even break out of the box of rationalization that so many architects have tried to put it in. Wood can, of course, be applied as a veneer, a simulacrum of nature's presence. Of course, some "wood" is actually plastic. We call it formica and a world of roadside American diners stretches as far as the eye can see. This book focuses on 100 examples of buildings that are partially or completely made of wood in its various forms. There is no risk in saying that wood is back, even in the guise of actual timber. Of course some of the "timber" beams seen in the projects published here may well be glulam (glued, laminated lumber), but the point is not to be more purist than the architects who employ wood.

THE DEATH OF THE ASSEMBLY LINE

Because of its warmth and also thanks to some of its inherent limitations, wood also seems to be encouraging a proliferation of new forms that are adapted to its strengths, such as its lightness. Wood can certainly be fashioned to geometric norms, but its fundamental nature is more unruly, less standardized, despite all that industry has done to shape and mold it. Wood is also reaching into new areas with a capacity to span ever-larger spaces thanks to designs like gridshells, or in combination with new materials like EFTE or Teflon-coated roofs.

The reasons for the resurgence of wood in contemporary architecture are multiple, and some may even be philosophically linked to the eternal appeal of the garden, the world of Arcadia where everything was simpler and nature was as close to heaven as most of us will ever get. The days of the modern tabula rasa are gone even as vast forests from the Amazon to Irian Jaya are slashed to make way for palm oil plantations or shopping centers. The strict grid, like the mass assembly line, was born of the industrial needs of another era when every part had to be standardized for reasons of economy. Today, computers used in design and milling make possible the fabrication of unique parts that need no longer be straight and soulless. Perhaps it is the call of the past that brings wood back into architecture; maybe it is ecological and economic common sense, or perhaps wood is a material that is closer to our own nature than steel or concrete.

[1] FSC Forest Stewardship Council, accessed on June 8, 2015, http://fsc.org.
[2] Roger Sathre and Jennifer O'Connor, *A Synthesis of Research on Wood Products & Greenhouse Gas Impacts*, 2nd Edition, FPInnovations, Vancouver, B.C., 2010.

EINLEITUNG

DIE UNBERECHENBARKEIT DES HOLZES

In diesen Plantagen Gottes herrschen Anstand und Heiligkeit, vollzieht sich ein ständiges Fest, und der Festgast vermag sich nicht vorzustellen, wie er selbst in 1000 Jahren all dessen müde werden könnte. In den Wäldern kehren wir zur Vernunft und zum Glauben zurück. Dort spüre ich, dass mir im Leben nichts zustoßen kann – keine Schande, kein Unglück (solange ich mein Augenlicht behalte), die die Natur nicht wiedergutmachen könnte. Ich stehe auf der nackten Erde, mein Haupt umweht von linden Lüften und erhoben in die Unendlichkeit des Raums, und alle niedrige Selbstsucht fällt von mir ab. Ich werde ganz zum durchscheinenden Auge; ich selbst bin nichts und sehe doch alles; Ströme des allumfassenden Seins durchfluten mich; ich bin Teil oder Bestandteil Gottes.

Ralph Waldo Emerson, *Die Natur*, 1836

Denken wir an Holz, kommen uns zunächst Wälder in den Sinn, die „Plantagen Gottes". Hier durchleben die Figuren aus Shakespeares *Sommernachtstraum* im Mondenschein eine Verwandlungskomödie, in der das Leben selbst mit jenem Stoff verglichen wird, aus dem Bäume gemacht sind. „We cannot fight for love, as men may do; We should be wood and were not made to woo" („Um Liebe kämpft ein Mann wohl mit den Waffen; Wir sind, um euch zu werben, nicht geschaffen"), sagt Helena in der ersten Szene des zweiten Akts, was im Englischen eine Anspielung an Holz implizieren mag.[1] Wie immer bei Shakespeare enthalten auch simple Aussagen gleich mehrere Bedeutungsebenen. Metaphorisch – und auch realiter – kann Holz als Ausdrucksform der Natur gesehen werden, als „Teil oder Bestandteil Gottes".

Auch die Architektur hat sich immer wieder von den Formen des Waldes inspirieren lassen – von der einfachen Säule zum Tempel und der Kathedrale. Holz ist ein grundlegender Bestandteil der ältesten menschlichen Wohnstätten, von Unterständen aus Astwerk bis hin zu übereinandergeschichteten Baumstämmen zum Schutz vor Stürmen. Ein Großteil dieser Artefakte hat keinerlei Spuren hinterlassen und ist längst zerfallen und wieder eins geworden mit dem Erdreich. Holzbauten gelten gemeinhin als kurzlebig. Je nach Klima und Instandhaltungsbemühungen können sie unter Umständen tatsächlich nur von kurzer Dauer sein. Bei entsprechender Behandlung aber hält Holz über Generationen und übersteht selbst dann noch ein ganzes Jahrtausend, wenn bisweilen die Erde bebt. Bäume leben, bevor sie gefällt und verwertet werden, länger als jeder andere Organismus auf unserer Erde. Nicht umsonst wurde ein Exemplar der sog. Langlebigen Kiefer (Pinus Longaeva) in den kalifornischen White Mountains auf den Namen „Methuselah" getauft. Ihr Alter beträgt schätzungsweise mehr als 4800 Jahre. Klonale Bäume wie der sog. Pando, eine in Utah befindliche Kolonie der Amerikanischen Zitterpappel (Populus tremuloides), keimen aus einem riesigen, zusammenhängenden Wurzelsystem, das mit geschätzten 80 000 Jahren weit älter ist als die Menschheit. Bäume bilden bildlich wie buchstäblich den Ursprung menschlichen Bauens. Sie bieten Schutz und Inspiration. Sie sind der Stoff, aus dem die Erde gemacht ist.

Während in Indonesien und anderswo auf der Welt weiterhin in großem Umfang Wälder abgeholzt werden – eine Praxis, die sich ganz und gar nicht mit ökologischen Bauprinzipien vereinbaren lässt –, erlebt Holz aus nachhaltiger Produktion in der Architektur des 21. Jahrhunderts eine Renaissance als geschätzter Baustoff. Aufgrund der Erneuerbarkeit von Nutzwäldern ist Holz eins der umweltverträglichsten Baumaterialien überhaupt, vor allem dann, wenn es nicht über allzu große Entfernungen transportiert wird.

Weil die Verwendung von Holz lange Zeit so weit verbreitet war, und beileibe nicht nur bei innovativer Architektur, hat es einen gewissen Ruf. Wozu ein Haus aus Holz bauen, wenn doch Beton und Aluminium so viel zeitgemäßer und solider sind? Dieser Band widmet sich einer neuen Generation von Gebäuden, die teilweise von traditionellen Formen des Bauens, vor allem aber von ökologischen Bautrends inspiriert sind. In einer Zeit, da die strenge Formensprache der Moderne und der noch freudlosere Minimalismus außer Mode geraten, sehnen sich viele Architekten und Auftraggeber wieder nach der Wärme und Natürlichkeit von Holz. Obwohl es sich um ein althergebrachtes Baumaterial handelt, lässt es sich mithilfe neuester computergestützter CNC-Fräsverfahren bearbeiten. So entstehen kostengünstig komplexe Formen oder Einzelstücke. Viele der in diesem Band vertretenen Architekten verwenden Holz für spezielle Zwecke oder bestimmte Teile ihrer Bauten. So kann ein Gebäude vollständig aus Stahlbeton bestehen, dafür aber holzverschalt sein. *100 Contemporary Wood Buildings* möchte einen Überblick darüber geben, was in den unterschiedlichsten Baustilen und -techniken derzeit an vielen Orten gebaut wird. Ohne den Anspruch auf Vollständigkeit zu erheben, konzentriert sich der Band auf das 21. Jahrhundert, schwerpunktmäßig auf die letzten fünf Jahre, und beweist, dass Holz als Baumaterial wieder von Relevanz ist.

HOLZ LEBT

Der Wandel, den die in diesem Band versammelten Projekte veranschaulichen, ist bemerkenswert. Moderne Architektur bestand zumeist aus Stahl und Beton und verbreitete sich über die Welt, als hätten Flüsse und Hügel nur darauf gewartet, eingeebnet zu werden. Fakt ist: Die Dampfwalzen rollen nach wie vor in großer Zahl. Die jüngste Vergangenheit ist nicht vollständig aus den zeitgenössischen Entwürfen verschwunden, aber man hat damit begonnen, neue Wege zu beschreiten. Eine der wichtigsten Neuerungen besteht in der Verwendung von Holz sowohl für kleinere als auch größere Bauprojekte. Zwar stehen „solide" Materialien wie Stahl und Stein nach wie vor für Dauerhaftigkeit. Dabei kommen schon seit Langem Steinfurniere und Verschalungselemente zum Einsatz – Solidität ist also lediglich eine Illusion. Kaum ein Gebäude der Gegenwart ist für die Ewigkeit gemacht, ganz gleich aus welchen Materialien es besteht. Glas und Aluminium finden genauso schnell ihren Weg auf die Müllhalde wie Holz. Nachdem in der zeitgenössischen Architektur die Illusion der Dauerhaftigkeit nach und nach an Bedeutung verloren hat, haben Architekten und Auftraggeber umgedacht. Schwindende Ressourcen und die wachsende Notwendigkeit, ökologische Aspekte in die Entwürfe einzubeziehen, haben dazu geführt, dass Holz wieder in Mode ist. Zwar nutzt es sich mit der Zeit ab, aber das gilt für jedes Material. Länder wie Japan beispielsweise haben den traditionellen Einsatz von Holz als Baumaterial nie aufgegeben. Teilweise auch deshalb, weil leichte Gebäudekonstruktionen bei sorgfältiger Planung besser gegen Erdbeben gewappnet sind als so manches scheinbar massivere Gebäude. Tadao Ando bringt einen weiteren Aspekt zur Sprache: „In Japan bestehen die Tempel aus Holz. Da schon der göttliche Geist im Innern des Tempels ewig währt, muss der Tempel selbst dies nicht." Um nur ein Beispiel zu nennen: Die 951 erbaute, fünfgeschossige Holzpagode der buddhistischen Tempelanlage Daigo-ji ist das älteste Bauwerk Kiotos.

ZURÜCK IN DIE ZUKUNFT

Damit Holz eine erneuerbare Ressource bleibt, müssen Wälder umsichtig bewirtschaftet und erhalten werden. Organisationen wie USGBC (United States Green Building Council) haben Standards eingeführt (LEED – Leadership in Energy and Environmental Design), mit deren Hilfe Holz zertifiziert werden kann, das sich für ökologisch nachhaltiges Bauen eignet. Das USGBC arbeitet mit dem FSC (Forest Stewardship Council) zusammen, einer „unabhängigen, gemeinnützigen Nichtregierungsorganisation zur weltweiten Förderung verantwortungsvoller Waldbewirtschaftung. Gegründet wurde das FSC 1993 als Antwort auf die weltweite Zerstörung der Wälder. Das FSC gilt als eine der wichtigsten Initiativen des letzten Jahrzehnts zur Förderung verantwortungsvoller Waldwirtschaft." Im August 2013 waren 181 Millionen ha Wald in 80 Ländern nach den FSC-Richtlinien zertifiziert.[2]

Über diese positiven Aspekte hinaus konnte zudem in zahlreichen Studien gezeigt werden, dass Produkte aus nachhaltig gewonnenem Holz einen positiven Einfluss auf die Erderwärmung haben dürften. In einer Übersicht zum aktuellen Stand der Forschungsliteratur über Holzprodukte und Treibhausgasemissionen, die 2010 von FPInnovations, einer gemeinnützigen kanadischen Organisation für die Erforschung der Wälder, veröffentlicht wurde, schließen die Autoren: „Diese Metaanalyse beziffert den positiven Effekt, den die Substitution mit Holz auf den Treibhausgaseffekt hat und liefert damit ein eindeutiges und für den Klimaschutz relevantes Argument für den bevorzugten Einsatz von Holz anstelle anderer Materialien. Voraussetzung hierbei ist eine nachhaltige Waldbewirtschaftung und ein verantwortungsvoller Umgang mit anfallenden Holzabfallprodukten. Eine wirksame und umfassende Strategie zur Entschärfung des Klimawandels und zum Übergang in ein CO_2-neutrales Wirtschaftssystem schließt also nachhaltige Forstwirtschaft mit ein. Erst sie ermöglicht die fortlaufende Produktion und den effizienten Einsatz von Holzprodukten."[3] Zwar ist ein wenig Zurückhaltung angezeigt, handelt es sich doch bei FPInnovations um eine Organisation mit Verbindungen zur Forstwirtschaft. Dennoch, mit sehr großer Wahrscheinlichkeit ist das Bauen mit Holz für die Zukunft unseres Planeten sehr viel verträglicher als der Einsatz von Produkten wie Stahl.

DAS PARADOX DER TOPFPFLANZE

Industrielle Bauverfahren waren wegen ihrer vielen Vorteile von grundlegender Bedeutung für die Durchsetzung der architektonischen Moderne. Auf sie gehen weltweit zahllose Bauwerke zurück, die ihrem Wesen nach „rational" sind und dementsprechend kalt anmuten. Nur wenigen Großmeistern der Moderne gelang es, Stahl und Glas trotz Rasterbauweise auf zeitlose Art zum Harmonieren zu bringen, so beispielsweise Ludwig Mies van der Rohe mit seinem Seagram Building in der Park Avenue in New York. Andere Architekten kleideten ihre Entwürfe in Granit, Marmor, Stahl und Glas und ließen den Menschen keine andere Wahl, als sich ihren Teil des Rasters so gemütlich wie möglich herzurichten. Gewiss, so mancher Architekt mag die Topfpflanzen in den Eingangshallen und Büros verfluchen. Was aber, wenn der Grund für die Topfpflanzen etwas anderes als schlechter Geschmack wäre? Was, wenn der Grund tiefer läge und mit etwas „Humanerem" zu tun hätte, als die Meister des Rasters vermuten? Zwar hat der Goldene Schnitt seine Gültigkeit nicht verloren, aber weder Körper noch Geist sind für eine Welt geschaffen, die auf geraden Linien und geometrischer Unbedingtheit beruht. Auch wenn bei Shakespeare Holz möglicherweise als Metapher für einen Mangel an Leidenschaft herhalten muss, handelt es sich um ein lebendiges, warmes Material, das zur Berührung einlädt, sogar den Geruchssinn anspricht.

So sehr es auch überraschen mag: Holz ist längst in der schönen neuen Welt digitaler Design- und CNC-Technologien angekommen. Holz kann alles. Es kann sich auch der Schublade der Rationalisierung entziehen, in die viele Architekten es zu stecken versuchten. Es kann in Form von Furnier die Gegenwart der Natur imitieren. So manches vermeintliche Holz ist in Wirklichkeit Kunststoff. Unter dem Markennamen Formica kennen wir es aus zahllosen amerikanischen Diners. Dieser Band präsentiert 100 Beispiele für Gebäude, die teilweise oder vollständig und auf ganz verschiedene Art und Weise aus Holz gefertigt sind. Holz erlebt fraglos eine Renaissance, sogar als wirkliche Holzbalken. Natürlich sind einige der vermeintlichen Massivholzbalken in diesem Band in Wahrheit verleimtes Brettschichtholz, aber man sollte nicht puristischer an die Sache herangehen als die Architekten, die Holz verwenden.

DER TOD DES FLIESSBANDS

Sowohl aufgrund seiner warmen Anmutung und seiner Vorzüge – geringes Gewicht ist einer davon – als auch wegen der ihm innewohnenden Beschränkungen inspiriert Holz zu einer Vielzahl neuer Bauformen. Zwar kann es problemlos an geometrische Normen angepasst werden, aber trotz aller Bemühungen der Industrie, es zu standardisieren, ist und bleibt Holz seinem Wesen nach unbändig und uneinheitlich. Als Rohstoff dringt es in neue Bereiche des Bauens vor. In Verbindung mit Materialien wie ETFE, teflonbeschichteten Dachkonstruktionen und Verfahren wie der Gitterschalenbauweise können mit ihm immer größere Flächen überspannt werden.

Es gibt viele verschiedene Gründe für die zunehmende Beliebtheit von Holz in der Architektur der Gegenwart. Manche mögen mit der uralten Anziehung zu tun haben, die Gärten auf uns ausüben, die Welt Arkadiens, wo alles einfacher und die Natur dem Paradies so unendlich nahe war. Nach wie vor fallen ausgedehnte Waldgebiete beispielsweise im Amazonasgebiet oder in West-Neuguinea Palmölplantagen und Einkaufszentren zum Opfer. Aber die Zeiten der großen Tabula rasa sind vorbei. Rasterbauweise und Massenproduktion am Fließband gehen auf die industriellen Bedürfnisse eines anderen Zeitalters zurück – als jedes Teil der Produktionskette aus Gründen der Wirtschaftlichkeit standardisiert sein musste. Heute ermöglicht der Einsatz von Computern sowohl im Entwurfsprozess als auch beim Fräsen die Anfertigung von maßgeschneiderten Bauteilen, die alles andere als rechtwinklig und seelenlos sind. Möglicherweise ist es der Ruf der Vergangenheit, der Holz in der Architektur derzeit wieder aufleben lässt, vielleicht ist es aber auch die allgemeine Einsicht in die ökologischen und wirtschaftlichen Vorteile, die sein Einsatz mit sich bringt. Allerdings könnte es auch sein, dass Holz unserem Wesen schlicht näher ist als Stahl und Beton.

[1] Das Wortspiel des Autors mit der Doppeldeutigkeit von wood (Wald und umworben) lässt sich nicht übersetzen.
[2] Vgl. http://www.fsc.org; Zugriff am 8. Juni 2015
[3] Roger Sathre, Jennifer O'Connor, *A Synthesis of Research on Wood Products & Greenhouse Gas Impacts*, 2. Auflage, FPInnovations, Vancouver, B. C., 2010

INTRODUCTION

LE BOIS, SUBSTANCE DE LA TERRE

Parmi ces plantations de Dieu règnent la grandeur et le sacré, une fête éternelle est apprêtée, et l'invité ne voit pas comment il pourrait s'en lasser en un millier d'années. Dans les bois, nous revenons à la raison et à la foi. Là, je sens que rien ne peut m'arriver dans la vie, ni disgrâce, ni calamité (mes yeux m'étant laissés) que la nature ne puisse réparer. Debout sur le sol nu, ma tête baignée par l'air joyeux et soulevée dans l'espace infini, tous nos petits égoïsmes s'évanouissent. Je deviens une pupille transparente ; je ne suis rien ; je vois tout ; tous les courants de l'Être universel circulent à travers moi ; je suis une partie ou une parcelle de Dieu.
Ralph Waldo Emerson, *La Nature*, 1836

Le bois, c'est avant tout la forêt, les « plantations de Dieu ». C'est dans les bois éclairés par la lune que les personnages du *Songe d'une nuit d'été* de Shakespeare jouent leur comédie transformatrice, là où la vie elle-même est comparée à la substance d'un arbre. C'est Héléna qui dit : « En amour, nous ne pouvons pas attaquer, comme les hommes ; nous devrions être de bois et n'étions pas faites pour courtiser » (*Le Songe d'une nuit d'été*, acte II, scène I), comme si le bois pouvait aussi être le symbole de la dureté ou du manque de passion [1]. Comme toujours avec Shakespeare, une affirmation aussi simple contient de nombreux niveaux de signification, vu qu'il paraît clair que ni les hommes, ni les femmes ne sont faits de bois. D'une manière métaphorique ou dans les faits, le bois peut être vu comme une expression de la nature, une « partie ou une parcelle de Dieu ».

C'est aussi dans la forêt que l'architecture, dans l'éventail déguisé qui va de la simple colonne au temple et à la cathédrale, trouve une grande partie de son inspiration. Sous forme de voûte de branches ou d'empilement de troncs offrant un abri contre la tempête, le bois constitue un élément essentiel des premières habitations, la plupart d'entre elles étant retournées à la terre au fil du temps et s'étant décomposées en ne laissant que quelques rares traces. L'architecture de bois a souvent la réputation d'être éphémère. Il est évident que les structures en bois peuvent, en fonction de facteurs comme le climat et l'entretien, ne pas résister très longtemps. Toutefois, bien traité, le bois peut traverser un millénaire, même si la terre tremble et que les générations se succèdent. Les arbres vivent – selon les espèces – plus longtemps qu'aucun autre organisme sur Terre. D'après les estimations, le pin de Bristlecone – le bien nommé Mathusalem –, dans les White Mountains en Californie, aurait plus de 4800 ans. Pando, la colonie clonale de peupliers faux-trembles située dans l'Utah, a germé à partir d'un seul système racinaire massif estimé à 80 000 ans, faisant d'eux des arbres bien plus âgés que la civilisation humaine. Au sens figuré comme au sens littéral, les arbres se trouvent à l'origine de la forme construite – refuge et inspiration, substance de la Terre.

Les forêts en Indonésie ou ailleurs continuent à subir une déforestation massive et de telles pratiques sont incompatibles avec une approche écologique de la construction ; le bois cependant, correctement exploité et récolté, aborde une nouvelle vie au XXIe siècle en tant que matériau de prédilection en architecture. Étant donné qu'une forêt gérée peut se renouveler, le bois – à condition de ne pas être transporté sur de trop longues distances – reste assurément l'un des matériaux de construction disponibles les plus écologiques.

Utilisé depuis longtemps à très grande échelle, pas seulement pour une architecture inventive, le bois est victime de sa réputation. Pourquoi opter pour une maison en bois alors que le béton et l'aluminium semblent tellement plus modernes et résistants ? Ce livre présente une toute nouvelle génération de bâtiments, certes inspirée en partie par les traditions, mais aussi par la vogue de la construction verte. Tandis que le modernisme strict ou le minimalisme encore plus aride sont passés de mode, de trop nombreux architectes et clients ont recherché la chaleur que dégage le bois, son caractère naturel. « Vieux » matériau de construction, le bois peut néanmoins être transformé par les techniques de fraisage de pointe CNC (Computer Numerical Control, machines à contrôle numérique) pour obtenir des formes complexes ou des pièces uniques à des coûts abordables. C'est ainsi qu'un grand nombre d'architectes présentés dans cet ouvrage ont recours au bois pour des besoins et des zones spécifiques de leurs bâtiments. Un bâtiment peut recevoir un bardage en bois tout en étant construit en béton ou en acier. L'objectif de ce livre est de proposer un aperçu des réalisations dans différents styles et techniques, à des endroits aussi variés que possible. Sans prétendre à l'exhaustivité, *100 Contemporary Wood Buildings* se focalise sur le XXIe siècle et, notamment, sur les cinq dernières années – une preuve que le bois est de retour en tant que matériau de construction contemporain.

LE BOIS EST VIVANT

Quel curieux changement expriment les constructions en bois dans ce livre. Généralement en acier et en béton, l'architecture moderne déroulait son inévitable trame sur la planète, comme si les collines et les cours d'eau n'attendaient que d'être nivelés. En toute impartialité, le rouleau compresseur est encore très actif. Non que le passé récent ait entièrement disparu des projets contemporains, mais d'autres voies ont été explorées. L'une des plus significatives et pertinentes d'entre elles est l'utilisation du bois dans les constructions, grandes et petites. Il est évident que des matériaux « résistants » tels que l'acier et la pierre parlent la langue de la longévité, mais la pierre, il y a longtemps, a cédé la place à des placages et des revêtements plus minces – la solidité n'était en fait qu'illusoire. Rares sont les bâtiments modernes, quelle que soit leur apparence extérieure, faits pour durer. Leurs éléments en verre et en aluminium rejoignent les tas de déchets aussi vite que n'importe quel bâtiment en bois. Une fois l'illusion de la permanence de l'architecture contemporaine dissoute – ce qui est déjà le cas dans l'ensemble –, les clients et les architectes ont été prêts à voir les choses sous un autre angle. Les ressources non renouvelables et la pression croissante pour intégrer des considérations écologiques dans toute conception ont permis le retour à la mode du bois. Le bois vieillit avec le temps, comme tout autre matériau. Certains pays, à l'instar du Japon, n'ont en réalité jamais vraiment abandonné leur usage ancestral du bois dans la construction. Ceci s'explique en partie par le fait qu'une construction légère bien conçue peut mieux résister aux tremblements de terre que nombre de constructions dites plus robustes. Comme l'a rappelé Tadao Ando : « Au Japon… le temple est construit en bois. L'esprit divin étant éternel au sein du bâtiment, l'enveloppe n'a pas à l'être. » Pour ne retenir qu'un exemple, la pagode en bois de cinq étages du temple de Daigo-ji, construite en 951, est le plus ancien bâtiment de Kyoto.

RETOUR VERS LE FUTUR

Que le bois reste une ressource renouvelable implique évidemment une exploitation et une gestion soigneuses des forêts. Des organisations comme l'USGBC (United States Green Building Council, Conseil américain pour les bâtiments verts) ont établi des standards (LEED ou Leadership in Energy and Environmental Design, Leadership en énergie et conception environnementale) permettant la certification du bois pour la construction soucieuse de l'environnement. Dans ce cas, l'USGBC travaille avec le Forest Stewardship Council (FSC). Le FSC « est une organisation indépendante, non gouvernementale et non lucrative créée pour promouvoir la gestion responsable des forêts dans le monde. Créé en 1993 en réponse à la déforestation dans le monde, le FSC est généralement considéré comme l'une des principales initiatives de la dernière décennie en faveur de la promotion de la gestion responsable des forêts dans le monde [2] ». En décembre 2013, 181 millions d'hectares de forêts ont été certifiés dans 80 pays selon les « principes et critères » du FSC – des normes strictes de gestion des forêts adaptées sur le plan écologique, répondant aux besoins sociaux et économiquement viables.

Outre leurs autres qualités, de nombreuses études ont également démontré que les produits forestiers – exploités et utilisés correctement – devraient exercer un impact positif sur le réchauffement climatique. Selon une étude publiée en 2010 dans une revue scientifique sur les produits forestiers et les émissions de gaz à effet de serre par FPInnovations, un centre de recherche canadien sur les forêts à but non lucratif : « Si l'on quantifie les effets positifs de la substitution par le bois sur les GES (gaz à effet de serre), cette métaanalyse fournit un argument climatique clair qui conduit à privilégier les produits forestiers au détriment des matériaux autres que le bois, à condition que les forêts soient gérées de façon durable et les résidus de bois de façon responsable. Une stratégie globale efficace en vue d'atténuer le changement climatique et une transition vers une économie neutre en carbone devraient par conséquent intégrer la gestion soutenable des terres forestières en vue de la production continue et de l'utilisation efficace des produits forestiers [3]. » Malgré les précautions à prendre avec un rapport publié par une organisation liée à l'industrie forestière, il reste très probable que la construction en bois constitue un meilleur pari pour le futur de la planète que celui proposé par des produits comme l'acier.

*Sou Fujimoto,
Final Wooden House, Kumamura,
Kumamoto, Japan, 2007–08*

LE PARADOXE DE LA PLANTE EN POT

Fort de ses nombreux avantages, le système de construction industrielle essentiel dans l'avènement du modernisme a recouvert le monde entier de bâtiments certes «rationnels», mais fondamentalement froids. Seuls quelques maîtres de la modernité comme Ludwig Mies van der Rohe avec son Seagram Building sur Park Avenue à New York sont parvenus à animer la trame et à faire chanter l'acier et le verre d'une manière réellement classique. Les autres se sont contentés d'habiller leurs bâtiments de granit et de marbre, d'acier et de verre, et n'ont laissé aux utilisateurs ou habitants d'autre choix que de rendre leur petit bout de trame aussi *cosy* que possible. Combien de fois les architectes maudissent-ils les locataires qui remplissent leurs entrées et bureaux de plantes en pot ? Et si la raison n'était pas simplement le mauvais goût du client ? Et si cela était lié à quelque chose de plus profond et de plus «humain» que ce que les maîtres de la trame soupçonnent ? Le nombre d'or existe toujours, mais ni le corps humain, ni l'esprit ne sont fondamentalement conçus pour un monde dominé par les lignes droites ou les certitudes euclidiennes. Même si Shakespeare l'utilisait comme métaphore du manque de passion, le bois est vivant ; il est chaud, il invite au toucher et convoque même l'odorat.

Au risque de surprendre, le bois est également très bien adapté au meilleur des mondes de la conception numérique et du fraisage CNC – le bois est capable de tout, même de s'évader du carcan rationnel dans lequel tant d'architectes ont essayé de l'enfermer. Bien sûr, le bois peut être utilisé comme placage, un simulacre de la présence de la nature. Il est vrai qu'un certain «bois» est vraiment artificiel, tel le formica qui évoque une succession de *diners* américains de bord de route à perte de vue. Ce livre se focalise sur 100 exemples de bâtiments entièrement ou partiellement en bois, sous diverses formes. Aucun risque donc de dire que le bois est de retour, même sous l'aspect de l'actuel bois de construction. Évidemment, certaines poutres en bois remarquées dans les projets publiés peuvent être en *glulam* (bois lamellé-collé), mais il ne s'agit pas d'être plus puristes que les architectes qui emploient le bois.

LA MORT DE LA CHAÎNE D'ASSEMBLAGE

En raison de son aspect chaleureux et aussi de certaines de ses limites inhérentes, le bois semble également favoriser une prolifération de nouvelles formes adaptées à ses forces, notamment sa légèreté. Le bois peut bien sûr être façonné selon des normes géométriques, mais sa nature fondamentale est plus indisciplinée et moins standardisée – malgré les efforts déployés par l'industrie pour le former et le mouler. Le bois explore également de nouveaux horizons grâce à son aptitude à franchir des portées toujours plus grandes au moyen de structures comme les *gridshells*, ou bien en s'associant à de nouveaux matériaux comme l'EFTE ou à des toitures recouvertes de téflon.

Les raisons de la résurgence du bois dans l'architecture contemporaine sont multiples ; certaines pourraient même avoir un lien philosophique avec l'appel éternel du jardin, le monde arcadien où tout était plus simple et où la nature était plus proche du paradis qu'aucun d'entre nous ne le sera jamais. Les jours de la *tabula rasa* moderne sont derrière nous. De vastes forêts – de l'Amazonie à l'Irian Jaya – sont abattues pour céder la place à des plantations d'huile de palme ou à des centres commerciaux. À l'instar de la production en série sur les chaînes d'assemblage, la trame rigide est née des besoins industriels d'une époque révolue où chaque partie devait être standardisée pour des motifs économiques. De nos jours, des ordinateurs chargés de la conception et du fraisage permettent la fabrication de pièces uniques qui peuvent désormais se passer d'être rectilignes et dépourvues d'âme. Peut-être est-ce l'appel du passé qui fait revenir le bois dans l'architecture, le bon sens écologique et économique, ou encore le fait que le bois est un matériau plus proche de notre propre nature que l'acier ou le béton.

1 Le jeu de mot original sur *wood* («bois», mais aussi «courtisé») est intraduisible.
2 FSC Forest Stewardship Council, consulté le 8 juin 2015, http://fsc.org.
3 Roger Sathre, Jennifer O'Connor, *A Synthesis of Research on Wood Products & Greenhouse Gas Impacts*, Vancouver, B.C., FPInnovations, 2e édition, octobre 2010.

ADJAYE ASSOCIATES

Adjaye Associates
223–231 Old Marylebone Road
London NW1 5QT / UK

Tel: +44 20 72 58 61 40 / Fax: +44 20 72 58 61 48
E-mail: info@adjaye.com / Web: www.adjaye.com

DAVID ADJAYE was born in 1966 in Dar es Salaam, Tanzania. He studied at the Royal College of Art in London (M.Arch, 1993), and worked in the offices of David Chipperfield and Eduardo Souto de Moura, before creating his own firm in London in 2000. He has been recognized as one of the leading architects of his generation in the United Kingdom, in part because of the talks he has given in various locations such as the Architectural Association, the Royal College of Art, and Cambridge University, as well as Harvard, Cornell, and the Universidade Lusíada in Lisbon. Some of his key works are a house extension (St. John's Wood, 1998); studio/home for Chris Ofili (1999); the SHADA Pavilion (2000, with artist Henna Nadeem); Siefert Penthouse (2001); Elektra House (2001); and a studio/gallery/home for Tim Noble and Sue Webster (2002), all in London. More recent work includes the Nobel Peace Center (Oslo, Norway, 2002–05); Bernie Grant Performing Arts Center (London, 2001–06); Stephen Lawrence Center (London, 2004–06); a visual arts building for the London-based organizations inIVA/Autograph at Rivington Place (London, 2003–07); the Museum of Contemporary Art Denver (Denver, Colorado, USA, 2004–07); "Sclera, Size + Matter" (London, UK, 2008, published here); and the Francis A. Gregory Library (Washington, D.C., USA, 2010–12), all in the UK unless stated otherwise. Current work includes participation in the ongoing Msheireb project (Doha, Qatar, 2015) and the National Museum of African American History and Culture (Smithsonian Institution, Washington, D.C., USA, 2015).

DAVID ADJAYE wurde 1966 in Daressalam, Tansania, geboren. Er studierte am Royal College of Art in London (M. Arch., 1993) und arbeitete für David Chipperfield und Eduardo Souto de Moura, bevor er 2000 in London sein eigenes Büro gründete. Er gilt weithin als einer der führenden Architekten seiner Generation in Großbritannien, auch wegen seiner Vorträge an Institutionen wie der Architectural Association, dem Royal College of Art, der Universität Cambridge, der Harvard und der Cornell University sowie der Universidade Lusíada in Lissabon. Zu seinen wichtigsten Projekten zählen eine Hauserweiterung (St. John's Wood, 1998), ein Atelier und Haus für Chris Ofili (1999), der SHADA Pavilion (2000, mit der Künstlerin Henna Nadeem), das Siefert Penthouse (2001), das Elektra House (2001) sowie ein Atelier mit Galerie und Haus für Tim Noble und Sue Webster (2002), alle in London. Jüngere Arbeiten sind u. a. das Friedensnobelpreiszentrum (Oslo, 2002–05), das Bernie Grant Performing Arts Center (London, 2001–06), das Stephen Lawrence Center (London, 2004–06), ein Haus für bildende Künste für die Londoner Organisation inIVA/Autograph am Rivington Place (London, 2003–07), das Museum of Contemporary Art Denver (Denver, Colorado, 2004–07), *Sclera, Size + Matter* (London, 2008, hier vorgestellt) sowie die Francis A. Gregory Library (Washington, D. C., 2010–12). Zu seinen aktuellen Projekten zählen sein Beitrag zum Msheireb-Projekt (Doha, Katar, 2015) und das National Museum of African American History and Culture (Smithsonian Institution, Washington, D. C., 2015).

DAVID ADJAYE est né en 1966 à Dar es-Salaam, en Tanzanie. Il étudie au Royal College of Art, à Londres (M.Arch., 1993), puis travaille dans les agences de David Chipperfield et d'Eduardo Souto de Moura, avant de créer sa propre agence à Londres, en 2000. Il est considéré comme l'un des plus importants architectes de sa génération au Royaume-Uni, en partie grâce à ses conférences en divers lieux, comme l'Architectural Association, le Royal College of Art et l'université de Cambridge, ainsi qu'à Harvard, Cornell, et à l'université Lusíada de Lisbonne. Parmi ses principales réalisations, on compte une extension d'habitation (St. John's Wood, 1998) ; un atelier/maison pour Chris Ofili (1999) ; le pavillon SHADA (2000, avec l'artiste Henna Nadeem) ; l'appartement de grand standing Siefert (2001) ; la Elektra House (2001) et un atelier/galerie/maison pour Tim Noble et Sue Webster (2002), tous situés à Londres. Ses projets récemment réalisés sont le Centre Nobel de la paix (Oslo, 2002–05) ; le Bernie Grant Performing Arts Centre (Londres, 2001–06) ; le Stephen Lawrence Centre (Londres, 2004–06) ; un immeuble dédié aux arts visuels pour les organisations inIVA/Autograph, à Rivington Place (Londres, 2003–07) ; le Museum of Contemporary Art de Denver (États-Unis, 2004–07) ; « Sclera, Size + Matter » (Londres, 2008, publié ici) et la bibliothèque Francis A. Gregory (Washington, 2010–12), tous situés au Royaume-Uni, sauf mention contraire. Ses projets en cours comprennent sa participation au projet Msheireb (Doha, Qatar, 2015) et le National Museum of African American History and Culture (Smithsonian Institution, Washington, 2015).

"SCLERA, SIZE + MATTER"

London Design Festival, London, UK, June–September 2008

Area: 40 m². Client: London Design Festival. Cost: not disclosed
Collaboration: American Hardwood Export Council (Sponsorship: tulipwood), Hess Wohnwerk (Fabricator),
Jochen A. Stahl, TU-Darmstadt FB Architektur (Structural Engineer)

This ephemeral pavilion was intended both to explore the ways in which the eye perceives light and to find new uses for tulipwood (Yellow Poplar). The elliptical structure measures 12 meters by 8 meters and was put in place on the South Bank Centre Square near the Thames. Adjaye explains that the name "sclera" means the "domain of parentheses, or the outer enclosure of the eyeball." The undulating pattern of wood appears random, but is in fact based on a loose system of varying timber lengths, with an open roof and gaps on the sides. Adjaye's work has often explored new uses for relatively common materials such as the wood employed here—and he has also played on the rules of perception in an innovative way, making apparently simple structures much more intriguing and challenging than they might at first appear. The very visible location selected for this installation also sought to bring intelligent design closer to the general public.

Bei dem temporären Pavillon setzte sich Adjaye sowohl mit der Lichtwahrnehmung des Auges als auch mit neuen Nutzungsmöglichkeiten für Rosenholz auseinander. Die elliptische, 8 x 12 m große Konstruktion wurde unweit des South Bank Centre Square nahe der Themse realisiert. Adjaye erläutert, dass „Sclera" das „Umschlossene oder die äußere Hülle des Augapfels" bezeichnet. Die wellenförmige Anordnung der Holzelemente wirkt wie zufällig, beruht jedoch auf einem lockeren System verschiedener Lattenlängen. Neben einem offenen Dach hat die Konstruktion auch seitlich Öffnungen. Adjaye befasst sich, wie so oft in seinem Werk, mit neuartigen Einsatzmöglichkeiten für eher gewöhnliche Baumaterialien wie das hier verwendete Holz. Zugleich spielt er auf innovative Weise mit den Gesetzmäßigkeiten der Wahrnehmung, wodurch scheinbar einfache Konstruktionen wesentlich faszinierender und anspruchsvoller wirken, als auf den ersten Blick zu vermuten wäre. Der prominente Standort der Installation wurde auch deshalb gewählt, um der Öffentlichkeit intelligentes Design näher zu bringen.

Ce pavillon éphémère avait pour objectifs d'explorer les manières dont l'œil perçoit la lumière et de trouver de nouveaux usages pour le bois de tulipier (Yellow Poplar). La structure elliptique de 12 m par 8 était installée sur le South Bank Centre Square, près de la Tamise. Adjaye explique que le nom « sclera » signifie « domaine de parenthèses, ou paroi externe du globe oculaire ». Le motif de bois ondulant semble aléatoire, mais est en fait basé sur un système relâché de poutres de longueurs variées, avec un toit ouvert et des vides sur les côtés. Dans ses projets, Adjaye explore souvent des usages nouveaux de matériaux relativement banals, comme le bois utilisé ici, et joue souvent de manière innovante avec les lois de la perception, pour rendre des structures apparemment simples beaucoup plus intrigantes et stimulantes qu'elles ne le semblent à première vue. L'emplacement très visible de cette installation visait aussi à mettre le grand public en contact avec un design éclairé.

The simple elliptical plan of the structure is rendered complex by the orchestration of the wooden slats that form the structure.

Der schlichte ellipsenförmige Grundriss des Pavillons gewinnt an Komplexität durch die ausgeklügelte Anordnung der Holzlatten, aus denen die Konstruktion besteht.

L'orchestration des lattes de bois de la structure enrichit le plan en simple ellipse du bâtiment.

Calling on imagery that might vary
between a forest and a cave with its
stalactites, there is also a musical
presence in the dense arrangement
of the wooden slats.

Der Raum erinnert an einen Wald
oder an Stalaktiten in einer Höhle.
Zugleich hat die dichte Anordnung
der Holzlatten etwas Musikalisches.

La structure évoque des images
de forêt ou de grotte à stalactites.
L'arrangement dense des lattes
de bois lui donne également une
présence musicale.

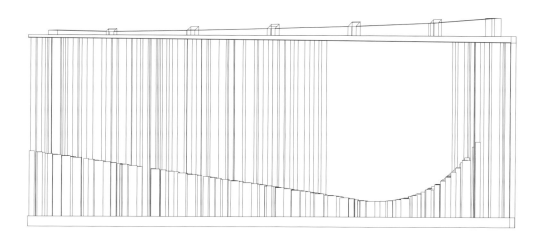

AI WEIWEI/FAKE DESIGN

Ai Weiwei/FAKE Design
Caochangdi 258 / Chaoyang District
Beijing 100102 / China

Tel/Fax: +86 10 8456 4194
E-mail: nobody@vip.sina.com
Web: blog.sina.com.cn/aiweiwei

The artist-architect **AI WEIWEI** was born in 1957 in Beijing, the son of the well-known Chinese poet Ai Qing. In 1978, after a 20-year period during which his family was banished from the capital for political reasons, Ai Weiwei returned to Beijing to study at the Film Institute. He went to New York in 1981 and studied at Parson's School of Design. He returned to China in 1994 and opened his studio in Beijing in 1999. This 500-square-meter home-studio, with a 1300-square-meter courtyard made of brick, was his first widely published work. It was built with the help of local workers. In 2000, he organized Shanghai's first independent art biennale under the evocative title "Fuck Off." His firm, FAKE Design, currently employs four architects, four designers, two photographers, and five assistants and interns, and works on landscape and interior design as well as on architecture and art projects. Their design philosophy is: "Make it simple." They participated with Herzog & de Meuron in the 2003 competition for the Beijing Stadium intended for the 2008 Olympic Games. Ai Weiwei is the coordinator and a participant in the Jinhua Architecture Park, inaugurated in 2007. Other recent work includes the Gowhere Restaurant, a renovation and construction project (2004); 9 Boxes-Taihe Complex (2004); the Photofactory (Caochangdi, 2007); 241 Art Corridor (2007); and Red No. 1, all in Beijing, as well as the installation "Template" realized for documenta 12 (Kassel, Germany, 2007, published here). More recently, Ai Weiwei completed the 2012 Serpentine Summer Pavilion (London, UK) with the architects Herzog & de Meuron.

Der Künstler und Architekt **AI WEIWEI** wurde 1957 in Peking als Sohn des bekannten Dichters Ai Qing geboren. Im Jahr 1978, nachdem seine Familie 20 Jahre lang aus politischen Gründen aus der chinesischen Hauptstadt verbannt gewesen war, kehrte Ai Weiwei nach Peking zurück, um ein Studium am dortigen Filminstitut aufzunehmen. 1981 ging Ai Weiwei nach New York, wo er an der Parson's School of Design studierte, um 1994 nach China zurückzukehren und 1999 in Peking ein Atelier zu eröffnen. Diese mithilfe lokaler Arbeitskräfte gebaute Kombination aus Wohnhaus und Atelier, mit 500 m² Innenfläche und einem 1300 m² großen Hof aus Ziegeln, war Ai Weiweis erste vielbeachtete Arbeit. Im Jahr 2000 organisierte er die erste unabhängige Kunstbiennale Schanghais unter dem provozierenden Titel „Fuck Off". Seine Firma FAKE Design beschäftigt derzeit vier Architekten, vier Designer, zwei Fotografen sowie fünf Assistenten und Praktikanten. Die Philosophie des Unternehmens, das sich mit Architektur, Innenarchitektur, Landschaftsgestaltung und Kunstprojekten beschäftigt, lautet: Mach es einfach. 2003 beteiligte FAKE Design sich gemeinsam mit Herzog & de Meuron an dem Wettbewerb für den Entwurf des Nationalstadions für die Olympischen Spiele 2008 in Peking. Zusätzlich zu einem eigenen Beitrag übernahm Ai Weiwei die Koordinierung des 2007 eröffneten Jinhua-Architekturparks. Weitere Projekte jüngeren Datums sind das Gowhere-Restaurant in Peking, entstanden durch die Renovierung und Erweiterung eines älteren Gebäudes (2004), die Wohnanlage 9 Boxes-Taihe (Peking, 2004), die Photofactory im Pekinger Stadtteil Cao Chang Di (2007), der 241 Art Corridor (Peking, 2007) und das Red No. 1 (Peking). Für die documenta 12 realisierte Ai Weiwei die nachfolgend vorgestellte Installation „Template" (Kassel, 2007). 2012 entwarf Ai Weiwei den Serpentine-Sommer-Pavillon in London mit den Architekten Herzog & de Meuron.

L'artiste et architecte **AI WEIWEI**, né en 1957 à Pékin, est le fils du célèbre poète Ai Qing. En 1978, après 20 années de bannissement de sa famille pour des raisons politiques, il revint à Pékin pour étudier à l'Institut du cinéma. Il part pour New York en 1981 et étudie à la Parson's School of Design. Il rentre en Chine en 1994 et ouvre son atelier à Pékin en 1999. Cet atelier-habitation de 500 m² construit avec l'aide d'artisans locaux dans une cour de brique de 1300 m² est sa première réalisation publiée. En 2000, il organise la première biennale d'art indépendante de Shanghai sous le titre évocateur de « Fuck Off ». Son agence, FAKE Design, emploie actuellement quatre architectes, quatre designers, deux photographes et cinq assistants et stagiaires. Elle intervient dans les domaines de l'architecture, l'architecture intérieure, le paysagisme et l'art. Sa philosophie de conception se résume à « Faire simple ». Elle a participé avec Herzog & de Meuron au concours de 2003 pour le stade de Pékin des Jeux olympiques de 2008. Ai Weiwei est le coordinateur et l'un des participants au projet du Jinhua Architecture Park, inauguré en 2007. Parmi ses autres travaux récents : le restaurant Gowhere, projet de rénovation et construction (2004) ; le complexe 9 Boxes-Taihe (2004) ; la Photofactory (Caochangdi, 2007) ; le 241 Art Corridor (2007) et Red No. 1, tous à Pékin, ainsi que l'installation *Template* réalisée pour la documenta 12 (Kassel, Allemagne, 2007, publiée ici). En 2012, Ai Weiwei a réalisé le Pavillon d'été de la Serpentine (Londres) avec les architectes Herzog & de Meuron.

"TEMPLATE"
Documenta 12, Kassel, Germany, 2007

Dimensions: 720 x 1200 x 850 cm (before collapsing);
422 x 1106 x 875 cm (after collapsing)

Made of wooden doors and windows from demolished Ming and Qing Dynasty houses (1368–1911), "**TEMPLATE**" might more easily be described as a work of art than a piece of architecture, and yet it employed elements derived from houses in a distinctly architectural form. Built in front of the "Crystal Palace," a temporary acrylic greenhouse designed by the French architects Lacaton & Vassal, the "architecture of 'Template'," according to Ai Weiwei, "is comprised of late Ming and Qing Dynasty wooden windows and doors which, joined together in five layers per side, form an open vertical structure having an eight-pointed base. In spite of its large size, from afar the installation conveys the illusion of being something foldable, like a gigantic three-dimensional paper cutout. Where the external framework is massive and regular, the internal part of each wall made out of windows and doors is shaped according to the volume of a hypothetical traditional Chinese temple, giving the impression that the whole wooden construction was assembled around a building that has later been removed." The artist goes on further to explain the connection of this work to architecture: "The windows and doors I employed used to belong to […] houses located in the Shanxi area of northern China, where entire old towns have been pulled down. We bought the fragments from different quarters, and these are probably the last pieces of that civilization. I like to use these leftovers as part of… not a sentiment, but evidence of our past activity. I like to carry these pieces into a completely contemporary context and I think it works well. It really is a mixed, troubled, questioning context, and a protest for its own identity. To me, the temple itself, you know I'm not religious, means a station where you can think about the past and the future; it's a void space. The selected area, not the material temple itself, tells you that the real physical temple is not there, but constructed through the leftovers of the past." At the end of June 2007, the structure, which had been intended to stand until the closure of the documenta on September 23, collapsed during a storm. Ai Weiwei said, "It's better than before; now the power of nature is in evidence, and art only becomes beautiful through this kind of emotion."

Ai Weiweis Documentabeitrag „**TEMPLATE**", zusammengesetzt aus Holztüren und -fenstern, die aus Abrisshäusern aus der Ming- und Qing-Dynastie (1368 bis 1911) stammen, erweckt zunächst eher den Eindruck eines Kunstwerks als den einer architektonischen Arbeit; trotzdem bilden die früheren Wohnhauselemente eine eindeutig architektonische Form. Ai Weiwei selbst erklärt zu seiner Installation, die vor dem temporären „Kristallpalast" – dem in Gewächshausbauweise errichteten Aue-Pavillon der französischen Architekten Lacaton & Vassal – aufgestellt wurde: „Die hölzernen Türen und Fenster aus der späten Ming- und der Qing-Dynastie, die die Architektur von ‚Template' ausmachen, sind auf jeder Seite in fünf Schichten übereinandermontiert und bilden eine offene vertikale Struktur mit einer achteckigen Basis. Trotz ihrer beachtlichen Größe erweckt die Installation aus der Ferne betrachtet den Eindruck, dass man sie so zusammenfalten könnte, als sei sie ein riesiger dreidimensionaler Papierschnitt. Während die Außenseite des Gebildes massiv und regelmäßig ist, ist der innere Teil der ganz aus Türen und Fenstern bestehenden Wände in der vermeintlichen Form eines traditionellen chinesischen Tempels ausgespart, sodass der Eindruck entsteht, die gesamte hölzerne Konstruktion sei um ein anderes Gebäude herum angelegt worden, das später entfernt wurde." Die Verbindung seiner Arbeit zur Architektur erläutert der Künstler wie folgt: „Die Fenster und Türen, die ich verwendet habe, gehörten früher zu […] Häusern in der Provinz Shanxi in Nordchina, wo man alte Städte komplett abgerissen hat. Die Fragmente, die wir gekauft haben, stammen aus verschiedenen Vierteln und sind vermutlich die letzten Relikte dieser Zivilisation. Diese Überreste möchte ich benutzen als Teil … nicht einer besonderen Sentimentalität, sondern als Zeugnis dessen, was wir früher getan haben. Ich möchte sie in einen ganz zeitgenössischen Kontext stellen und ich finde, das funktioniert recht gut. Natürlich ist es ein unübersichtlicher, schwieriger Kontext, der auch Fragen aufwirft – und ein Protest für eine eigene Identität. Für mich, der ich ja selbst nicht religiös bin, ist der Tempel ein Ort, an dem man über die Vergangenheit und die Zukunft nachdenken kann; es ist ein leerer Raum. Der ausgewählte Bereich – kein materieller Tempel als solcher – zeigt an, dass hier der konkrete Tempel nicht real vorhanden ist, sondern durch die Überreste der Vergangenheit konstruiert wird." Ende Juni 2007 fiel das Gebilde, das der Planung nach bis zum Abschluss der documenta am 23. September hätte stehenbleiben sollen, durch einen Sturm in sich zusammen, wozu Ai Weiwei erklärte: „Es ist jetzt besser als vorher – die Macht der Natur tritt in Erscheinung und nur durch diese Form der Emotion kommt die Kunst zu ihrer Schönheit."

Réalisée à partir de portes et de fenêtres de maisons démolies des dynasties Ming et Qing (1368–1911), « **TEMPLATE** » est peut-être plus une œuvre d'art qu'une réalisation architecturale, mais elle emploie des éléments de maisons dans une forme à l'évidence architecturée. Édifiée devant le « Crystal Palace », serre temporaire en acrylique conçue par les Français Lacaton & Vassal, « l'architecture de *Template*, selon Ai Weiwei, se compose de fenêtres et de portes en bois des anciennes dynasties Ming et Qing, réunies en cinq strates par côté pour former une structure verticale sur une base octogonale. Malgré ses importantes dimensions, l'installation vue de loin donne l'impression d'être repliable, tel un gigantesque découpage en papier. Alors que le cadre externe est plein et régulier, chaque paroi interne est composée de portes et de fenêtres rappelant le volume d'un hypothétique temple chinois ancien, donnant l'impression que cette construction en bois a été assemblée autour d'un bâtiment supprimé ultérieurement ». L'artiste éclaire également le lien de cette œuvre avec l'architecture : « Les fenêtres et les portes employées appartenaient à […] des maisons de la région du Shanxi dans le Nord de la Chine où des villes anciennes ont été démolies. Nous avons acheté ces fragments en différents endroits et ce sont probablement les dernières traces de cette civilisation. J'ai aimé les remonter dans un contexte contemporain entièrement différent et je pense que la proposition fonctionne bien. C'est un contexte de questionnements mêlés et troublés et la protestation d'une identité. Pour moi qui ne suis pas croyant, le temple est un lieu où chacun peut penser au passé et au futur. C'est un espace vide. La zone choisie, pas le temple matériel lui-même, vous enseigne que le vrai temple n'est pas là, mais construit avec les vestiges du passé. » À la fin du mois de juin 2007, la structure qui devait durer jusqu'à la clôture de la documenta, lë 23 septembre, s'est effondrée lors d'une tempête. Pour Ai Weiwei : « C'est mieux qu'avant, maintenant la puissance de la nature est mise en évidence et l'art ne devient vraiment magnifique qu'à travers ce type d'émotion. »

Photographed before (top right) and after its collapse in a storm at the end of June 2007, Ai Weiwei's "Template" assumes two different forms, both of which remain valid for the artist.

Ai Weiweis Kunstwerk vor (rechts oben) und nach seiner Zerstörung durch einen Sturm im Juni 2007 – beide Zustandsformen erklärte der Künstler für gültig.

Photographiée avant (à droite, en haut) et après son effondrement lors d'une tempête fin juin 2007, l'œuvre d'Ai Weiwei s'est présentée sous deux formes très différentes.

WERNER AISSLINGER

Studio Aisslinger
Heidestr. 46–52
10557 Berlin
Germany

Tel: +49 30 31 50 54 00
Fax: +49 30 31 50 54 01
E-mail: studio@aisslinger.de
Web: www.aisslinger.de

WERNER AISSLINGER was born in Nördlingen, Germany, in 1964. He studied design at the University of Arts (Hochschule der Künste, 1987–91), Berlin. From 1989 to 1992, he freelanced with the offices of Jasper Morrison and Ron Arad in London and at the Studio de Lucchi in Milan. In 1993, he founded Studio Aisslinger in Berlin, focusing on product design, design concepts, and brand architecture. From 1998 to 2005, he was a Professor of Product Design at the Design College (Hochschule für Gestaltung) in Karlsruhe (Department of Product Design). He has developed furniture with Italian brands such as Cappellini and Zanotta and office furniture with Vitra in Switzerland. He works on product designs and architectural projects with brands like Interlübke, Mercedes-Benz, Adidas, and Hugo Boss. In 2003, he designed the Loftcube, a temporary residence intended for rooftop installation (Berlin), which would appear to have a conceptual relation to the Fincube (Ritten, Italy, 2010) published here.

WERNER AISSLINGER wurde 1964 in Nördlingen geboren und studierte Design an der Hochschule der Künste Berlin (1987–91). Zwischen 1989 und 1992 arbeitete er als freier Mitarbeiter für die Büros von Jasper Morrison und Ron Arad in London sowie für das Studio de Lucchi in Mailand. 1993 gründete er das Studio Aisslinger in Berlin, das sich auf Produktdesign, Designkonzepte und Markenarchitektur spezialisiert hat. Von 1998 bis 2005 war Aisslinger Professor für Produktdesign an der Hochschule für Gestaltung in Karlsruhe. Er entwickelte Möbel für italienische Hersteller wie Cappellini und Zanotta sowie Büromöbel für Vitra in der Schweiz. Aisslinger arbeitet an Produktentwürfen für Firmen wie Interlübke, Mercedes-Benz, Adidas und Hugo Boss. 2003 entwarf er den Loftcube, eine temporäre Wohneinheit, die sich auf Dächern installieren lässt (Berlin) und vom Konzept her erkennbar mit dem hier vorgestellten Fincube (Ritten, Italien, 2010) verwandt ist.

WERNER AISSLINGER, né à Nördlingen (Allemagne) en 1964, a étudié le design à l'Université des arts de Berlin (Hochschule der Künste,1987–91). De 1989 à 1992, il collabore en free-lance avec les agences de Jasper Morrison et Ron Arad à Londres et le Studio de Lucchi à Milan. En 1993, il fonde le Studio Aisslinger à Berlin, qui se consacre au design produit, aux concepts de design et à l'architecture de marques. De 1998 à 2005, il a été professeur de design produit à l'École supérieure de Design de Karlsruhe (Hochschule für Gestaltung). Il a créé des meubles pour des marques italiennes comme Cappellini et Zanotta, et du mobilier de bureau pour Vitra en Suisse. Il travaille aussi bien sur des projets de design que d'architecture pour des marques comme Interlübke, Mercedes-Benz, Adidas ou Hugo Boss. En 2003, il a conçu le Loftcube, résidence temporaire destinée à une toiture berlinoise, projet non sans lien conceptuel avec son Fincube (Ritten, Italie, 2010), publié ici.

FINCUBE

Winterinn, Ritten, South Tyrol, Italy, 2010

Address: not applicable; www.fincube.eu. Area: 47 m². Client: Josef Innerhofter, Fincube
Cost: €150 000 (basic version). Collaboration: Tina Bunyaprasit (Studio Aisslinger, Interior Design),
Markus Lobis (Interior Wood Structure), Matthias Prast (Finishes)

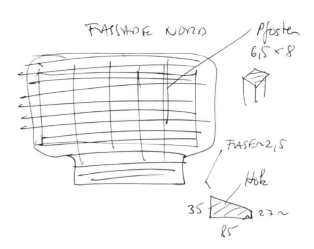

The extensive use of locally harvested larch and a double skin assure that this easily transportable house is also ecologically sound.

Dank der Nutzung lokaler Lärchenholzbestände und einer doppelten Außenhaut ist das transportable Haus auch ökologisch nachhaltig.

Le recours intensif au mélèze local et la double peau assurent à cette maison facilement transportable de réelles qualités écologiques.

According to the designer: "Natural high tech is the concept of this new modular, sustainable, and transportable low-energy house." The structure was installed at an altitude of 1200 meters above sea level in the South Tyrol and made with local collaboration. Built with locally harvested larch, the structure employs "long-lasting and recyclable materials," and so the **FINCUBE** can be dismantled and reassembled on another site. Triple glazing and a double façade are formed into a "unique overall mushroom-like monoshape." The client has envisaged placing a group of these residences in temporary locations, given that minimum preparation of the site is required.

Der Designer erklärt: „Das Konzept dieses neuen modularen, nachhaltigen und transportablen Niedrigenergiehauses ist naturverbundenes Hightech." Der Bau wurde in Tirol auf einer Höhe von 1200 m über N.N. errichtet und in Zusammenarbeit mit lokalen Firmen realisiert. Die Konstruktion aus regional geschlagenem Lärchenholz nutzt „langlebige und recyclebare Materialien", weshalb sich der **FINCUBE** demontieren und an anderen Standorten wieder errichten lässt. Dreifachverglasung und Doppelfassade sind zu einem „außergewöhnlichen, pilzähnlichen fließenden Gesamtkörper" geformt. Da der Baugrund nur minimal vorbereitet werden muss, plant der Auftraggeber, eine ganze Gruppe dieser Wohnbauten vor Ort zu errichten.

Selon le designer : « Le concept de cette nouvelle maison modulaire, durable, transportable, à faible consommation d'énergie est le high-tech naturel. » Cette structure en « cube » a été installée à une altitude de 1200 m dans le Tyrol du Sud en collaboration avec des entreprises locales. Réalisé en mélèze de la région, il fait appel à « des matériaux de longue durabilité et recyclables ». Le **FINCUBE** peut être démonté et réassemblé ailleurs. Sa double façade à triple vitrage présente une « forme monocoque originale de champignon ». Intéressé par le faible coût de préparation du terrain, le client a envisagé de réaliser un groupe de ces résidences destinées à la location temporaire.

Despite its double skin, the house remains quite open to its environment, as seen in the image above.

Trotz seiner doppelten Außenhaut öffnet sich das Haus zur Umgebung, wie die Aufnahme oben belegt.

Malgré sa double peau, la maison reste ouverte sur son environnement, comme le montre l'image ci-dessus.

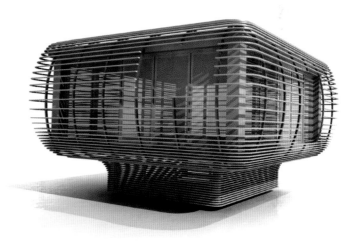

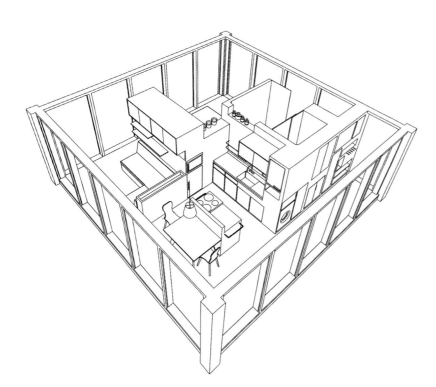

Renderings show the way the volume of the house sits above the site. An axonometric drawing of the interior renders explicit the compact, square design. Above, a walkway behind the larch outer frame, and an interior view.

Renderings verdeutlichen die minimale Bodenversiegelung durch den Baukörper. Eine Axonometrie des Innenraums bietet Einblicke in den kompakten Entwurf auf quadratischem Grundriss. Oben eine hinter dem äußeren Lärchenrahmen verlaufende Holzgalerie sowie eine Innenaufnahme.

Ces images de synthèse montrent comment la maison repose sur son terrain. La vue axonométrique de l'intérieur précise la compacité des aménagements dans la forme carrée. En haut, une coursive entre les deux peaux et une vue de l'intérieur.

AL BORDE

AL BORDE
Los Ríos N11–206 y Briceño
Quito
Pichincha
Ecuador

Tel: +593 9 8463 6428
E-mail: contact@albordearq.com
Web: www.albordearq.com

Al Borde was founded in 2007 by **PASCUAL GANGOTENA**, born in 1971, and **DAVID BARRAGÁN**, born in 1981, in Quito, Ecuador. They both graduated from the Architecture School of the Catholic University of Ecuador, respectively in 2005 and 2006. Prior to creating their firm, David Barragán worked with the architect José María Sáez, and Pascual Gangotena was Principal of the non-profit organization "Un Techo Para Ecuador," whose main work was focused in design and construction of community infrastructure and low-income housing with the support of volunteers from all over the country. Their work includes the Pentimento House (Quito, 2006); the Atelier-Greenhouse (Machachi, 2007); Entre Muros House (Tumbaco, Quito, 2007–08, published here); Kay Pacha Yaku Hukuma (Yasuni, 2009); the Itala House (Puembo, 2009); Nueva Esperanza School (Manabí, 2009); Houses 001 and 002 (Quito, 2010); and UEM North (Quito, 2011), all in Ecuador.

Das Büro Al Borde wurde 2007 von **PASCUAL GANGOTENA**, geboren 1971, und **DAVID BARRAGÁN**, geboren 1981, in Quito, Ekuador, gegründet. Beide studierten Architektur bis 2005 bzw. 2006 an der Katholischen Universität von Ekuador. Vor Gründung des gemeinsamen Büros arbeitete David Barragán bei dem Architekten José María Sáez, und Pascual Gangotena war Leiter der Non-Profit-Organisation Un Techo Para Ecuador, deren Tätigkeit vorwiegend in Planung und Bau von kommunaler Infrastruktur und sozialem Wohnungbau mithilfe von Freiwilligen aus dem ganzen Land bestand. Zu den Arbeiten des Büros zählen das Haus Pentimento (Quito, 2006), ein Atelier- und Gewächshaus (Machachi, 2007), das Haus Entre Muros (Tumbaco, Quito, 2007–08, hier veröffentlicht), Kay Pacha Yaku Hukuma (Yasuni, 2009), das Haus Itala (Puembo, 2009), die Schule Nueva Esperanza (Manabí, 2009), die Häuser 001 und 002 (Quito, 2010) sowie UEM North (Quito, 2011), alle in Ekuador.

L'agence Al Borde a été fondée en 2007 par **PASCUAL GANGOTENA**, né en 1971, et **DAVID BARRAGÁN**, né en 1981, à Quito (Équateur). Tous deux sont diplômés de l'école d'architecture de l'Université catholique de l'Équateur, en 2005 et en 2006 respectivement. Avant de créer cette agence, David Barragán travaillait avec l'architecte José María Sáez et Pascual Gangotena était l'un des dirigeants de l'association « Un Techo Para Ecuador » (Un toit pour l'Équateur), dont l'objectif principal est la conception et la construction d'infrastructures communautaires et de logements sociaux avec le soutien de bénévoles de toutes les régions du pays. Parmi leurs réalisations, toutes situées en Équateur, on peut citer la maison Pentimento (Quito, 2006) ; un atelier-serre (Machachi, 2007) ; la maison Entre Muros (Tumbaco, Quito, 2007–08, publiée ici) ; Kay Pacha Yaku Hukuma (Yasuni, 2009) ; la maison Itala (Puembo, 2009) ; l'école Nueva Esperanza (Manabí, 2009) ; les maisons 001 et 002 (Quito, 2010) et le projet UEM North (Quito, 2011).

ENTRE MUROS HOUSE

Tumbaco, Quito, Ecuador, 2007–08

Address: not disclosed. Area: 180 m²
Client: Carla Flor. Cost: $50 400

Built on a 5000 m² site on a hillside of the Ilaló volcano, this house was built with rammed earth, wood, and stone. The architects describe it as the result of a "search for living in harmony with nature, the need of autonomy for each one of the three members of the family, the low budget," and the phrase: "There is always another way of doing things and another way for living." A long corridor was used as an element that isolates the project from neighbors and includes furniture "worked inside the thick adobe walls." Gray water is used for irrigation, and solar energy to heat water. The raw materials of the adobe walls come from the site itself. The architects have also paid careful attention to customs such as a ceremony requesting the permission of the volcano to build on the site, and cutting wood and reeds at the appropriate phase of the moon.

Dieses auf einem 5000 m² großen Hanggrundstück am Vulkan Ilaló errichtete Haus wurde aus Stampflehm, Holz und Naturstein erbaut. Die Architekten beschreiben es als Ergebnis der „Suche nach einem Leben in Harmonie mit der Natur, des Bedürfnisses nach Autonomie für jedes einzelne der drei Familienmitglieder, des geringen Etats" sowie der Überzeugung: „Es gibt immer eine Möglichkeit, etwas auf andere Weise auszuführen und sich für einen anderen Lebensstil zu entscheiden." Ein langer Korridor, „in dessen dicke Lehmwände die Möblierung eingefügt wurde", trennt das Gebäude von den Nachbarhäusern. Grauwasser dient zur Bewässerung, Solarenergie zum Erwärmen des Wassers. Das Rohmaterial für die Lehmwände stammt vom Grundstück. Die Architekten haben zudem Rücksicht auf traditionelle Bräuche genommen und z. B. eine Zeremonie abgehalten, mit welcher der Vulkan um Erlaubnis gebeten wurde, auf dem Gelände zu bauen, sowie Holz und Schilf in den entsprechenden Mondphasen zu schneiden.

Construite sur un terrain de 5000 m² à flanc de colline du volcan Ilaló, cette maison est en adobe, bois et pierre. Les architectes la présentent comme « le résultat d'une recherche de vie en harmonie avec la nature, la réponse au besoin d'autonomie de chacun des trois membres de la famille et à un budget limité ». Ils précisent « qu'il y a toujours une autre façon de faire les choses et une autre façon de vivre ». Un long corridor a été utilisé pour isoler la résidence du voisinage, il intègre des meubles « travaillés dans l'épaisseur des murs d'adobe ». Les eaux usées sont utilisées pour l'irrigation et l'énergie solaire pour chauffer l'eau. Les matériaux qui ont servi à préparer les murs d'adobe proviennent du site même. Les architectes ont également porté la plus grande attention aux coutumes locales, telle que celle qui consiste à organiser une cérémonie pour demander au volcan la permission de construire sur ses pentes ou celle qui consiste à abattre le bois et les roseaux en fonction des phases de la lune.

The house appears to be articulated, as though it had fully absorbed the forms of the hilly terrain.

Die Gliederung des Hauses scheint die Formen des hügeligen Geländes vollständig aufzunehmen.

La maison semble articulée, comme si elle avait absorbé le profil mouvementé du terrain.

Strips of light and bands of glazing give a generous continuity to the appearance of the house. This aspect of the design is emphasized in the drawing on the right.

Lichtstreifen und Fensterbänder verleihen dem Erscheinungsbild des Hauses großzügige Kontinuität. Dieser Aspekt der Planung kommt in der Zeichnung rechts deutlich zum Ausdruck.

Des bandeaux de lumière et de vitrages participent à la continuité visuelle de la maison. Cet aspect du projet est mis en valeur dans le dessin de droite.

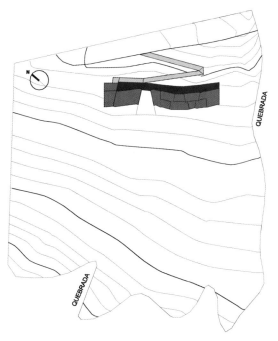

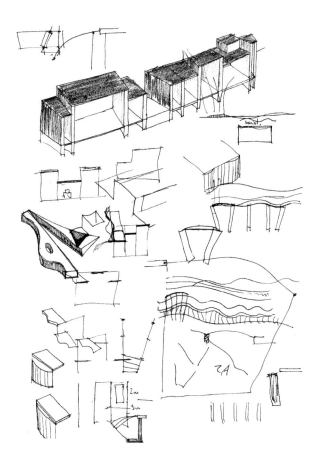

Contrasting with the more apparent sophistication of the exterior pictures on the previous pages, these interior views emphasize the rustic textures inside the structure.

Im Gegensatz zur deutlicher erkennbaren Raffinesse der Außenansichten auf den vorherigen Seiten zeigen diese Aufnahmen die rustikalen Oberflächen im Innern des Gebäudes.

Contrastant avec la sophistication plus marquée de l'extérieur (pages précédentes), ces vues de l'intérieur font ressortir les textures rustiques choisies pour l'intérieur.

AND

AND: Architecture of Novel Differentiation
 # 301, 919–7, Bangbae-dong, Seocho-gu
Seoul 137–843
South Korea

Tel: +82 70 8771 9668
Fax: +82 2 6499 9668
E-mail: andemail@naver.com
Web: www.a-n-d.kr

Born in 1976 in Janggye (South Korea), **EUI YEOB JEONG** received a Bachelor of Engineering in Architecture from Inha University (Incheon, South Korea, 2002), and an M.Arch from the University of Toronto (2006). He worked as an intern at Morphosis Architects (Los Angeles, 2004), MJM Architects in Toronto (2006), and Space Group in Seoul (2007–10) where he was a junior architect. In 2010, he established his own practice AND (Architecture of Novel Differentiation), and has worked on architecture, interiors, and furniture design. In 2011, AND won the Architecture of the Year Award from the Korean Institute of Architects (KIA, for Topoject, Gyeonggi-do, 2010, published here). **TAE KYOUNG LEE** was born in 1981 in South Korea. She received her B.A. degree from the University of Toronto (2006) and her M.Arch from Yale University (2010). She has been a Senior Researcher at AND since 2010. Aside from Topoject, the work of AND includes Skinspace (Gyeonggi-do, 2010, also published here); and Aggrenad (Gyeongsangnam-do, 2011). Three houses in Gangwon-do are in the process of design and construction.

EUI YEOB JEONG wurde 1976 in Janggye (Südkorea) geboren und schloss sein Studium an der Inha-Universität (Incheon, Südkorea, 2002) mit einem Bachelor of Engineering im Fach Architektur und einem M. Arch. an der University of Toronto (2006) ab. Er machte Praktika bei Morphosis Architects (Los Angeles, 2004) sowie bei MJM Architects in Toronto (2006) und arbeitete bei Space Group in Seoul (2007–10) als Juniorarchitekt. 2010 gründete er AND (Architecture of Novel Differentiation), ein Büro für Architektur, Innenarchitektur und Möbeldesign, das 2011 mit dem Architecture of the Year Award des Korean Institute of Architects (KIA) ausgezeichnet wurde (für Topoject, Gyeonggi-do, 2010, hier vorgestellt). **TAE KYOUNG LEE** wurde 1981 in Südkorea geboren. Sie absolvierte einen B. A. an der University of Toronto (2006) und einen M. Arch. an der Yale University (2010). Seit 2010 ist sie als Senior Researcher für AND tätig. Neben Topoject gehören zu den Projekten von AND u. a. Skinspace (Gyeonggi-do, 2010, ebenfalls hier vorgestellt) und Aggrenad (Gyeongsangnam-do, 2011). Drei Häuser in Gangwon-do befinden sich derzeit in der Planung und Ausführung.

Né à 1976 à Janggye (Corée-du-Sud), **EUI YEOB JEONG** a obtenu un Bachelor d'ingénierie en architecture à l'université Inha (Incheon, Corée-du-Sud, 2002) et un M.Arch. à l'université de Toronto (2006). Il a travaillé comme stagiaire pour Morphosis Architects (Los Angeles, 2004), MJM Architects à Toronto (2006) et comme architecte junior pour Space Group à Séoul (2007–10). En 2010, il a créé sa propre agence AND (Architecture of Novel Differentiation) et réalisé des projets d'architecture, d'aménagement intérieur et de design de mobilier. En 2011, AND a remporté le Prix d'architecture de l'année de l'Institut coréen des architectes (KIA, pour Topoject, Gyeonggi-do, 2010, publié ici). **TAE KYOUNG LEE** est née en 1981 en Corée-du-Sud. Elle a obtenu son B.A. à l'université de Toronto (2006) et son M.Arch. à l'université de Yale (2010). Elle est directrice de recherche chez AND depuis 2010. Outre le Topoject, figurent parmi les projets d'AND le Skinspace (Gyeonggi-do, 2010, également publié ici) et Aggrenad (Gyeongsangnam-do, 2011). Trois maisons sont en cours de conception et de construction dans le Gangwon-do.

SKINSPACE

Yangpyeong-gun, Gyeonggi-do, South Korea, 2010

Address: not disclosed. Area: 130 m²
Client: Il Young Jeong. Cost: $80 000

This house was designed for the artist Il Young Jeong, who originally proposed a budget of just $30 000 for a living space and studio. The client agreed to double the budget, and the final figure was a bit higher. The architect used cast concrete and ordinary plywood shaped into "scales" on a site not more than one hour from Seoul. AND used a computer program to design the wooden and metal parts for the project which permitted them to be manufactured with a laser-cutting process. In an article published by *The New York Times*, the artist is quoted as saying: "The building invites nature inward. It allows me to feel nature's changes and observe them more vividly." The architect describes the project in rather poetic terms: "The skin of the façade is gently rolled inward as it breaks up the boundary between the interior and the exterior. The rolled-in surfaces lift up as they enter the interior, and they traverse the interior toward the opposite side of the wall. During the crossing, the panels of the skin are split and distorted, creating a loose crack. The landscape permeates through the crack, and so does light. The light colors the space with every moment in time. As a body moves, the space of the crack changes sensitively. Skin becomes space, and space becomes skin."

Dieses Haus wurde im Auftrag des Künstlers Il Young Jeong entworfen. Ursprünglich war ein Budget von lediglich 30 000 $ für ein Wohnatelier vorgesehen. Il Young Jeong war einverstanden, das Budget zu verdoppeln. Die Endsumme lag noch etwas höher. Für das Projekt, das sich eine Stunde von Seoul entfernt befindet, kamen Gussbeton und einfache, schuppenartig angeordnete Schichtholzplatten zum Einsatz. AND verwendete ein Computerprogramm für den Entwurf der Holz- und Metallteile, die anschließend mithilfe von Lasertechnologie zugeschnitten werden konnten. In einem in der *New York Times* veröffentlichten Artikel sagt der Künstler: „Das Haus lädt die Natur ins Innere ein und erlaubt mir, ihre Veränderlichkeit hautnah mitzuerleben." Der Architekt beschreibt das Projekt auf recht poetische Weise folgendermaßen: „Die Fassadenhaut rollt sich sacht ins Innere und hebt die Grenze zwischen innen und außen auf. Im Innern hebt sie sich empor und durchläuft den Raum hin zur gegenüberliegenden Wand. Nach und nach teilen und drehen sich die Platten und bilden einen weiten Riss, durch den Licht und Natur dringen. In jedem Moment färbt Licht den Raum. Bewegt man sich, verändert sich das Erscheinungsbild des Risses. Die Oberfläche wird zum Raum, der Raum zur Oberfläche."

Cette maison a été conçue pour l'artiste Il Young Jeong qui disposait à l'origine d'un budget limité à 30 000 $ pour un séjour et un atelier. Le client a accepté de doubler son budget, mais le prix final a été légèrement supérieur. L'architecte a utilisé du béton coulé et du contreplaqué ordinaire sous forme d'« écailles » sur un site à moins d'une heure de Séoul. AND a eu recours à un logiciel pour concevoir les pièces métalliques et en bois du projet, ce qui a permis leur fabrication par découpe au laser. Un article publié dans le *New York Times* cite l'artiste : « Le bâtiment invite la nature à pénétrer à l'intérieur. Cela me permet de ressentir les changements de la nature et de les observer de façon plus vivante. » L'architecte décrit le projet en termes plutôt poétiques : « La peau de la façade est délicatement roulée vers l'intérieur lorsqu'elle brise la frontière entre l'intérieur et l'extérieur. Les surfaces enroulées s'élèvent au moment où elles entrent, puis traversent l'intérieur pour rejoindre le côté opposé du mur. Pendant la traversée, les panneaux de la peau sont séparés et déformés, créant ainsi une large césure. Le paysage pénètre à travers la césure, de même que la lumière. La lumière colore l'espace à chaque instant. L'espace de la césure se modifie imperceptiblement à mesure que le corps progresse. La peau se fait espace et l'espace devient peau. »

To the left, a plan of the site showing a roof view of the house. Below, a section drawing shows the same kind of transparency that is visible in the images on these two pages.

Links ein Geländeplan mit einer Dachansicht des Hauses. Die Schnittzeichnung spiegelt die auf den Fotos zu erkennende Transparenz des Gebäudes wider (unten).

À gauche, un plan du site avec la toiture de la maison. Ci-dessous, une coupe révèle le même type de transparence visible sur les illustrations de ces deux pages.

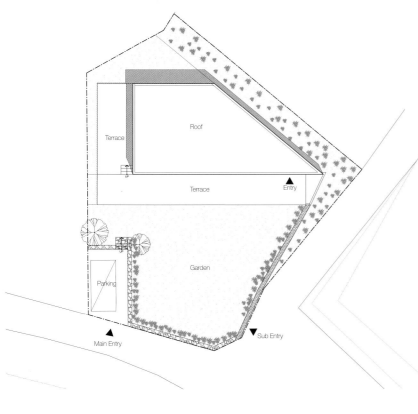

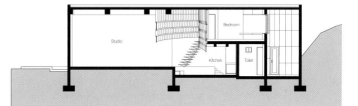

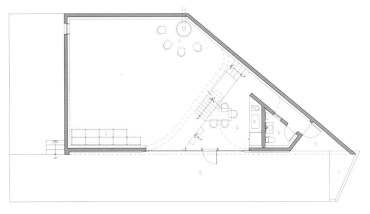

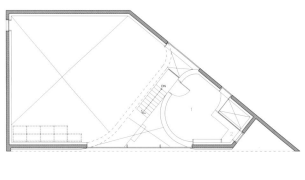

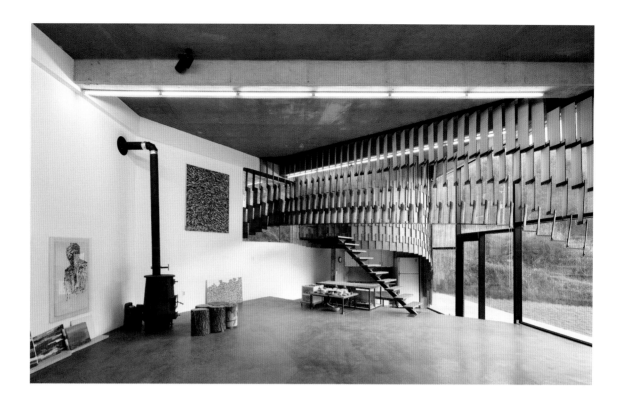

Left page, the ground- and upper-floor plans and an image showing the wooden fins that curve away from the glazed façade. The light wooden stairway is also seen on this page, with a view of the generous open space on the ground floor.

Grundrisse des Erd- und Oberge-schosses sowie ein Foto der schup-penförmig angeordneten Holzplatten, die sich von der Glasfassade in den Raum krümmen (linke Seite). Erkenn-bar sind auch die leichte Treppe und das großzügige Erdgeschoss.

Page de gauche, les plans du rez-de-chaussée et de l'étage avec une image montrant les ailettes de bois qui décrivent une courbe s'éloignant de la façade vitrée. Tout en légèreté, l'escalier en bois est également visible sur cette page avec une vue sur le généreux espace du rez-de-chaussée.

TOPOJECT

Yangpyeong-gun, Gyeonggi-do, South Korea, 2010

Address: not disclosed. Area: 197 m²
Client: not disclosed. Cost: $450 000

This single-family house for a couple from Seoul was built on a 600-square-meter plot of land near a narrow road. The house opens to the south where there is a view of the natural setting and a creek. The architect explains that his design is a "mutant" combination of an "object building" and a "landscape building," whence its curious name. The "topography becomes an object, creating semi-private outdoor spaces," while the "continuous exterior spaces meet the interior spaces at all levels adding compact, yet rich spatial qualities. The boundary between exterior and interior, land and building, subject and object becomes ambiguous," according to the architect. The exterior of the house is finished in stained red cedar panels and a Dryvit exterior insulation and finishing system.

Dieses Einfamilienhaus für ein Paar aus Seoul liegt auf einem 600 m² großen Grundstück unweit einer schmalen Straße und öffnet sich nach Süden auf eine Landschaft mit Bach. Der Architekt erklärt, bei dem Entwurf handele es sich um einen „hybride" Verbindung aus „Objektgebäude" und „Landschaftsgebäude". Daher auch der eigenwillige Name. Die „Topografie wird zum Objekt, wodurch halbprivate Räume unter freiem Himmel entstehen", während die „Außenbereiche des Hauses auf allen Ebenen auf die Innenräume treffen und kompakte, aber eindrucksvolle Raumsituationen entstehen lassen. Die Grenze zwischen innen und außen, Landschaft und Gebäude, Subjekt und Objekt verschwimmt", so der Architekt. Die Fassade ist mit gebeizten Paneelen aus dem Holz des Riesenlebensbaums verkleidet und verfügt über ein Dryvit-Wärmedämmverbundsystem.

Cette maison de week-end a été construite pour un couple de Séoul sur une parcelle de 600 m² près d'une route étroite. Elle s'ouvre au sud sur le cadre naturel et une crique. L'architecte explique que son parti consiste en une combinaison « mutante » entre un « bâtiment-objet » et un « bâtiment-paysage », d'où son étrange nom. La « topographie devient un objet, créant des espaces extérieurs semi-privés », tandis que les « espaces extérieurs continus rencontrent les espaces intérieurs à tous les niveaux en ajoutant des qualités spatiales certes compactes, mais riches. La frontière entre extérieur et intérieur, paysage et bâtiment, sujet et objet, devient ambiguë » selon l'architecte. La maison est revêtue de panneaux de cèdre rouge teinté avec un système d'isolation et de finition de parois extérieures Dryvit.

The contrast between the dark wood façade, the broad glazed surfaces of the house, and the white interior is evident in this view taken at nightfall.

Auf diesem bei Dämmerung aufgenommenen Foto ist der Kontrast zwischen der dunklen Holzfassade, den großen Glasflächen und den weißen Innenräumen gut erkennbar.

Le contraste entre la façade sombre en bois, les larges baies vitrées de la maison et l'intérieur blanc frappe dans cette vue prise à la tombée du jour.

Below, a site plan and an image showing how the lawn seems to come right up on top of the house. Above, the larger upper volume hangs over the swimming pool and the smaller, transparent lower floor.

Unten ein Geländeplan und eine Ansicht der Rasenfläche, die sich geradewegs aufs Dach zu erstrecken scheint. Im Bild oben ragt der obere größere Teil des Gebäudes über den Swimmingpool und das kleinere, transparente Untergeschoss.

Ci-dessous, un plan du site et une image qui révèle comment la pelouse semble monter jusqu'au sommet de la maison. Ci-dessus, le vaste volume supérieur est suspendu au-dessus de la piscine et de l'étage inférieur, plus petit et transparent.

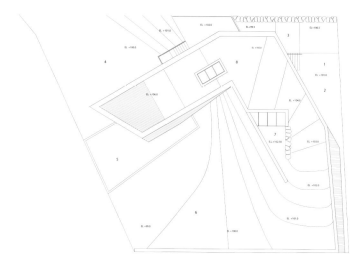

Combining wood, metal, concrete, and glass, the architects obtain an interesting contrast between the hard materials and the soft outdoor landscape. Right page, section drawings and an interior view that emphasizes the bright atmosphere.

Holz, Metall, Beton und Glas: Die Architekten erzielen einen interessanten Kontrast zwischen der Solidität dieser Materialien und der Weichheit der Landschaft. Rechts zwei Querschnitte und eine Ansicht der hellen Innenräume.

En associant bois, métal, béton et verre, les architectes réussissent à créer un contraste intéressant entre la dureté des matériaux et la douceur du paysage. Page de droite, des coupes et une vue intérieure soulignent la luminosité des espaces.

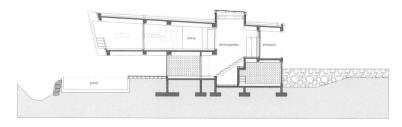

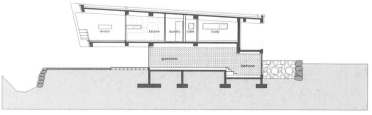

TADAO ANDO

Tadao Ando Architect & Associates
Osaka, Japan

Born in Osaka in 1941, **TADAO ANDO** was self-educated as an architect, largely through his travels in the United States, Europe, and Africa (1962–69). He founded Tadao Ando Architect & Associates in Osaka in 1969. He has received the Alvar Aalto Medal, Finnish Association of Architects (1985); the Medaille d'or, French Academy of Architecture (1989); the 1992 Carlsberg Prize; and the 1995 Pritzker Prize. Notable buildings include Church on the Water (Hokkaido, Japan, 1988); Japan Pavilion Expo '92 (Seville, Spain, 1992); Forest of Tombs Museum (Kumamoto, Japan, 1992); the Suntory Museum (Osaka, Japan, 1994); Museum of Wood (Mikata, Hyogo, Japan, 1991–94, published here); Rokko Housing (Kobe, Japan, 1983–99); Awaji Yumebutai (Awajishima, Hyogo, Japan, 1997–2000); the Pulitzer Foundation for the Arts (St. Louis, Missouri, USA, 1997–2000); Komyo-ji Temple (Saijo, Ehime, Japan, 1998–2000, also published here); the Modern Art Museum of Fort Worth (Fort Worth, Texas, USA, 1999–2002); and the Chichu Art Museum on the island of Naoshima in the Inland Sea (Japan, 2004). He also completed the Naoshima Benesse House Park and Beach (Naoshima, Kagawa, Japan, 2004–06); the Omote Sando Hills complex (Tokyo, Japan, 2006); 21_21 Design Sight (Tokyo, Japan, 2004–07); Tokyu Toyoko Line Shibuya Station (Shibuya-ku, Tokyo, Japan, 2006–08); an expansion of the Clark Art Institute (Williamstown, Massachusetts, USA, 2006–08); and the renovation of the Punta della Dogana (Venice, Italy, 2007–09). Most recently, Tadao Ando completed the Stone Sculpture Museum (near Bad Kreuznach, Germany, 1996–2010); the Shiba Ryotaro Memorial Museum (Higashiosaka, Osaka, Japan, 1998–2001/2010); the WSJ-352 Building on the Novartis Campus (Basel, Switzerland, 2004–10); the Lee Ufan Museum (Naoshima, Kagawa, Japan, 2007–10); and the Ando Museum (Naoshima, Kagawa, Japan, 2012–13, also published here). He is working on the Abu Dhabi Maritime Museum (Abu Dhabi, UAE, 2006–); and a house for the designer Tom Ford near Santa Fe (New Mexico, USA).

TADAO ANDO wurde 1941 in Osaka geboren. Als architektonischer Autodidakt hat er sich vor allem durch Reisen in die USA sowie nach Europa und Afrika (1962–69) weitergebildet. Tadao Ando Architect & Associates gründete er 1969 in Osaka. Er wurde mit der Alvar-Aalto-Medaille des Finnischen Architektenverbands (1985), der Medaille d'or der Französischen Akademie für Architektur (1989), dem Carlsberg-Preis (1992) und dem Pritzker-Preis (1995) ausgezeichnet. Bedeutende Projekte sind die Kirche am Wasser (Hokkaido, Japan, 1988), der Japanische Pavillon auf der Expo '92 (Sevilla, 1992), das Museum Wald der Gräber (Kumamoto, Japan, 1992), das Suntory Museum (Osaka, 1994), das Holzmuseum (Mikata, Hyogo, Japan, 1991–94, hier vorgestellt), die Wohnanlage Rokko (Kobe, Japan, 1983–99), Awaji Yumebutai (Awajishima, Hyogo, Japan, 1997–2000), die Pulitzer Foundation for the Arts (St. Louis, Missouri, USA, 1997–2000), der Tempel Komyo-ji (Saijo, Ehime, Japan, 1998–2000, ebenfalls hier vorgestellt), das Modern Art Museum in Fort Worth (Texas, 1999–2002) sowie das Chichu-Kunstmuseum auf der Insel Naoshima im Seto-Binnenmeer (Japan, 2004). Zu Andos in der jüngeren Vergangenheit abgeschlossenen Projekten zählen Park und Strand des Naoshima Benesse House (Naoshima, Kagawa, Japan, 2004–06), Omote Sando Hills (Tokio, 2006), 21_21 Design Sight (Tokio, 2004–07), die Station Shibuya der Tokyu-Toyoko-Linie (Shibuya-ku, Tokio, 2006–08), eine Erweiterung des Clark Art Institute (Williamstown, Massachusetts, 2006–08) sowie ein Umbau der Punta della Dogana (Venedig, 2007–09). 2010 beendete Ando das Steinskulpturenmuseum (nahe Bad Kreuznach, 1996–2010), das Shiba-Ryotaro-Gedenkmuseum (Higashiosaka, Osaka, 1998–2001/10), das WSJ-352-Gebäude auf dem Novartis Campus (Basel, 2004–10), das Lee-Ufan-Museum (Naoshima, Kagawa, 2007–10) sowie das Ando-Museum (Naoshima, Kagawa, 2012–13, ebenfalls hier vorgestellt). Ando arbeitet derzeit am Meeresmuseum von Abu Dhabi (VAE, seit 2006) und an einem Haus für den Designer Tom Ford bei Santa Fe (New Mexico, USA).

Né à Osaka en 1941, **TADAO ANDO** a étudié l'architecture en autodidacte, en grande partie lors de voyages aux États-Unis, en Europe et en Afrique (1962–69). Il a fondé Tadao Ando Architect & Associates à Osaka en 1969. Il a reçu la médaille Alvar Aalto de l'Association finlandaise des architectes en 1985, la médaille d'or de l'Académie française d'architecture en 1989, le prix Carlsberg en 1992 et le prix Pritzker en 1995. Ses réalisations les plus notables comprennent l'Église sur l'eau (Hokkaido, Japon, 1988) ; le pavillon du Japon à l'Expo' 92 de Séville ; le musée de la Forêt des tombes (Kumamoto, Japon, 1992) ; le musée Suntory (Osaka, 1994) ; le musée du Bois (Mikata, Hyogo, Japon, 1991–94, publié ici) ; les immeubles de logement Rokko (Kobe, Japon, 1983–99) ; le complexe Awaji Yumebutai (Awajishima, Hyogo, Japon, 1997–2000) ; la Fondation Pulitzer pour les arts (Saint Louis, Missouri, 1997–2000) ; le temple Komyo-ji (Saijo, Ehime, Japon, 1998–2000, également publié ici) ; le Musée d'art moderne de Fort Worth (Texas, 1999–2002) et le Musée d'art Chichu sur l'île de Naoshima dans la mer Intérieure (Japon, 2004). Il a également réalisé le complexe Benesse House Park and Beach (Naoshima, Kagawa, Japon, 2004–06) ; le complexe Omote Sando Hills (Tokyo, 2006) ; le centre dédié au design 21_21 Design Sight (Tokyo, 2004–07) ; la station Shibuya de la ligne de métro Tokyu Toyoko (Shibuya-ku, Tokyo, 2006–08) ; une extension du Clark Art Institute (Williamstown, Massachusetts, 2006–08) et la rénovation de la Punta della Dogana (Venise, 2007–09). Plus récemment, Tadao Ando a achevé le musée de la Sculpture sur pierre (près de Bad Kreuznach, Allemagne, 1996–2010) ; le musée du Mémorial Shiba Ryotaro (Higashiosaka, Osaka, 1998–2001/2010) ; l'immeuble WSJ-352 du campus Novartis (Bâle, 2004–10) ; le musée Lee Ufan (Naoshima, Kagawa, 2007–10) et le musée Ando (Naoshima, Kagawa, Japon, 2012–13, également publié ici). Il travaille actuellement sur le Musée maritime d'Abou Dhabi (EAU, 2006–) et sur une maison pour le designer Tom Ford près de Santa Fe (Nouveau-Mexique, États-Unis).

ANDO MUSEUM

Naoshima, Kagawa, Japan, 2012–13

Address: 736–2 Naoshima, Kagawa 761–3110, Japan, +81 87 892 3754 (Fukutake Foundation),
www.benesse-artsite.jp/en/ando-museum. Area: 126 m²
Client: Naoshima Fukutake Art Museum Foundation. Cost: not disclosed

This structure is actually based on the reuse of an old wooden house situated on the island of Naoshima in the Seto Inland Sea of Japan, where the architect has worked frequently in the past at the request of the head of the Benesse Corporation, Soichiro Fukutake. Tadao Ando states: "There are many houses on the island built more than one hundred years ago. The continuous tiled roofs of the houses that look as if they had been folded and stacked on top of each other, the exterior walls of yakisugi (blackened fire-treated cedar), and the earthen walls represent the passage of time and the mark left by generations of inhabitants and have become part of the scenery of Naoshima, just like the natural environment…" It was Soichiro Fukutake who decided to restore a number of these houses and to turn them into spaces for contemporary art (Art Houses), as was the case with the interventions of Tatsuo Miyajima and Rei Naito among others. The **ANDO MUSEUM** was conceived in the same way. Ando explains that the building is intended "to create a multilayered exhibition space that changes its expression at every moment with strong light penetrating through a slit opening between the old and new architecture." The exhibition focuses on Tadao Ando's projects on Naoshima, but also on the history of the island. The structure includes office space as well as the gallery. Interior floors are in exposed concrete with a trowel finish. Exposed concrete is also used for interior walls and ceilings, but the blackened cedar board exterior of the house as well as the exposed timber roof frame make the presence of wood significant.

Diesem Projekt liegt ein altes Holzhaus auf der im japanischen Seto-Binnenmeer gelegenen Insel Naoshima zugrunde, auf der Ando im Auftrag von Soichiro Fukutake, dem Vorstand der Benesse Corporation, in der Vergangenheit häufig tätig war. Tadao Ando: „Es gibt auf der Insel viele Häuser, die vor mehr als 100 Jahren errichtet wurden. Die Ziegeldächer erwecken den Eindruck, sie seien gefaltet und übereinandergestapelt. Die aus *yakisugi* (schwarzem, feuerbehandeltem Zedernholz) bestehenden Außenwände und die Erdwände stehen für das Vergehen der Zeit und die Spuren, die von Generationen von Inselbewohnern hinterlassen wurden. Sie sind Teil der Inselkulisse, so wie die Landschaft …" Es war Soichiro Fukutakes Idee, einige dieser Häuser instandzusetzen und für die Präsentation zeitgenössischer Kunst zu nutzen, wie geschehen bei den Interventionen von Tatsuo Miyajima und Rei Naito. Das **ANDO-MUSEUM** wurde genauso geplant. Ando erklärt, das Gebäude solle „ein vielschichtiger Ausstellungsraum sein, dessen Anmutung sich von einem Moment auf den nächsten wandeln kann, wenn durch eine Spaltöffnung zwischen der alten und der neuen Architektur helles Licht fällt". Die Ausstellung konzentriert sich auf Andos Projekte auf Naoshima, geht aber auch auf die Geschichte der Insel ein. In dem Gebäude befinden sich neben den Ausstellungs- auch Büroräume. Die Böden im Innenbereich bestehen aus geglättetem Sichtbeton. Auch die Innenwände und Decken sind aus Sichtbeton gefertigt. Außenwände aus geschwärztem Zedernholz und das offenliegende Dachgebälk geben dem Holz jedoch eine große Präsenz.

Ce bâtiment s'appuie en fait sur une ancienne maison en bois située sur l'île de Naoshima dans la mer Intérieure de Seto au Japon, île où l'architecte a autrefois fréquemment travaillé à la demande du directeur de la Benesse Corporation, Soichiro Fukutake. Tadao Ando précise : « Il y a sur l'île de nombreuses maisons dont la construction remonte à plus de cent ans. Les toitures continues en tuiles des maisons qui semblent avoir été pliées et empilées les unes sur les autres, les murs extérieurs de yakisugi (cèdre noirci traité par le feu) et les murs de terre représentent le passage du temps et l'empreinte des générations d'habitants ; ils font partie du décor de Naoshima au même titre que l'environnement naturel… » C'est Soichiro Fukutake qui a pris la décision de restaurer une partie de ces maisons et de les transformer en espaces dédiés à l'art contemporain (maisons d'art), comme cela fut le cas pour les interventions, entre autres, de Tatsuo Miyajima et Rei Naito. Le **MUSÉE ANDO** est d'une conception similaire. Ando explique que le bâtiment est censé « créer un espace d'exposition multicouche dont l'expression change à tout moment sous l'effet d'une forte lumière pénétrant à travers une fente entre l'ancienne et la nouvelle architecture ». L'exposition se focalise sur les projets de Tadao Ando à Naoshima, mais aussi sur l'histoire de l'île. Le bâtiment comprend des bureaux, mais aussi la galerie. Les sols intérieurs sont en béton apparent lissé à la truelle. On retrouve le béton apparent sur les murs et les plafonds intérieurs, tandis que l'extérieur en planches de cèdre noirci révèle autant la forte présence du bois que la charpente visible du toit.

Set in an old fishing village where the typical architecture has sloping tile roofs and charred cedar walls, the Ando Museum features a modern interior space, seen in the section drawing below.

Das Ando-Museum liegt in einem alten Fischerdorf, dessen typische Architektur sich durch Ziegeldächer und feuergeschwärztes Zedernholz auszeichnet. Der Querschnitt unten zeigt den modernen Innenraum des Museums.

Situé dans un ancien village de pêcheurs où l'architecture typique est faite de toitures inclinées en tuiles et de murs en cèdre carbonisé, le musée Ando se caractérise par son espace intérieur moderne que dévoile la coupe ci-dessous.

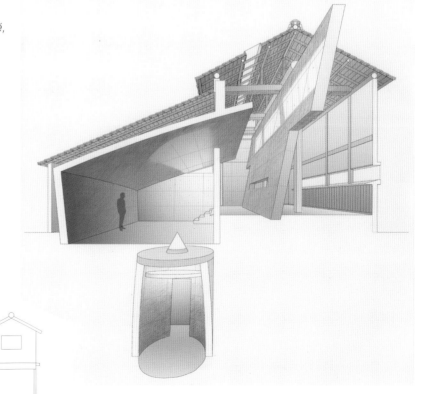

As he has in other historic buildings like the much larger Punta della Dogana in Venice (Italy), Ando contrasts the old wood of the original building with his strong, smooth concrete walls.

Wie bei der Neugestaltung anderer historischer Gebäude auch, darunter die sehr viel größere Punta della Dogana in Venedig, kontrastiert Ando das alte Holz des Originalgebäudes mit massiven, glatten Betonwänden.

À l'image de ce qu'il a déjà fait pour d'autres bâtiments historiques comme le Punta della Dogana à Venise (Italie) plus grand, Tadao Ando oppose l'ancien bois du bâtiment d'origine aux murs en béton robustes et tendres.

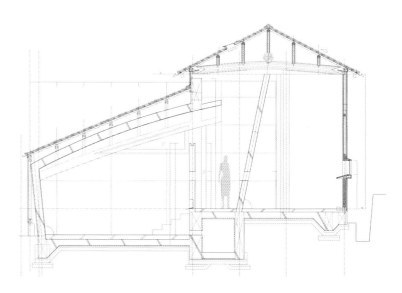

Even in a small space, the architect is able to engender a feeling of monumentality. Here natural light filters down from above into the new gallery.

Selbst in kleinen Räumen gelingt es dem Architekten, einen Eindruck von Monumentalität zu erzeugen. Von oben fällt Tageslicht in die neuen Galerieräume.

Même dans un petit espace, l'architecte est capable de créer un sentiment de monumentalité. Ici, la lumière naturelle tombe du haut dans la nouvelle galerie.

KOMYO-JI TEMPLE

Saijo, Ehime, Japan, 1998–2000

Address: 550 Omachi Saijo-shi, Ehime, Japan,
+81 897 53 4583, www.koumyouji.com. Site area: 3221.8 m², Floor area: 1284.1 m²
Client: Komyo-ji Temple. Cost: not disclosed

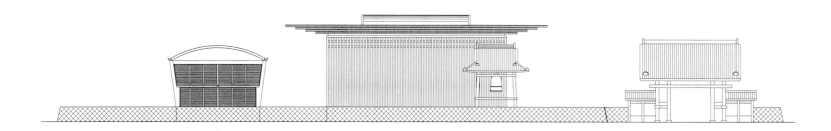

Although permission was given to the architect to demolish the existing main gate and bell tower of the temple, he chose to conserve both, and set the new structure on a spring-fed pond.

Obwohl der Architekt das bestehende Haupttor und den Glockenturm des Tempels hätte abreißen dürfen, entschied er sich, beides zu erhalten und den Neubau umgeben von einem Quellwasserbecken zu errichten.

Bien que l'architecte avait obtenu l'autorisation de démolir la porte principale et le campanile du temple, il a décidé de les conserver tous deux et de les entourer d'un bassin alimenté par une source.

Located on the island of Shikoku, the small town of Saijo (Ehime) has the particularity of being one of the only places in Japan where each home has running spring water all year long. Intended as the reconstruction of an existing 250-year-old temple, **KOMYO-JI** was to be "a place where people would come to gather together." Although the design does not specifically adhere to religious tradition, its wooden forms are not entirely alien to temple architecture. The architect insisted that his design, consisting of three layers of interlocking beams supported by 16 columns in four groups for the temple itself, should represent something of a return to the founding principles of wooden temple structures. Open lattice walls allow ample daylight to penetrate into the main sanctuary hall and, as is often the case in the architecture of Ando, light from the surrounding reflecting pool gives variety and liveliness to the otherwise inanimate forms. The pool is of course a clear reference to the omnipresence of spring water in Saijo. Ando is still better known for his use of concrete than for wood, but as he did in the Japanese Pavilion for Expo '92 or in other later buildings such as the Museum of Wood, he shows a mastery of this traditional Japanese building material that contributes to a renewal of its aesthetic and structural usefulness in architecture. The wooden temple at Komyo-ji is flanked by a reinforced concrete structure that houses the residence of the priest, and a consecrated area where the ashes of community members are stored by their families. Ando designed a surprising large-scale plastic curtain for the walls of the hall that leads to the burial area, again echoing ancient traditions in a very modern context. The walls of the concrete volume, angling out toward the roof, make space for the ash repositories but also imply an upward movement that does not belie the spiritual function of this place.

Die auf der Insel Shikoku gelegene Kleinstadt Saijo (Ehime) ist einer der wenigen japanischen Orte, in denen jeder Haushalt das ganze Jahr über mit fließendem Quellwasser versorgt wird. Als Rekonstruktion eines bestehenden, 250 Jahre alten Tempels sollte **KOMYO-JI** ein Ort sein, „an dem Menschen zusammenkommen können". Obgleich sich der Entwurf nicht besonders eng an religiöse Traditionen hält, sind seine hölzernen Formen der klassischen Tempelarchitektur nicht fremd. Das Bauwerk ist aus drei Schichten ineinander greifender Balken konstruiert, welche durch vier Gruppen aus jeweils 16 Säulen gestützt werden, und bedeutet nach Aussage des Architekten eine Rückkehr zu den ursprünglichen Konstruktionsprinzipien von Holztempelbauten. Gitterförmig durchbrochene Trennwände sorgen für eine ausreichende Belichtung des großen Sanktuariums, und – wie häufig in Andos Architektur – auch hier verleihen die Lichtreflexe des umlaufenden Wasserbeckens den ansonsten eher statischen Formen Abwechslung und Lebendigkeit. Das Bassin selbst nimmt offensichtlich Bezug auf das in Saijo allgegenwärtige Quellwasser. Ando ist zwar eher für die Verwendung von Beton als von Holz bekannt, aber wie schon in seinem Japanischen Pavillon für die Expo '92 in Sevilla und jüngeren Bauten wie dem Holzmuseum in Hyogo, beweist er auch hier eine Meisterschaft im Umgang mit diesem traditionellen japanischen Baumaterial, die zu einer Erneuerung der ästhetischen und bautechnischen Qualitäten von Holz in der Architektur beiträgt. Der Holztempel in Komyo-ji wird von einem Gebäude aus Stahlbeton flankiert, das die Wohnräume des Priesters und einen geweihten Bereich beherbergt, in dem die Gefäße mit der Asche der verstorbenen Gemeindemitglieder von deren Hinterbliebenen aufbewahrt werden. In dem überraschend großformatigen Plastikvorhang, den Ando für die Wände der Halle vor dem Beisetzungsbereich gestaltet hat, finden wiederum alte Traditionen ihren Nachhall in einem modernen Kontext. Die sich zum Dach hin weitenden Wände des Betongebäudes schaffen nicht nur Raum für die Urnen, sondern symbolisieren eine Aufwärtsbewegung, die der spirituellen Funktion dieses Ortes entspricht.

Situé sur l'île de Shikoku, la petite ville de Saijo (Ehime) présente la particularité d'être l'un des rares lieux au Japon où chaque maison bénéficie de sa propre source d'eau permanente. Reconstruction d'un temple existant vieux de 250 ans, **KOMYO-JI** se veut « un lieu où viennent les gens pour se réunir». Bien que le projet ne relève pas spécifiquement de la tradition religieuse, sa forme n'est pas entièrement étrangère à celle des temples japonais. L'architecte précise que ce plan consistant en trois strates de poutres entrecroisées soutenues par 16 colonnes réparties en quatre groupes pour le temple lui-même, représente une sorte de retour aux principes fondateurs des structures des temples en bois. Des murs en lattis de bois à claire-voie permettent à la lumière naturelle de pénétrer dans le sanctuaire et, comme souvent chez Ando, les reflets du bassin qui les entourent animent et font varier la perception des formes par ailleurs austères. Le bassin est une référence à l'omniprésence de l'eau de source à Saijo. Ando est davantage connu pour ses réalisations en béton qu'en bois, mais comme pour le Pavillon japonais de l'Expo '92, ou le musée du Bois, il témoigne ici d'une maîtrise de ce matériau traditionnel qui contribue au renouvellement de son esthétique et de son utilisation structurelle en architecture. Le temple en bois Komyo-ji est flanqué d'une construction en béton armé qui abrite la résidence du prêtre et une zone consacrée dans laquelle sont déposées les cendres des membres de la communauté. Ando a conçu un vaste rideau en plastique étonnant pour les murs du hall qui conduit à ce columbarium, là encore en rappel contemporain d'une très ancienne tradition. Les murs du volume en béton dans lequel sont déposées les urnes cinéraires s'évasent vers le toit en un mouvement ascensionnel qui renforce la fonction spirituelle du lieu.

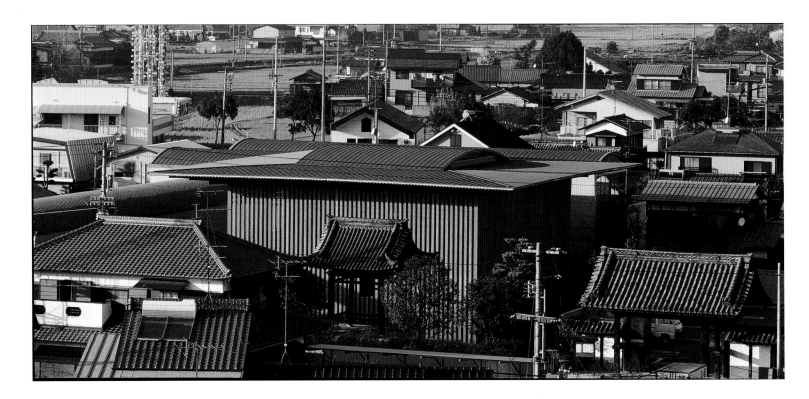

Left page, the new temple structure is visible rising above the roofs of the older precinct buildings.

Linke Seite: Der neue Tempelbau erhebt sich weithin sichtbar über die Dächer des alten Tempelbezirks.

Page de gauche : la nouvelle structure du temple s'élève bien au-dessus des toits des bâtiments plus anciens du quartier.

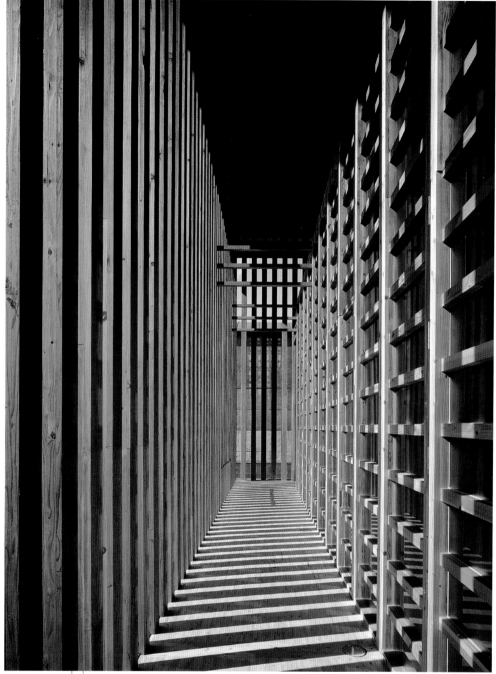

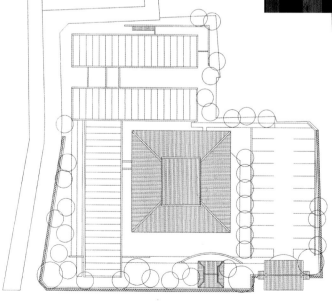

Left, a site plan shows the new structures in context. Above, the vertical wooden slats employed by the architect admit ample natural light while remaining in the spirit of Japanese temples.

Der Lageplan links zeigt die neuen Bauten im Kontext. Die vertikalen Holzlatten (oben) lassen reichlich natürliches Licht in den Tempel und erzeugen eine für japanische Tempel typische Stimmung.

Le plan de situation de gauche montre les nouveaux bâtiments en contexte. Ci-dessus, les lattes de bois verticales utilisées par l'architecte laissent généreusement passer la lumière du jour tout en restant dans l'esprit des temples japonais.

Inside the concrete volume, this waiting area is used by grieving families during funerals. The unusual plastic curtain over the window is echoed by a symmetrical curtain on the opposite wall. Ando's geometric (and surely not Christian) cross shows through the curtain.

Im Innern des Betongebäudes wird der Wartebereich während der Beisetzung von den Trauergästen benutzt. Dem ungewöhnlichen Kunststoffvorhang entspricht ein gleicher Vorhang an der gegenüberliegenden Wand. Andos geometrisches (und gewiss nicht christliches) Kreuz ist durch den Vorhang zu sehen.

À l'intérieur du volume en béton, cette aire d'attente est à la disposition de familles pendant les funérailles. Le curieux rideau de plastique devant la baie possède sa réplique sur le mur opposé. La « croix » d'Ando, qui n'est pas chrétienne, se retrouve en transparence.

Left: Inside the actual funerary area, where ashes are preserved in niches in the wooden volume to the right of the image. The concrete is varnished and reflects the low light coming from the far end of the space.

Links: Innenansicht des eigentlichen Beisetzungsraums, wo die Asche der Verstorbenen in hölzernen Nischen (rechts im Bild) aufbewahrt wird. Der Beton ist lackiert und reflektiert das am äußersten Ende des Raums einfallende Licht.

À gauche : intérieur du columbarium où l'on conserve les cendres dans des niches du volume en bois, à droite de la photo. Le béton verni reflète la lumière assourdie venant de l'extrémité de la salle.

MUSEUM OF WOOD

Mikata, Hyogo, Japan, 1991–94

Address: 951 Muraokaku Wachi, Kami, Mikata,
Hyogo 667–1347, Japan +81 796 96 1388. Site area: 168 310 m², Floor area: 2694.6 m²
Client: Museum of Wood. Cost: not disclosed

This remarkable museum was built to commemorate the 45th National Wood Festival held in Hyogo Prefecture, which occurs on Arbor Day, a ceremony founded by the emperor of Japan in the 1950s following the wartime destruction of the forests. Located three hours by car from Osaka near a ski resort, the remote wooded site covers an area of 168 310 m². Built of wood with a steel frame and reinforced concrete, the museum features a ring-shaped exhibit hall with a 46-meter outer diameter and a 22-meter void within. The access bridge cuts directly through the structure, bridging over a central fountain, and leading visitors 200 meters further to an observation deck and guesthouse. Inside the museum, a sloping floor guides visitors down along a spiral path, which takes them twice into the central void. Locally milled Hyogo cedar was used for the posts and beams. The enormous laminated wood columns, rising to a height of 16 meters, are arranged in a manner that recalls the forest. Unfortunately, the quality of the exhibits, with models of wooden houses and light-box images, is not equivalent to the extraordinary quality of the architecture. Although not reminiscent of any particular temple, this structure does give at the very least an impression of communion with nature, and recalls that Japan's rich forests are the source of its traditional interest in wooden architecture. Like a number of his other museums (Chikatsu-Asuka Historical Museum, for example), the **MUSEUM OF WOOD** is a homage by the architect to the sources of Japan's culture and history.

Das bemerkenswerte Museum wurde zum Gedenken an das 45. Staatliche Holzfestival der Präfektur Hyogo errichtet, das traditionell am Tag des Baums stattfindet. Dieser Nationalfeiertag wurde vom japanischen Kaiser in den 1950er-Jahren nach der kriegsbedingten Zerstörung der Wälder ins Leben gerufen. Das abgelegene, bewaldete Gelände liegt etwa drei Autostunden von Osaka entfernt in der Nähe eines Skigebiets und umfasst eine Fläche von 168 310 m². Das in Stahlskelettbauweise aus Holz und Stahlbeton erbaute Museum besteht aus einer ringförmigen Ausstellungshalle mit einem Außenradius von 46 m und einem zentralen Hohlraum von 22 m Durchmesser. Die Zugangsrampe, die über einen zentralen Springbrunnen führt, durchschneidet das gesamte Gebäude und bringt die Besucher zu einer 200 m entfernt liegenden Aussichtsplattform sowie einem Gästehaus. Im Innern des Museums führt ein leicht abschüssiger Boden die Besucher in zwei Spiralwindungen bis hinunter zum Erdgeschoss des zentralen Hohlraums. Die Pfeiler und Balken bestehen aus einheimischer Hyogo-Zeder; dazu sind die bis zu 16 m hohen Säulen aus Schichtholz so angeordnet, dass sie an einen Wald erinnern. Leider entspricht die Qualität der Ausstellungsstücke – Modelle von Holzhäusern und Bilder in Leuchtkästen – nicht dem hohen Niveau der Architektur. Auch wenn das Gebäude an keinen bestimmten Tempel anknüpft, erweckt es dennoch den Eindruck einer innigen Verbundenheit mit der Natur. Damit erinnert es daran, dass die üppigen Wälder Japans die Quelle seiner traditionellen Holzarchitektur sind. Ebenso wie eine Reihe anderer von Ando entworfener Museen, etwa das Historische Museum Chikatsu-Asuka in Osaka, ist auch das **HOLZMUSEUM** eine Hommage des Architekten an die japanische Kultur und Geschichte.

Ce remarquable musée a été édifié à l'occasion de la 45ᵉ Fête nationale du bois de la préfecture de Hyogo, dont le point culminant est le jour de l'Arbre, institué par l'empereur dans les années 1950 à la suite des destructions de forêts pendant la guerre. Située à trois heures de voiture d'Osaka, près d'une station de ski, le site isolé et boisé couvre 168 310 m². Construit en bois sur une ossature d'acier et de béton armé, le musée comprend une salle d'exposition en forme d'anneau de 46 m de diamètre extérieur, autour d'un vide de 22 m de diamètre. La passerelle d'accès traverse entièrement la construction en passant par-dessus une fontaine centrale pour conduire 200 m plus loin à une terrasse d'observation et une résidence d'accueil. À l'intérieur, le sol incliné guide les visiteurs vers un cheminement en spirale, qui les fait traverser deux fois le vide central. Les poutres et les piliers sont en cèdre local. Les énormes colonnes de bois lamellé de 16 m de haut, rappellent la forêt avoisinante. Malheureusement, la qualité des expositions – des maquettes de maisons en bois et des images sur visionneuses – n'est pas au niveau de la qualité architecturale. Bien qu'elle ne rappelle aucun temple précis, cette construction laisse une impression de communion avec la nature et évoque les denses forêts de l'archipel qui sont à la source des traditions locales de l'architecture en bois. Comme un certain nombre d'autres institutions (Musée historique de Chikatsu-Asuka, par exemple), ce **MUSÉE DU BOIS** est un hommage d'Ando aux sources de la culture et de l'histoire de son pays.

Left page, a long approach bridge leads away from the main structure of the museum. Above, the double entrance openings lead visitors into a largely open central space seen on the next pages.

Linke Seite: Eine lange Zugangsbrücke führt vom Hauptgebäude des Museums fort. Die doppelte Pforte (oben) leitet die Besucher in einen großen zentralen Raum (folgende Doppelseite).

Page de gauche : une longue passerelle d'accès mène du bâtiment principal au musée. Ci-dessus, la double porte introduit les visiteurs dans un espace central largement ouvert (voir pages suivantes).

Inside the museum, a spiraling inner walkway greets the visitor. Laminated wooden columns, much like those used in Seville, symbolically recall both the neighboring forest and the very purpose of the museum.

Im Innern des Museums empfängt eine spiralförmige Rampe den Besucher. Laminierte Holzstützen, die den in Sevilla verwendeten gleichen, erinnern symbolisch an den benachbarten Wald und den Zweck des Museums.

À l'intérieur du musée, une passerelle intérieure en spirale attend le visiteur. Des colonnes en bois lamellé, proches de celles utilisées à Séville, rappellent symboliquement la forêt voisine et l'objet même du musée.

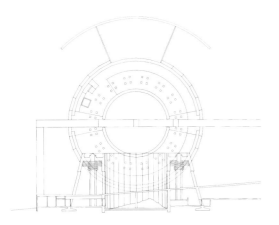 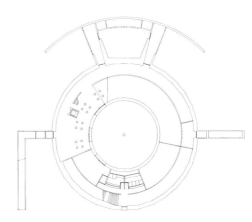 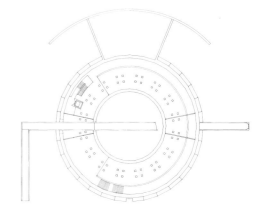

Plans show the distribution of interior spaces and the essential role played by the empty core of the structure. Right: A view looking up from the level of the fountain in the round interior courtyard.

Die Grundrisse zeigen die Aufteilung der Innenräume und die wichtige Rolle, welche der offene Kern des Gebäudes spielt. Rechte Seite: Blick von der Ebene des Springbrunnens in den runden Innenhof.

Plans de distribution des espaces intérieurs et du rôle essentiel joué par le noyau vide central. Page de droite : vue vers le ciel prise de la fontaine, dans la cour intérieure circulaire.

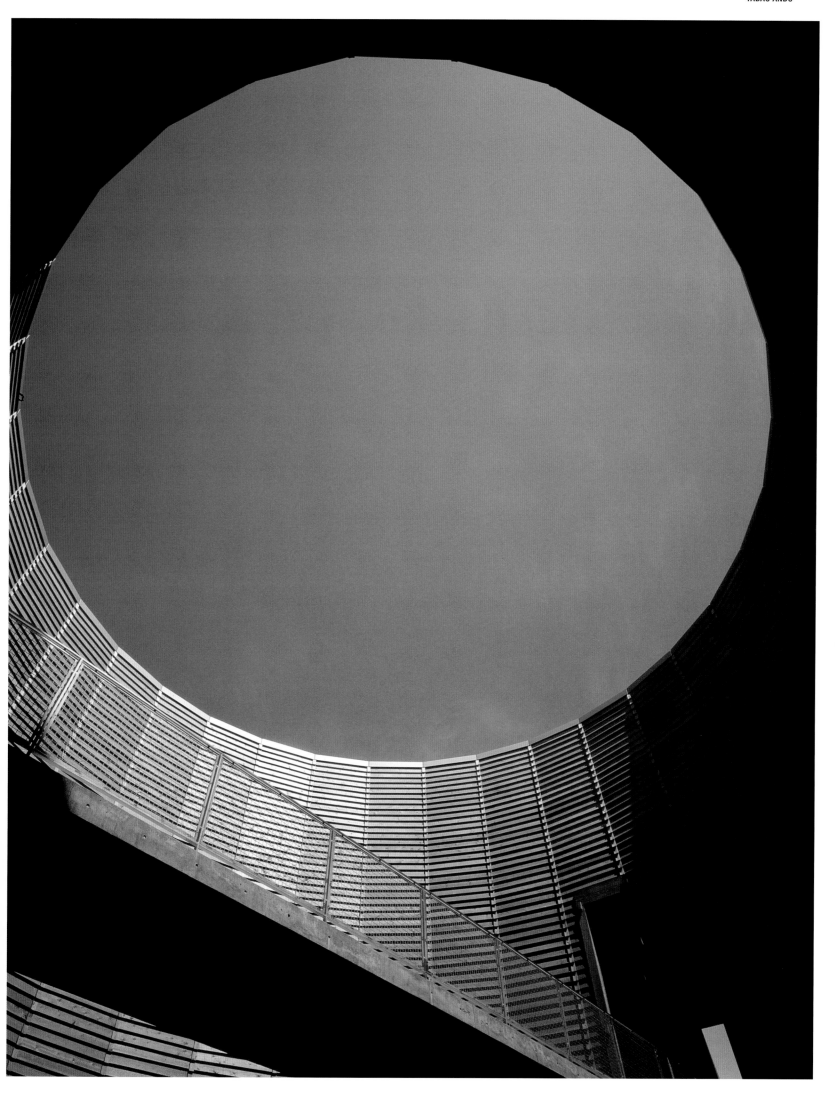

ATELIER BOW-WOW

Atelier Bow-Wow
8–79 Suga-cho
Shinjuku-ku
Tokyo 160–0018
Japan

Tel/Fax: +81 3 3226 5336
Web: www.bow-wow.jp

Atelier Bow-Wow was established in 1992 by Yoshiharu Tsukamoto and Momoyo Kaijima. **YOSHIHARU TSUKAMOTO** was born in 1965 in Tokyo and studied at, among others, the École d'architecture de Paris-Belleville (1987–88), before graduating from the Tokyo Institute of Technology (Doctorate in Engineering, 1994). He was a Visiting Associate Professor at UCLA (2007–08). **MOMOYO KAIJIMA** was born in 1969 in Tokyo, and graduated from Japan Women's University (1991), the Graduate School of the Tokyo Institute of Technology (1994), and studied at the ETH (Zurich, 1996–97). Their work includes the Hanamidori Cultural Center (Tokyo, Japan, 2005); the House and Atelier Bow-Wow (Tokyo, Japan, 2005); Mado Building (Tokyo, Japan, 2006); Pony Garden (Kanagawa, Japan, 2008); Machiya Guesthouse (Kanazawa, Japan, 2008); Mountain House (Nevada, USA, 2008, published here); Four Boxes Gallery (Skive, Denmark; 2009); Machiya Tower (Tokyo, Japan, 2010); the BMW Guggenheim Lab (New York, New York, USA, 2010; Berlin, Germany, 2012; Mumbai, India, 2012–13); and housing on Rue Rebière (Paris, France, 2012).

1992 gründeten Yoshiharu Tsukamoto und Momoyo Kaijima ihr Büro Atelier Bow-Wow. **YOSHIHARU TSUKAMOTO**, 1965 in Tokio geboren, studierte u. a. an der École d'Architecture (Paris, Belleville, UP8, 1987–88) und promovierte 1994 am Tokyo Institute of Technology in Bauingenieurwesen. 2007/08 war er Gastprofessor an der UCLA. **MOMOYO KAIJIMA** wurde 1969 in Tokio geboren und absolvierte ihr Studium an der Japan Women's University (1991), der Graduiertenfakultät des Tokyo Institute of Technology (1994) sowie der ETH Zürich (1996–97). Zu ihren Projekten zählen das Kulturzentrum Hanamidori (Tokio, 2005), Haus und Atelier Bow-Wow (Tokio, 2005), das Mado-Gebäude (Tokio, 2006), der Pony Garden (Kanagawa, Japan, 2008), das Gästehaus Machiya (Kanazawa, Japan, 2008), das Mountain House (Nevada, USA, 2008, hier vorgestellt), die Four Boxes Gallery (Skive, Dänemark, 2009), der Machiya Tower (Tokio, 2010), das BMW Guggenheim Lab (New York, 2010; Berlin, 2012; Mumbai, 2012–13) und ein Wohnbauprojekt an der Rue Rebière (Paris, 2012).

Atelier Bow-Wow a été créé en 1992 par Yoshiharu Tsukamoto et Momoyo Kaijima. Né en 1965 à Tokyo, **YOSHIHARU TSUKAMOTO** est diplômé de l'Institut de technologie de Tokyo (doctorat en ingénierie, 1994). Il a également étudié à l'École d'architecture de Paris-Belleville (Paris, 1987–88). Il a été professeur associé à l'UCLA (2007–08). Née en 1969 à Tokyo et diplômée de l'Université pour les femmes du Japon (1991) et de la faculté d'études supérieure de l'Institut de technologie de Tokyo (1994), **MOMOYO KAIJIMA** a étudié à l'ETH (Zurich, 1996–97). Leurs réalisations comprennent le Centre culturel Hanamidori (Tokyo, 2005) ; la maison et atelier Bow-Wow (Tokyo, 2005) ; l'immeuble Mado (Tokyo, 2006) ; le Pony Garden (Kanagawa, Japon, 2008) ; la pension Machiya (Kanazawa, Japon, 2008) ; la Mountain House (Nevada, 2008, publiée ici) ; la galerie Four Boxes (Skive, Danemark, 2009) ; la tour Machiya (Tokyo, 2010) ; le BMW Guggenheim Lab (New York, 2010 ; Berlin, 2012 ; Bombay, 2012–13) et des logements rue Rebière (Paris, 2012).

MOUNTAIN HOUSE

Nevada, USA, 2008

Address: not disclosed. Area: 115 m²
Client: not disclosed. Cost: not disclosed

This small retreat in an isolated site in Nevada is quite unexpected, with its large-scale timber upper terrace. Wood is also present on the lower level, with a timber ceiling. Beds are inserted into alcoves, and there is even an exterior bathtub for those who dare use it. There is a sense of economy in this architecture, and also of symbiosis with the natural environment; the architects have surely not been directly inspired by local residences, but have brought with them their very specific sense of surprising volumes and an ability to integrate architecture into a natural setting that clearly has a relationship to Japanese thinking, despite the US site involved here.

Das kleine, einsam gelegene Wochenendhaus in Nevada überrascht mit seiner großen Dachterrasse aus Holz. Der gleiche Werkstoff ist in Form einer Holzdecke auch in der unteren Ebene präsent. Die Betten wurden in Alkoven integriert, und für die Mutigen gibt es sogar eine Badewanne unter freiem Himmel. Die Architektur wirkt zurückhaltend und scheint sich geradezu symbiotisch in die landschaftliche Umgebung zu fügen. Ganz offensichtlich wurden die Architekten hier nicht von lokalen Bauten inspiriert. Vielmehr brachten sie ihr höchst eigenes Gespür für unerwartete Baukörper und die Einbindung von Architektur in ihr natürliches Umfeld mit – ein Ansatz, der zweifellos im japanischen Denken wurzelt, trotz des amerikanischen Bauplatzes.

Avec sa vaste terrasse couverte en bois, cette petite retraite édifiée dans un site isolé du Nevada est assez surprenante. Ce matériau est également présent dans les aménagements du rez-de-chaussée et dans les plafonds. Les lits sont logés dans des alcôves et l'on trouve même une baignoire extérieure pour ceux qui ont le courage de l'utiliser. On note un certain sens de l'économie dans cette architecture, mais aussi une recherche de symbiose avec l'environnement naturel. Les architectes ne se sont pas directement inspirés de l'habitat local, mais ont appliqué leur sens très particulier du volume et montré leur habileté à intégrer l'architecture dans un cadre naturel – attitude clairement en relation avec la pensée architecturale japonaise, bien que l'on soit ici aux États-Unis.

Plans, a section, and photos show how wood is used to shelter space while leaving it in good part open to the outside.

Grundrisse, ein Schnitt und die Aufnahmen veranschaulichen, wie mit Holz schützende Räume geschaffen wurden, diese aber zugleich überwiegend zum Außenraum offen bleiben.

Les plans, une coupe et les photographies montrent comment une structure en bois vient abriter le vaste espace supérieur tout en le laissant en grande partie ouvert sur l'extérieur.

Wood is present throughout, even in the old-style wood burning stove (left). Simple hanging light bulbs, or such architectural details as the bed surrounded by bookshelves seen below, emphasize a feeling of rural simplicity.

Holz ist überall präsent, selbst in Gestalt des altmodischen Holzofens (links). Schlichte herabhängende Glühbirnen und architektonische Details wie das von Bücherregalen gerahmte Bett (unten) unterstreichen die schlichte Rustikalität.

Le bois est omniprésent, y compris par la présence d'un ancien poêle à bois (à gauche). De simples ampoules suspendues ou des détails architecturaux comme l'alcôve du lit entouré de rayonnages (ci-dessous) soulignent la sobriété rustique.

ATELIER OSLO + AWP

Atelier Oslo, A. Filipstadveien 5, 0250 Oslo, Norway / Tel: +47 21 66 34 22
E-mail: jonas@www.atelieroslo.no / Web: www.atelieroslo.no

AWP, 25 Rue Henry Monnier, 75009 Paris, France / Tel: +33 1 53 20 92 15
E-mail: awp@awp.fr / Web: www.awp.fr

ATELIER OSLO was created in 2006 by Nils Ole Bae Brandtzæg (born in 1975), Thomas Liu (born in 1978), Marius Mowe (born in 1973), and Jonas Norsted (born in 1973). The Partners all graduated from the Oslo School of Architecture, and worked in the offices of Sverre Fehn, Knut Hjeltnes, Jensen & Skodvin, and Lund Hagem. They were awarded First Prize in a competition for a residential high rise (Lervig, with Lund Hagem, 2008). They completed the Leilighetshotell Medical Spa (Verdens Ende, Tjøme, in collaboration with Lund Hagem, 2007); the Skihotel (Geilo, in collaboration with Lund Hagem); and The Lantern (Sandnes, with AWP, 2008–09, published here), all in Norway. Atelier Oslo was nominated for The Lantern, with AWP, for the 2009 Mies van der Rohe Award. **AWP** was created in 2003. The three current Partners are Matthias Armengaud, an architect and urban planner (ENSA Versailles), Marc Armengaud, a philosopher (Paris I, Sorbonne), and Alessandra Cianchetta, an architect and landscape architect ("La Sapienza," Rome; ETSA Barcelona; ETSA Madrid). Their focus is on a renewed relationship between master planning, landscape architecture, and architecture. Alessandra Cianchetta explains that AWP was the team leader in the competition phase for The Lantern, and that Atelier Oslo was the team leader for the development and construction phase of the project. The project is the result of a "co-conception." The work of AWP includes the French Pavilion for the Architecture Biennale in São Paulo (São Paulo, Brazil, 2007); the landscape design for the Museum of Modern Art of Villeneuve D'Ascq (France, 2010); and the enlargement of a water purification plant (Évry, France, 2003–12).

ATELIER OSLO wurde 2006 von Nils Ole Bae Brandtzæg (geboren 1975), Thomas Liu (geboren 1978), Marius Mowe (geboren 1973) und Jonas Norsted (geboren 1973) gegründet. Alle Partner schlossen ihr Studium an der Oslo School of Architecture ab und waren für die Büros von Sverre Fehn, Knut Hjeltnes, Jensen & Skodvin und Lund Hagem tätig. Das Team gewann den ersten Preis in einem Wettbewerb für ein Wohnhochhaus (Lervig, mit Lund Hagem, 2008). Darüber hinaus realisierten die Architekten das Leilighetshotell Medical Spa (Verdens Ende, Tjøme, in Zusammenarbeit mit Lund Hagem, 2007), das Skihotel (Geilo, ebenfalls mit Lund Hagem) sowie das Projekt Laterne (Sandnes, mit AWP, 2008–09, hier vorgestellt), alle in Norwegen. Für Laterne wurden Atelier Oslo + AWP 2009 für den Mies-van-der-Rohe-Preis nominiert. **AWP** wurde 2003 gegründet. Aktuell hat das Büro mit dem Architekten und Stadtplaner Matthias Armengaud (ENSA Versailles), dem Philosophen Marc Armengaud (Paris I, Sorbonne) und der Architektin und Landschaftsarchitektin Alessandra Cianchetta (La Sapienza, Rom, ETSA Barcelona, ETSA Madrid) drei Partner. Ihr Hauptanliegen ist es, ein neues Verhältnis zwischen Masterplanung, Landschaftsarchitektur und Architektur zu gestalten. Alessandra Cianchetta zufolge übernahm AWP die Teamleitung für das Lantern-Projekt während des Wettbewerbs, während Atelier Oslo die Entwicklungs- und Bauphase leitete. Somit ist das Projekt Ergebnis einer „Co-Entwicklung". Zu den Arbeiten von AWP zählen der Französische Pavillon für die Architekturbiennale in São Paulo (Brasilien, 2007), die Landschaftsgestaltung für das Museum für moderne Kunst in Villeneuve d'Ascq (Frankreich, 2010) sowie die Erweiterung einer Wasseraufbereitungsanlage (Evry, Frankreich, 2003–12).

ATELIER OSLO a été créé en 2006 par Nils Ole Bae Brandtzæg (né en 1975), Thomas Liu (né en 1978), Marius Mowe (né en 1973) et Jonas Norsted (né en 1973). Les associés sont tous diplômés de l'École d'architecture d'Oslo et ont travaillé dans les agences de Sverre Fehn, Knut Hjeltnes, Jensen & Skodvin et Lund Hagem. Ils ont remporté le premier prix d'un concours pour une tour d'habitations (Lervig, avec Lund Hagem, 2008), ont réalisé l'hôtel thermal Leilighetshotell (Verdens Ende, Tjøme, en collaboration avec Lund Hagem, 2007) ; l'hôtel Skihotel (Geilo, en collaboration avec Lund Hagem) ; et la Lanterne (Sandnes, avec AWP, 2008–09, projet publié ici), tous situés en Norvège. Atelier Oslo, a été sélectionné, avec AWP, pour la Lanterne, pour le prix Mies van der Rohe 2009. **AWP** a été créé en 2003. Les trois collaborateurs actuels sont Matthias Armengaud, architecte et urbaniste (ENSA Versailles), Marc Armengaud, philosophe (Paris I, Sorbonne) et Alessandra Cianchetta, architecte et architecte paysagiste (« La Sapienza », Rome, ETSA Barcelone, ETSA Madrid). Ils mettent l'accent sur un nouveau type de relations entre plan directeur, architecture du paysage et architecture. Alessandra Cianchetta explique qu'AWP a joué un rôle moteur dans la phase de compétition pour le projet de la Lanterne, et Atelier Oslo dans sa phase de développement et de construction. Ce projet est le fruit d'une « coconception ». Les projets d'AWP incluent le pavillon de la France de la Biennale d'architecture de São Paulo (Brésil, 2007) ; le traitement paysager du Musée d'art moderne de Villeneuve d'Ascq (France, 2010) et l'agrandissement de la station d'épuration d'Évry (Évry, France, 2003–12).

THE LANTERN

Sandnes, Norway, 2008–09

Address: Langgata, Sandnes, Norway. Area: 140 m². Client: Sandnes Municipality
Cost: €1.1 million. Collaboration: Atelier Oslo: Thomas Liu (Project Leader),
Nils Ole Bae Brandtzæg, Marius Mowe, Jonas Norsted, Bosheng Gan AWP: Matthias Armengaud,
Marc Armengaud, Alessandra Cianchetta, Arnaud Hirschauer

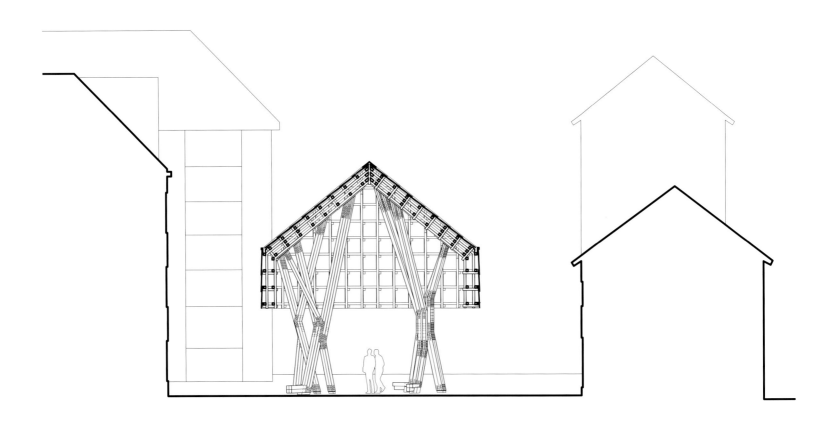

Subsequent to the selection of Sandnes and Stavanger as the European cultural capitals for 2008, a series of competitions called Norwegian Wood was initiated, to promote "contemporary, sustainable timber architecture." The city of Sandnes sought, in this context, to create a canopy over a small pedestrian square. The aim was to revitalize the square and to provide a location for a market, informal concerts, or simple meetings. The competition for a structure intended to be visible from a certain distance was won by Atelier Oslo and the French firm AWP. The design, completed in November 2008, is meant to echo a traditional wooden house, whose transparency allows it to glow from within at night, hence the name—**THE LANTERN.** Laminated pine elements measuring 90 x 90 millimeters are used for most of the structure with steel reinforcement for the joints. Glass panels mounted directly on the wood in an overlapping pattern replace the traditional slate roof. Individual "sculptural" oak columns, which turn into benches at the juncture with the ground, hold up the structure.

Nach der gemeinsamen Ernennung der norwegischen Städte Sandnes und Stavanger zur Europäischen Kulturhauptstadt 2008 wurde eine Reihe von Wettbewerben unter dem Arbeitstitel „Norwegian Wood" zur Förderung „zeitgenössischer, nachhaltiger Holzarchitektur" initiiert. In diesem Zusammenhang beschloss die Stadt Sandnes, eine Pavillonkonstruktion auf einem kleinen Platz der örtlichen Fußgängerzone zu realisieren. Ziel war es, den Platz neu zu beleben und einen Standort für Märkte, spontane Konzerte oder kleinere Versammlungen zu schaffen. Den Wettbewerb für die Konstruktion, die auch aus einiger Entfernung sichtbar sein sollte, konnten Atelier Oslo und das französische Büro AWP gemeinsam für sich entscheiden. Der im November 2008 fertiggestellte Bau erinnert an ein traditionelles Holzhaus, das dank der transparenten Konstruktion nachts von innen leuchtet – daher der Name **DIE LATERNE.** Konstruktives Hauptelement sind 90 x 90 mm starke Kiefernschichtholzstreben mit stahlverstärkten Verbindungsstücken. Statt eines traditionellen Schieferdachs wurden einander überlappende Glasplatten direkt auf das Holz montiert. „Skulpturale" Eichenholzpfeiler, die sich am Boden zu Bänken verbreitern, stützen den Bau.

Le choix de Sandnes et Stavanger comme capitales culturelles européennes 2008 a donné lieu au lancement d'un ensemble de concours baptisé Norwegian Wood, destiné à promouvoir une « architecture en bois contemporaine et durable ». Dans ce contexte, la ville de Sandnes souhaitait couvrir une petite place piétonne. Le but était de revitaliser la place en offrant un lieu pour un marché, des concerts informels ou de simples rencontres. Ce sont Atelier Oslo et l'agence française AWP qui ont remporté le concours pour une structure qui devait être visible de loin. Le projet, achevé en novembre 2008, évoque une maison en bois traditionnelle. Sa transparence lui permet d'irradier de l'intérieur dans la nuit, d'où son nom, **LA LANTERNE.** Des éléments en pin lamellé de 90 x 90 mm sont utilisés pour la majorité du bâtiment, avec des renforts en acier pour les joints. Des panneaux vitrés, montés directement sur le bois et se chevauchant, remplacent le traditionnel toit d'ardoise. La structure est supportée par des colonnes « sculpturales » individuelles en chêne, formant des banquettes au niveau du sol.

A drawing (left) and two photos show the full structure in its setting, echoing the sloped roofs of neighboring structures.

Eine Zeichnung (linke Seite) und zwei Fotos zeigen den Bau, der die Satteldächer der Nachbarbauten aufgreift, in seinem baulichen Umfeld.

Un dessin (page de gauche) et deux photos montrent l'implantation de l'ensemble du bâtiment répondant aux toits en pente des édifices voisins.

SHIGERU BAN

Shigeru Ban Architects, 5–2–4 Matsubara,
Setagaya, Tokyo 156–0043, Japan
Tel: +81 3 3324 6760 / Fax: +81 3 3324 6789
E-mail: tokyo@shigerubanarchitects.com
Web: www.shigerubanarchitects.com

Born in 1957 in Tokyo, **SHIGERU BAN** studied at SCI-Arc from 1977 to 1980. He then attended the Cooper Union School of Architecture, where he studied under John Hejduk (1980–82). He worked in the office of Arata Isozaki (1982–83), before founding his own firm in Tokyo in 1985. He designed the Japanese Pavilion at Expo 2000 in Hanover. His work includes the Atsushi Imai Memorial Gymnasium (Odate, Akita, Japan, 2000–02, published here); the Hanegi Forest Annex (Setagaya, Tokyo, Japan, 2004); Mul(ti)houses (Mulhouse, France, 2001–05); the Takatori Church (Kobe, Hyogo, Japan, 2005); the disaster relief Post-Tsunami Rehabilitation Houses (Kirinda, Hambantota, Sri Lanka, 2005); the Papertainer Museum (Seoul Olympic Park, Songpa-Gu, South Korea, 2006); the Nicolas G. Hayek Center (Tokyo, 2007); the Paper Teahouse (London, 2008); Haesley Nine Bridges Golf Clubhouse (Yeoju, South Korea, 2009); the Paper Tube Tower (London, UK, 2009); and the Metal Shutter Houses on West 19th Street in New York (New York, USA, 2010). He installed his Paper Temporary Studio on top of the Centre Pompidou in Paris to work on the new Centre Pompidou-Metz (Metz, France, 2006–10, also published here). Recent work includes the Camper Pavilion (Alicante, Spain; Sanya, China; Miami, Florida, USA; Lorient, France, prefabrication June to September 2011); Kobe Kushinoya (Osaka, Japan, 2011); L'Aquila Temporary Concert Hall (L'Aquila, Italy, 2011); Container Temporary Housing, disaster relief project for the east Japan earthquake and tsunami (Miyagi, Japan, 2011); the Camper NY SoHo store (New York, USA, 2012); and Tamedia (Zurich, Switzerland, 2011–13). Current work includes the Swatch Group Headquarters and Production Facility (Bienne, Switzerland, 2012–14); and the Oita Prefecture Museum of Art (Oita, Japan, 2012–14).

SHIGERU BAN, 1957 in Tokio geboren, studierte von 1977 bis 1980 am Southern California Institute of Architecture (SCI-Arc). Anschließend besuchte er die Cooper Union School of Architecture, wo er bei John Hejduk studierte (1980–82). Bevor er 1985 sein eigenes Büro in Tokio gründete, arbeitete er bei Arata Isozaki (1982 bis 1983). Er plante den Japanischen Pavillon für die Expo 2000 in Hannover. Zu seinen Entwürfen zählen das Atsushi Imai Memorial Gymnasium (Odate, Akita, Japan, 2000–02, hier vorgestellt), eine Erweiterung der Wohnanlage Hanegi Forest (Setagaya, Tokio, 2004), Mul(ti)houses (Mulhouse, Frankreich, 2001–05), die Takatori-Kirche (Kobe, Hyogo, Japan, 2005), Häuser für die Katastrophenhilfe nach dem großen Tsunami (Kirinda, Hambantota, Sri Lanka, 2005), das Papertainer Museum (Olympiapark Seoul, Songpa-Gu, Südkorea, 2006), das Nicolas G. Hayek Center (Tokio, 2007), das Paper Teahouse (London, 2008), das Clubhaus für den Haesley Nine Bridges Golfclub (Yeoju, Südkorea, 2009), der Paper Tube Tower (London, 2009) und die Metal Shutter Houses an der West 19th Street in New York (2010). Auf dem Dach des Centre Georges Pompidou in Paris hatte Ban sich ein temporäres Atelier aus Papphöhren eingerichtet, um dort am neuen Centre Pompidou-Metz (2006–10, ebenfalls hier vorgestellt) arbeiten zu können. Jüngere Projekte sind der Camper-Pavillon (Alicante, Spanien; Sanya, China; Miami, Florida; Lorient, Frankreich, Vorfertigung Juni–September 2011), Kobe Kushinoya (Osaka, Japan, 2011), ein temporärer Konzertsaal in L'Aquila (Italien, 2011), temporäre Container-Notunterkünfte für das Erdbeben- und Tsunamigebiet in Ostjapan (Miyagi, 2011), der Camper Store in SoHo (New York, 2012) und Tamedia (Zürich, 2011–13). Zu den aktuellen Projekten zählen die Firmenzentrale und neue Fertigungsgebäude für die Swatch-Gruppe (Biel, Schweiz, 2012–14) und das Kunstmuseum für die Präfektur Oita (Oita, Japan 2012–14).

Né à Tokyo en 1957, **SHIGERU BAN** étudie au SCI-Arc (1977–80) puis suit l'enseignement de John Hejduk à la Cooper Union School of Architecture (1980–82). Il travaille dans l'agence d'Arata Isozaki (1982–83) avant de créer la sienne à Tokyo, en 1985. Il conçoit le Pavillon japonais pour Expo 2000, à Hanovre. Ses réalisations comprennent le gymnase Atsushi Imai Memorial (Odate, Akita, Japon, 2000–02, publié ici) ; l'annexe Hanegi Forest (Setagaya, Tokyo, 2004) ; l'ensemble de logements sociaux Mul(ti)houses (Mulhouse, 2001–05) ; l'église de Takatori (Kobé, Hyogo, 2005) ; les Post-Tsunami Rehabilitation Houses pour les sinistrés du tsunami (Kirinda, Hambantota, Sri Lanka, 2005) ; le Papertainer Museum (parc Olympique de Séoul, Songpa-Gu, Corée-du-Sud, 2006) ; le Centre Nicolas G. Hayek (Tokyo, 2007) ; la Paper Teahouse (Londres, 2008) ; le Haesley Nine Bridges Golf Clubhouse (Yeoju, Corée-du-Sud, 2009) ; la tour Paper Tube (Londres, 2009) et l'ensemble Metal Shutter Houses sur la 19e Rue Ouest, à New York (2010). Il installe un atelier provisoire, le Paper Temporary Studio, au sommet du Centre Pompidou-Paris, pour travailler au projet du nouveau Centre Pompidou-Metz (2006–10, publié ici). Parmi ses réalisations récentes : le pavillon Camper (Alicante ; Sanya, Chine ; Miami ; Lorient) ; le restaurant Kobe Kushinoya (Osaka, 2011) ; la salle de concert provisoire de L'Aquila (L'Aquila, Italie, 2011) ; Container Temporary Housing, logements d'urgence pour les sinistrés du séisme et du tsunami de 2011 (Miyagi, Japon, 2011) ; la boutique Camper NY SoHo (New York, 2012) et le siège de Tamedia (Zurich, 2011–13). Ses projets en cours : le siège et centre de production du groupe Swatch (Bienne, Suisse, 2012–14) et le Musée d'art de la préfecture d'Oita (Oita, Japon 2012–14).

CENTRE POMPIDOU-METZ

Metz, France, 2006–10

Address: Avenue de l'Amphithéâtre, 57000 Metz, France, +33 3 8756 5524,
www.centrepompidou-metz.fr. Area: 11 176 m². Client: City of Metz. Cost: not disclosed
Collaboration: Jean de Gastines, Philip Gumuchdjian

Shigeru Ban Architects (Tokyo) in association with Jean de Gastines (Paris) and Philip Gumuchdjian (London) won the design competition to build a new Centre Pompidou in the city of Metz on November 26, 2003. In this instance, Ban's surprising woven timber roof, based on a hexagonal pattern, was the most visible innovation, but his proposal to suspend three 90 x 15-meter gallery "tubes" above the required Grand Nef (nave) and Forum spaces was also unexpected and inventive. Working at the time of the competition on the Japan Pavilion (Expo 2000, Hanover, Germany, 1999–2000), Shigeru Ban purchased a Chinese hat in a crafts shop in Paris in 1998. "I was astonished at how architectonic it was," says Shigeru Ban. "The structure is made of bamboo, and there is a layer of oil-paper for waterproofing. There is also a layer of dry leaves for insulation. It is just like a roof for a building. Since I bought this hat, I wanted to design a roof in a similar manner." Ban was anxious to participate in the original competition because of the involvement of the Centre Pompidou, whose architecture he had admired as being audacious for its time. Aside from its spectacular interior spaces, the **CENTRE POMPIDOU-METZ** opens broadly onto its surrounding piazza, echoing the architect's frequent interest in the ambiguity of interior and exterior.

Shigeru Ban Architects (Tokio) in Zusammenarbeit mit Jean de Gastines (Paris) und Philip Gumuchdjian (London) gewannen am 26. November 2003 den Wettbewerb für ein neues Centre Pompidou in der Stadt Metz. In diesem Fall war Bans erstaunliches geflochtenes Holzdach, das auf einem sechseckigen System basiert, die auffallendste Innovation. Doch auch sein Vorschlag, drei 90 x 15 m große Galerie-„Röhren" über dem geforderten Grand Nef (Schiff) und dem Forum aufzuhängen, war überraschend und einfallsreich. Shigeru Ban, der damals am Wettbewerb für den japanischen Pavillon (Expo 2000, Hannover, 1999–2000) arbeitete, kaufte 1998 in einem Pariser Kunstgewerbegeschäft einen chinesischen Hut: „Ich war erstaunt, wie architektonisch er war", sagt der Architekt. „Er besteht aus Bambus, mit einer wasserdichten Schicht aus Ölpapier darüber. Zur Isolierung hat er auch eine Schicht aus getrockneten Blättern. Das ist genauso wie bei einem Hausdach. Seit ich diesen Hut gekauft habe, wollte ich ein Dach auf ähnliche Weise planen." Ban wollte unbedingt an dem Wettbewerb teilnehmen, weil er vom Centre Pompidou ausgelobt worden war, das er für seine damals kühne Architektur bewunderte. Von seinen spektakulären Innenräumen abgesehen, öffnet sich das **CENTRE POMPIDOU-METZ** weit zur umgebenden Piazza und spiegelt die anhaltende Auseinandersetzung des Architekten mit der Doppeldeutigkeit von Innen- und Außenraum.

Shigeru Ban Architects (Tokyo) en association avec Jean de Gastines (Paris) et Philip Gumuchdjian (Londres) a remporté le concours pour la construction d'une antenne du Centre Pompidou à Metz le 26 novembre 2003. Si sa surprenante couverture en entrelacs de bois de forme hexagonale est l'innovation la plus perceptible, la suspension des trois galeries tubulaires de 90 x 15 m au-dessus de la grande nef et du forum prévus par le programme est une solution tout aussi novatrice et inattendue. Travaillant au moment du concours sur le projet du Pavillon japonais d'Expo 2000 (Hanovre, 1999–2000), Ban avait acheté un chapeau de paille dans une boutique d'artisanat chinois : « Ce chapeau m'a surpris par son caractère architectonique. C'est une structure en bambou, sur laquelle est tendue une feuille de papier huilé imperméable. Des feuilles séchées en renforcent l'isolation. C'est exactement comme un toit de bâtiment. Depuis, j'ai eu envie de construire un toit de nature similaire. » Ban avait envie de participer à ce concours car il appréciait l'implication du Centre Pompidou dont il avait admiré l'architecture, si audacieuse pour son temps. Le **CENTRE POMPIDOU-METZ**, aux volumes intérieurs spectaculaires, s'ouvre sur un parvis qui illustre l'intérêt que porte Ban à l'ambiguïté entre intérieur et extérieur.

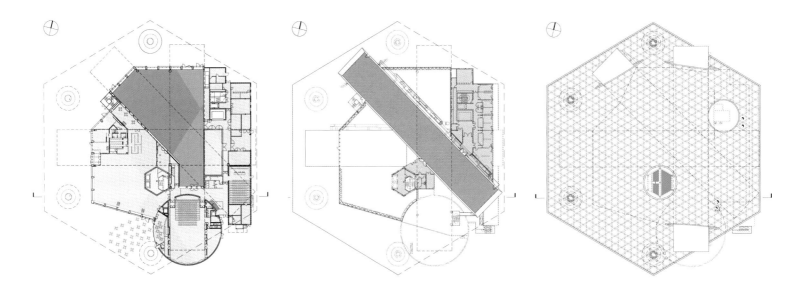

Plans of the successive levels of the structure reveal that, despite the "organic" appearance of the building as seen from ground level, it is in reality carefully organized according to the main hexagonal shape most visible in the roof plan (right).

Die Grundrisse der Geschosse zeigen, dass das Gebäude, obwohl es von unten betrachtet ganz „organisch" wirkt, sorgfältig auf der Basis der achteckigen Form geplant ist, die am besten auf dem Grundriss des Dach-geschosses zu erkennen ist (rechts).

En dépit de l'apparence « organique » du bâtiment vue au niveau du sol, les plans des différents niveaux de la structure révèlent qu'en réalité, son organisation suit scrupuleusement la forme octogonale principale, plus visible sur le plan du toit (à droite).

Above, the roof of the Centre Pompidou-Metz, inspired by a Chinese hat bought by the architect, is seen during the day. Right, a night view shows the translucent nature of the roof, which also reveals its woven wood pattern in this image.

Das Dach des Centre Pompidou-Metz, inspiriert von einem chinesischen Hut, den der Architekt sich gekauft hatte, ist oben bei Tag zu sehen. Rechts illustriert eine nächtliche Ansicht die Lichtdurchlässigkeit des Dachs und zugleich die „geflochtene" Holzkonstruktion.

Ci-dessus, la toiture du Centre Pompidou-Metz, inspirée d'un chapeau chinois acheté un jour par l'architecte, vue ici de jour. À droite, vue nocturne montrant le caractère translucide de la toiture et révélant sa structure tressée en bois.

The architect's idea was to have generous spaces that would be covered and yet open out onto the surrounding square.

Das Ziel des Architekten war es, großzügige Räume zu schaffen, die sowohl überdacht als auch zum benachbarten Platz geöffnet sind.

L'idée de l'architecte était de créer de généreux volumes qui soient à la fois couverts et ouverts sur le parvis entourant le bâtiment.

Right, a drawing shows the suspended exhibition "tubes."

Die Zeichnung rechts zeigt die aufgehängten Ausstellungs-„Rohre".

Le plan à droite illustre les « tubes » d'exposition suspendus.

The most spectacular interior space of the Centre Pompidou-Metz is this soaring gallery with the elevator structure seen in the center and the wooden roof.

Der spektakulärste Innenraum des Centre Pompidou-Metz ist die hoch aufragende Galerie mit dem Aufzug in der Mitte und dem Holzdach darüber.

L'espace intérieur le plus spectaculaire du Centre Pompidou-Metz est cette immense galerie avec l'ascenseur en son centre et le toit de bois au-dessus.

ATSUSHI IMAI MEMORIAL GYMNASIUM

Odate, Akita, Japan, 2000–02

Address: 3–12–30 Katayama, Odate City, Akita Prefecture, Japan. Site area: 2041.9 m², Building area: 940.6 m², Total floor area: 980.9 m². Client: Obayashi Tohoku. Cost: ¥450 million

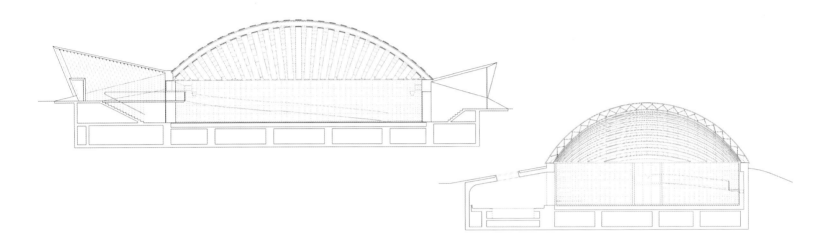

The oval dome of the gymnasium has an open span of 20 x 28 meters made with laminated veneer lumber arches.

Die ovale Kuppel der Sporthalle hat eine stützenfreie Spannweite von 20 x 28 m und wurde mit Bogenträgern aus Furnierschichtholz realisiert.

La coupole ovale du gymnase couvre une surface de 20 x 28 m. Les arcs sont en bois lamellé plaqué.

This timber building, also called Plywood Structure 04, is a sports facility designed between February 2000 and August 2001. Located in the far north of the island of Honshu, this one-story timber and reinforced-concrete structure is in the same town as Toyo Ito's Odate Jukai Dome Park (1995–97). The total floor area of the building is 981 square meters, and the site measures 2042 square meters. Intended as a gymnasium and swimming pool, the building uses a laminated veneer lumber (LVL) structural system. Creating a 20 x 28-meter oval dome with the capacity to resist heavy snow loads in the winter was a challenge for Shigeru Ban. He chose to create an LVL space frame with successive wooden arches, proving that thin plywood can be used more effectively on larger spans than might be expected. In much the same way, Ban has shown that paper tubes can be employed as structural elements. An added advantage of the system is that it uses much less wood than other systems of lamination. He does not shy away from questioning some of the most firmly rooted beliefs of the architectural profession, in particular its reliance on tried and true, but often expensive, construction methods. In this he is almost unique, going far beyond the traditional issues of design, dealing, too, with fundamental questions of the use of space. He succeeds in mastering form even as he innovates in other areas.

Der Holzbau, auch Plywood Structure 04 genannt, ist eine zwischen Februar 2000 und August 2001 entworfene Sporthalle. Der eingeschossige Bau aus Holz und Stahlbeton liegt im äußersten Norden der Insel Honshu und zudem in derselben Stadt wie Toyo Itos Odate Jukai Dome Park (1995–97). Die Gesamtfläche des Gebäudes beläuft sich auf 981 m², das Grundstück ist 2042 m² groß. Beim Bau der Sport- und Schwimmhalle kam ein Konstruktionssystem aus LVL (Furnierschichtholz) zum Einsatz. Der Entwurf eines 20 x 28 m großen ovalen Kuppelbaus, der im Winter hohen Schneelasten standhalten muss, war eine Herausforderung für Ban. Er entschied sich für ein Tragwerk aus LVL mit hintereinander geschalteten Holzbogenträgern und bewies damit, dass dünnes Sperrholz effektiver über größere Spannweiten einsetzbar ist, als bisher angenommen. Auf dieselbe Weise hatte Ban bereits gezeigt, dass sich auch Pappröhren als Konstruktionselement eignen. Ein weiterer Vorteil des Systems ist, dass weitaus weniger Holz verbraucht wird, als bei anderen Verbundsystemen. Shigeru Ban scheut sich nicht, einige der grundlegendsten Glaubenssätze der Architektur zu hinterfragen, besonders das Vertrauen auf altbewährte, wenn auch kostspielige Konstruktionsverfahren. In dieser Hinsicht ist er unerreicht. Er geht weit über übliche Designfragen hinaus und setzt sich zudem mit essenziellen Problemen der Raumnutzung auseinander. Es gelingt ihm, formale Fragen zu meistern und zugleich auf anderen Gebieten innovativ zu sein.

Ce bâtiment, également appelé « Plywood Structure 04 », est une installation sportive conçue entre février 2000 et août 2001 et édifiée à l'extrême nord de l'île de Honshu. En bois et béton armé, d'un seul niveau, elle se trouve dans la même ville que le parc du stade d'Odate Jukai (1995–97) dû à Toyo Ito. La surface utile totale de ce gymnase et cette piscine est de 981 m² pour un terrain de 2042 m². La construction fait appel à un système structurel en LVL (bois lamifié). La création d'une coupole ovale de 20 x 28 m capable de résister à fortes chutes de neige représentait un défi pour l'architecte. Il opta alors pour une structure spatiale en LVL faite d'une succession d'arcs en bois, prouvant ainsi qu'un contreplaqué mince pouvait servir à des portées plus longues que ce que l'on pensait. Dans le même esprit, il avait déjà démontré que les tubes en carton pouvaient être utilisés comme éléments de structures. L'avantage supplémentaire de ce système était de consommer beaucoup moins de bois que les autres techniques de lamification. Ban n'a pas craint de remettre en cause certaines des pratiques les plus profondément ancrées de la profession architecturale, en particulier lorsqu'elle se cantonne à des méthodes de constructions éprouvées, mais souvent coûteuses. Il est pratiquement seul dans cette démarche, et n'hésite pas à dépasser les problématiques traditionnelles de la conception pour remettre en question les fondements de l'utilisation de l'espace. Il réussit à maîtriser la forme tout en innovant dans d'autres domaines.

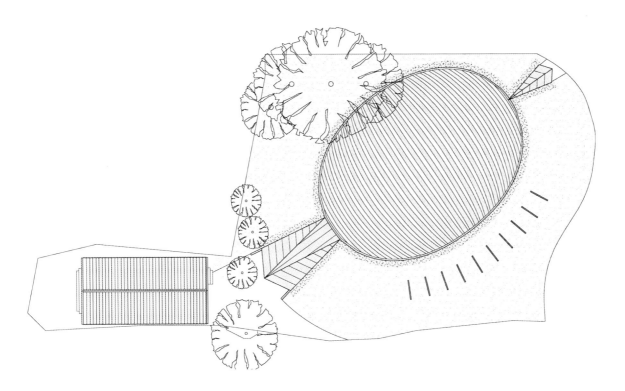

Left page, a site drawing shows the precise elliptical form of the structure. The exterior of the structure has an almost hermetic, tortoise-like appearance.

Der Lageplan links oben zeigt die präzise, elliptische Form des Baus. Von außen wirkt der Bau geradezu hermetisch geschlossen, wie eine Schildkröte.

Le plan de situation de la page de gauche montre la forme elliptique précise de la structure. L'extérieur qui semble assez hermétique rappelle une carapace de tortue.

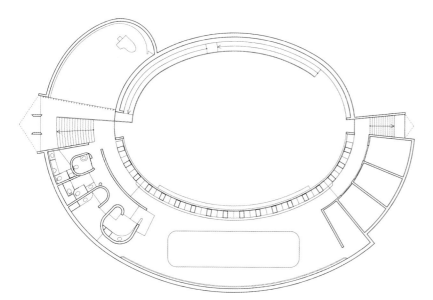

A lower-level pool area uses curves, V-shaped supports, and a combination of screens and ceiling lights to animate space that might otherwise have been more ordinary.

Im unteren Schwimmbeckenbereich kommen Kurven, V-förmige Stützen und eine Kombination aus Wandschirmen und Oberlichtern zum Einsatz und beleben den Raum, der sonst womöglich gewöhnlich gewirkt hätte.

L'espace inférieur de la piscine est animé par des courbes, des poteaux de soutien en forme de V et une combinaison d'écrans et de luminaires en plafond.

BEHNISCH ARCHITECTS

Behnisch Architekten
Rotebühlstr. 163a
70197 Stuttgart
Germany

Tel: +49 711 60 77 20
Fax: +49 711 6077 29 9
E-mail: ba@behnisch.com
Web: www.behnisch.com

STEFAN BEHNISCH was born in 1957 in Stuttgart. He studied Philosophy at the Philosophische Hochschule der Jesuiten, Munich (1976–79), Economics at the Ludwig Maximilian University, Munich, and Architecture at the University of Karlsruhe (1979–87). He worked at Stephen Woolley & Associates (Venice, California, 1984–85), and has been a Principal Partner at Behnisch since 1989. Born in Manchester in 1966, **DAVID COOK** studied Architecture at the Polytechnic in Manchester and obtained his diploma at the University of East London in 1992. Since 1993, he has been working with Behnisch Architekten and, since 2006, has been a Partner in the office. Together with Stefan Behnisch and Martin Haas, he has been heading the practice Behnisch Architekten since 2006. **MARTIN HAAS** was born in 1967 in Waldshut. After working as a cameraman, he began studying Architecture at the Technical University of Stuttgart in 1988, where he obtained his diploma in 1995. He studied at South Bank University, worked with Alan Brookes Associates in London, and produced advertising films. In 1995, he started working with Behnisch Architekten and has been a Partner in the firm since 2006. Recent work includes Thermal Baths (Bad Aibling, 2007); the Römerbad Thermal Spa Extension (Bad Kleinkirchheim, Carinthia, Austria, 2006–07, published here); the Kovner Residence (Sebastopol, California, USA, 2008); and the Deutsches Meeresmuseum "Ozeaneum" (Stralsund, 2008), all in Germany unless stated otherwise.

STEFAN BEHNISCH wurde 1957 in Stuttgart geboren. Er studierte Philosophie an der Philosophischen Hochschule der Jesuiten, München (1976–79), Wirtschaftswissenschaften an der Ludwig-Maximilians-Universität München und Architektur an der Universität Karlsruhe (1979–87). Er arbeitete für Stephen Woolley & Associates (Venice, Kalifornien, 1984–85) und ist seit 1989 Hauptgesellschafter von Behnisch Architekten. **DAVID COOK** wurde 1966 in Manchester geboren, studierte Architektur an der Polytechnischen Hochschule Manchester und machte sein Diplom 1992 an der University of East London. Seit 1993 ist er für Behnisch Architekten tätig und dort seit 2006 Partner. Seit 2006 leitet er das Büro mit Stefan Behnisch und Martin Haas. **MARTIN HAAS** wurde 1967 in Waldshut geboren. Nach anfänglicher Tätigkeit als Kameramann studierte er ab 1988 Architektur an der Technischen Hochschule Stuttgart, wo er 1995 sein Diplom machte. Er studierte an der South Bank University, arbeitete für Alan Brookes Associates in London und produzierte Werbefilme. Seit 1995 ist er für Behnisch Architekten tätig und seit 2006 Partner. Neuere Projekte sind u. a. die Thermalbäder in Bad Aibling (2007), die Erweiterung des Römerbads (Bad Kleinkirchheim, Kärnten, Österreich, 2006–07, hier vorgestellt), die Kovner Residence (Sebastopol, Kalifornien, 2008) sowie das Deutsche Meeresmuseum „Ozeaneum" (Stralsund, 2008).

STEFAN BEHNISCH est né en 1957 à Stuttgart. Il a étudié la philosophie à l'École supérieure de philosophie des Jésuites, à Munich (1976–79), l'économie à l'université Ludwig-Maximilian de Munich, et l'architecture à l'université de Karlsruhe (1979–87). Il a travaillé chez Stephen Woolley & Associates (Venice, Californie, 1984–85), et est associé principal de l'agence Behnisch depuis 1989. Né à Manchester en 1966, **DAVID COOK** a étudié l'architecture à l'École polytechnique de Manchester et a obtenu son diplôme à l'université de Londres-Est en 1992. Depuis 1993, il collabore avec Behnisch Architekten, dont il devient associé en 2006. Avec Stefan Behnisch et Martin Haas, il dirige le cabinet Behnisch Architekten depuis 2006. **MARTIN HAAS** est né en 1967 à Waldshut. Après avoir travaillé comme cameraman, il étudie l'architecture à l'Université technique de Stuttgart en 1988, où il obtient son diplôme en 1995. Il étudie à la South Bank University, travaille avec Alan Brookes Associates à Londres, et réalise des films publicitaires. Il commence en 1995 à collaborer avec Behnisch Architekten dont il devient associé en 2006. Leurs réalisations récentes incluent les thermes de Bad Aibling (2007) ; l'extension de l'établissement thermal Römerbad (Bad Kleinkirchheim, Carinthie, Autriche, 2006–07, publié ici) ; la résidence Kovner (Sebastopol, Californie, États-Unis, 2008) et Ozeaneum, le Musée océanographique de Stralsund (2008), toutes situées en Allemagne, sauf mention contraire.

RÖMERBAD THERMAL SPA EXTENSION

Bad Kleinkirchheim, Carinthia, Austria, 2006–07

Address: Dorfstr. 74, 9546 Bad Kleinkirchheim, Austria,
+43 240 8282 301, www.therme-badkleinkirchheim.at. Area: 10 260 m²
Client: Bad Kleinkirchheimer Thermen GmbH. Cost: €15 million

The Römerbad Thermal Spa opened in 1979 and was considered at the time to be an innovative departure in thermal spa architecture. The multistory main hall brought Roman baths to mind. Behnisch Architekten and five other architects were commissioned in 2005 to propose ways to renew the facility, and to add a wellness and sauna area, a rest room, a beauty area, and a children's space. Service spaces are concentrated on the northern side of the complex, while views of a stream and the mountains are privileged on the south. Thirteen new sauna and steam rooms were added in three different "landscape" configurations. The first of these, the Romanum, is on the lower level and "reflects the bathing culture of Ancient Rome." Near the entrance area, the Noricum "reflects the regional level of the spa—the water, forests and cliffs…" The so-called Maximum area is at the top of the spa, and is connected by a glazed spiral passage to the treatment area. Roof terraces are "integrated in the comprehensive graphic design of the roof as a fifth façade." A high atrium is included in the new wellness wing, while a sauna garden, new façades, and the general palette of materials and colors used harmonizes with the preexisting structure. The architects conclude: "As the name itself suggests, the atmosphere and ambience of this 'Roman Bath' is achieved not by merely ornamental means but by conscious abstraction, based on a limited number of essentially sculptural forms and colors."

Die Architektur des Römerbads galt 1979 bei seiner Eröffnung als ausgesprochen innovativ für Thermalbäder dieser Art – mit seiner mehrstöckigen Haupthalle erinnerte es an römische Bäder. 2005 bat man Behnisch Architekten sowie fünf andere Teams um einen Entwurf zur Sanierung des Komplexes und zum Anbau eines Wellness- und Saunabereichs, eines Ruheraums, eines Kosmetik- und eines Kinderbereichs. Betriebsräume wurden an der Nordseite des Komplexes gebündelt, während sich im Süden Ausblicke zum Fluss und zu den Bergen bieten. 13 neue Sauna- und Dampfbadeinrichtungen wurden hinzugefügt und verteilen sich über drei verschiedene „Landschaften". Das Romanum liegt auf der untersten Ebene und „spiegelt die Badekultur des alten Rom". Das Noricum hingegen befindet sich unweit des Eingangs und reflektiert „den regionalen Kontext des Spas – Wasser, Wälder und Felsen …" Das sogenannte Maximum schließlich liegt auf der obersten Ebene der Therme und ist durch eine verglaste Wendeltreppe mit den Behandlungsräumen verbunden. Dachterrassen wurden bei der betont grafischen Gestaltung des Dachs als fünfte Fassade integriert. Im neuen Wellnessbereich wurde ein hohes Atrium realisiert. Der Saunagarten, die neuen Fassaden und die allgemeine Farb- und Materialpalette harmonisieren mit dem bestehenden Altbau. Die Architekten fassen zusammen: „Wie schon der Name sagt, werden Atmosphäre und Flair des ‚Römerbads' nicht allein durch dekorative Elemente geschaffen, sondern durch bewusste Abstraktion, auf Grundlage einer begrenzten Anzahl im Grunde skulpturaler Formen und Farben."

L'établissement thermal Römerbad était considéré, à l'époque de son inauguration en 1979, comme une rupture innovante dans le domaine de l'architecture thermale. Le bâtiment principal de plusieurs étages évoquait les thermes romains. Behnisch Architekten et cinq autres architectes ont été invités, en 2005, à proposer un projet de rénovation de l'établissement, en y ajoutant un espace bien-être et sauna, des toilettes, un espace beauté, et un espace enfants. Les espaces de service sont concentrés dans la partie nord du complexe, tandis que la partie sud privilégie la vue sur un cours d'eau et les montagnes. Treize nouveaux saunas et bains de vapeur ont été rajoutés dans trois configurations « paysagères » différentes. La première, le Romanum, situé au niveau inférieur, « évoque la culture des bains de la Rome antique ». Situé à proximité de l'entrée, le Noricum « évoque l'aspect régional des thermes – l'eau, les forêts et les à-pics… ». Enfin, le Maximum, situé au niveau supérieur, est relié à l'espace de soins par un passage vitré en spirale. Des toits-terrasses sont « intégrés dans la conception globale du dessin du toit comme une cinquième façade… ». Un atrium élevé est inclus dans la nouvelle aile de l'espace bien-être, tandis que le jardin du sauna, les nouvelles façades et la gamme générale des matériaux et des couleurs utilisés s'harmonisent avec le bâtiment préexistant. Les architectes concluent ainsi : « Comme le suggère leur nom, l'atmosphère et l'ambiance de ces "bains romains" ne sont pas simplement créés par le décor, mais par une abstraction consciente fondée sur un nombre restreint de formes sculpturales et de couleurs. »

A site plan (right) and photos of the spa suggest a careful integration of the architecture into the topography of the location. A section drawing (below) brings to mind the form of a cruise ship.

Wie der Lageplan (rechts) und Ansichten der Therme zeigen, wurde die Architektur einfühlsam in die ört-liche Topografie integriert. Der Gebäudeschnitt (unten) erinnert an ein Kreuzfahrtschiff.

Un plan de situation (à droite) et des photos de l'établissement thermal suggèrent une intégration attentive de l'architecture dans la topographie du lieu. Une coupe (ci-dessous) évoque la forme d'un bateau de croisière.

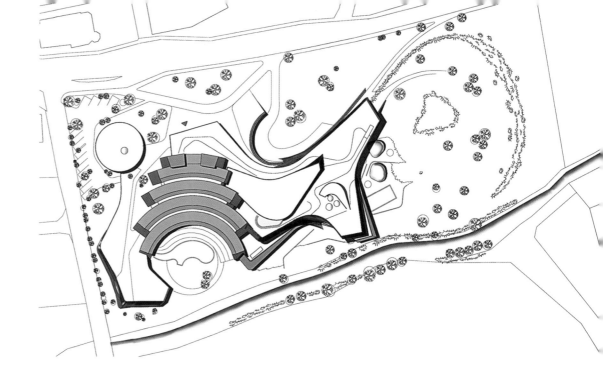

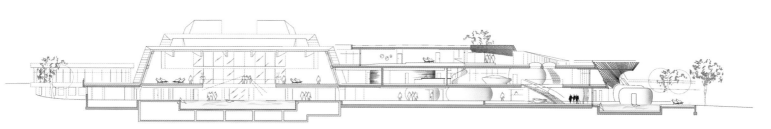

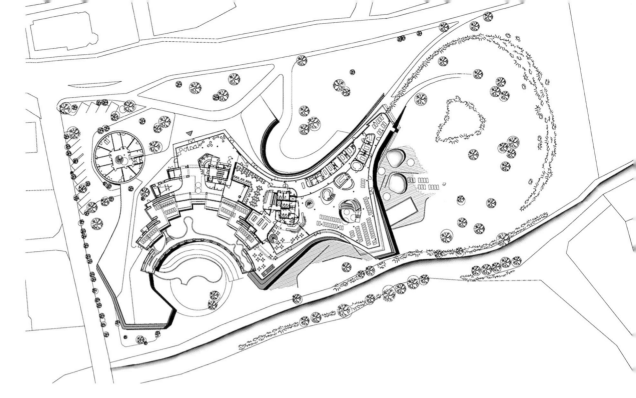

The sinuous curves of the baths and other architectural elements reinforce the impression that the building is almost carved out of its surroundings.

Die geschwungenen Formen der Becken und anderer architektonischer Elemente verstärken den Eindruck, das Gebäude sei geradezu aus seinem Umfeld herausgeschnitten worden.

Les courbes sinueuses des thermes et des autres éléments architecturaux renforcent l'impression d'un bâtiment presque sculpté dans son environnement.

HAGY BELZBERG

Belzberg Architects
2321 Main Street
Santa Monica, CA 90405
USA

Tel: +1 310 453 9611
Fax: +1 310 453 9166
E-mail: hb@belzbergarchitects.com
Web: www.belzbergarchitects.com

HAGY BELZBERG received his M.Arch degree from the Harvard GSD and began his professional career with explorations of non-standardized construction methodology involving digital manufacturing. In 2000, he was awarded the contract to design the interior space of Frank Gehry's Walt Disney Concert Hall (Los Angeles, 2003), where he utilized digital machining and prefabrication to work within the complex existing structure. In 2008, he was selected as an "Emerging Voice" by the Architectural League of New York. His work includes 20th Street Offices (Santa Monica, California, 2009); Skyline Residence (Los Angeles, California, 2008–10); Kona Residence (Kona, Hawaii, 2010, published here); Los Angeles Museum of the Holocaust (Los Angeles, California, 2010); 9800 Wilshire Boulevard Offices (Beverly Hills, California, 2012); City of Hope Cancer Research Museum (Duarte, California, 2013); and the Occidental College Center for Global Affairs (Los Angeles, 2013), all in the USA.

HAGY BELZBERG schloss sein Studium mit einem M. Arch. an der Harvard GSD ab und forschte zu Beginn seiner Laufbahn zu Konstruktionsmethoden mit nicht-standardisierten Bauteilen und digitaler Fertigung. 2000 gewann er die Ausschreibung für den Innenausbau der Walt Disney Concert Hall von Frank Gehry (Los Angeles, 2003). Dort arbeitete er mit digitalen Fertigungsmethoden und digitaler Vorfertigung, um dem komplexen Bau gerecht zu werden. 2008 zeichnete ihn der Architektenverband New York als „Neues Talent" aus. Zu seinen Projekten zählen Büros an der 20th Street (Santa Monica, Kalifornien, 2009), die Skyline Residence (Los Angeles, Kalifornien, 2008–10), das Holocaust-Museum in Los Angeles (2010), die Kona Residence (Kona, Hawaii, 2010, hier vorgestellt), Büros am 9800 Wilshire Boulevard (Beverly Hills, Kalifornien, 2012), das City of Hope Museum für Krebsforschung (Duarte, Kalifornien, 2013) sowie das Occidental College am Center for Global Affairs (Los Angeles, 2013), alle in den USA.

HAGY BELZBERG a obtenu son diplôme de M.Arch. à la Harvard GSD et entamé sa carrière professionnelle par l'exploration de méthodologies de constructions non standard dont les techniques de fabrication pilotées par ordinateur. En 2000, il a été chargé de l'aménagement intérieur du Walt Disney Concert Hall de Frank Gehry (Los Angeles, 2003) où il a utilisé des techniques d'usinage numérique et de préfabrication pour s'adapter à une structure complexe. En 2008, il a été désigné «Voix émergente» par l'Architectural League de New York. Parmi ses réalisations, toutes aux États-Unis : les bureaux de la 20e Rue (Santa Monica, Californie, 2009) ; la Skyline Residence (Los Angeles, Californie, 2008–10) ; la Kona Residence (Kona, Hawaï, 2010, publiée ici) ; le musée de l'Holocauste de Los Angeles (Los Angeles, 2010) ; les bureaux du 9800 Wilshire Boulevard (Beverly Hills, Californie, 2012), le musée de la Recherche sur le cancer City of Hope (Duarte, Californie, 2013) et l'Occidental College Center for Global Affairs (Los Angeles, 2013).

KONA RESIDENCE

Kona, Hawaii, USA, 2010

Address: not diclosed. Area: 725 m². Client: not disclosed. Cost: not disclosed
Collaboration: Barry Gartin (Project Manager), David Cheung, Cory Taylor

Wood and stone finishes are juxta-
posed in the exterior design. The
warm interiors, where wood domi-
nates, can be seen through the gen-
erously glazed façades.

Am Außenbau, rechts im Bild, kontrastieren Fassadenelemente aus Holz
und Stein. Durch die großzügige Verglasung fällt der Blick auf das warme
Interieur, in dem Holz dominiert.

À l'extérieur, on retrouve la juxtaposi-
tion de la pierre et du bois. L'intérieur chaleureux, où prédomine le
bois, se perçoit à travers les
immenses baies vitrées.

The architect based the alignments of this house, built between hardened lava flows, on the viewing axis of volcanic mountains to the east and the ocean to the west. According to the designers: "The program is arranged as a series of pods distributed throughout the property, each having its own unique features and view opportunities. The pods are programmatically assigned as two sleeping pods with common areas, media room, master suite, and main living space. An exterior gallery corridor becomes the organizational and focal feature for the entire house, connecting the two pods along a central axis." Rooftop photovoltaic panels, rainwater collection, and drywells are part of the environmental aspects of the design. Recycled teak wood and local cut lava make reference to local building tradition, as does the entry pavilion inspired by Hawaiian basket weaving. Wood ceilings and screen sculpted with digital technology "continue the abstract approach to traditional Hawaiian wood carving, further infusing traditional elements into the contemporary arrangement."

Der Architekt plante das Haus, das zwischen erstarrten Lavafeldern liegt, entlang von Sichtachsen zu den Vulkanbergen im Osten und zum Meer im Westen. Die Planer erklären: „Das Programm wurde in einer Reihe von Raumeinheiten untergebracht, die über das gesamte Gelände verteilt sind und jeweils besondere Highlights und Ausblicke bieten. Die Einheiten gliedern sich programmatisch in zwei Schlafeinheiten mit Gemeinschaftsbereichen, Medienzimmer, Hauptschlafzimmer mit Nebenräumen und Hauptwohnraum. Ein als Galerie gestalteter Außenkorridor bildet den organisatorischen Kern des gesamten Hauses und verbindet die zwei Raumeinheiten entlang einer Mittelachse." Ökologische Aspekte des Entwurfs sind Solarmodule auf dem Dach, Regenwassernutzung sowie Vorfluter. Mit recyceltem Teakholz, vor Ort gebrochenem Lavagestein und dem Eingangspavillon, einer Reminiszenz an hawaiianische Korbflechttechniken, erweist der Entwurf lokalen Bautraditionen seine Reverenz. Holzdecken und ein digital gefertigter Wandschirm „setzen die abstrakte Interpretation traditioneller hawaiianischer Holzschnitztechniken fort und lassen weitere traditionelle Elemente in das zeitgenössische Ensemble einfließen".

Les axes de cette maison, construite entre d'anciennes coulées de lave, matérialisent des vues sur une chaîne de volcans à l'est et l'océan à l'ouest. « Le programme est décliné en une série d'unités réparties sur la parcelle, chacune possédant ses caractéristiques et ses perspectives propres. Chacune remplit en effet une fonction : deux chambres avec des espaces communs, un salon média, une grande chambre et un séjour principal. Une galerie extérieure constitue l'axe visuel et organisationnel de la maison toute entière en reliant les unités le long de son axe central. » Des panneaux photovoltaïques en toiture, la collecte des eaux de pluie et des puits secs illustrent le caractère écologique du projet. Le bois de teck recyclé et la pierre de lave renvoient aux traditions constructives locales, de même que le pavillon d'entrée inspiré de l'art du cannage hawaïen. Des plafonds et des écrans sculptés par technologies numériques « reprennent l'approche abstraite de la sculpture du bois hawaïenne, ce qui renforce la présence des éléments traditionnels dans cet aménagement contemporain ».

Above, dining and sunning areas come together in space that takes advantage of the warm local climate. The distinction between interior and exterior is absent.

Essbereich und Sonnenterrasse profitieren vom warmen Klima der Region und gehen fließend ineinander über. Auf eine Trennung von Innen- und Außenraum wurde verzichtet.

Ci-dessus, la terrasse-salle à manger couverte et le solarium bénéficient pleinement de la douceur du climat local. La distinction entre l'intérieur et l'extérieur a été gommée.

Above, the angled exterior forms of the house contrast materials and surfaces, some completely opaque, others transparent or reflective.

Oben: Die winklingen äußeren Formen des Hauses bilden einen Kontrast zu den Materialien und Oberflächen, die mal ganz opak, mal transparent oder reflektierend sind.

Ci-dessus, les formes anguleuses extérieures de la maison contrastent avec les matériaux et les surfaces, certaines opaques, d'autres transparentes ou réfléchissantes.

Below, the asymmetric entrance archway of the house, apparently inspired by local crafts. A drawing of the entrance canopy is seen on the right page.

Unten der asymmetrische Bogengang am Eingang, inspiriert von lokalen Handwerkstraditionen (rechts unten in einer Zeichnung).

Ci-dessous, la pergola asymétrique de l'entrée, apparemment inspirée de traditions artisanales locales. À droite, dessin de cette même arche.

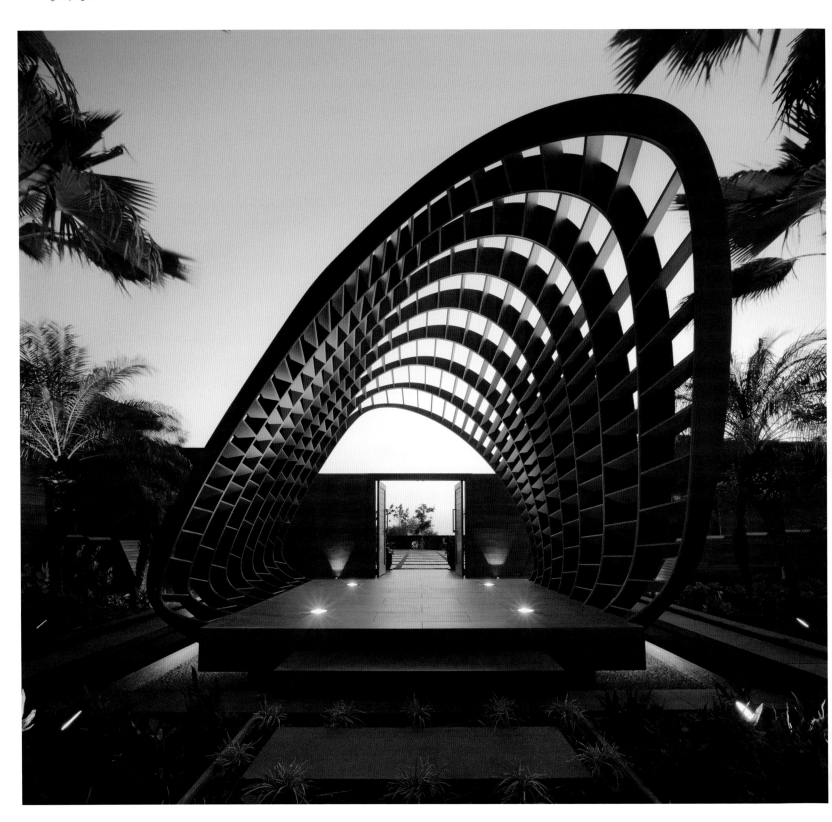

Fully opening walls allow private space to be almost entirely outside, while still within the protection of the house.

Private Wohnbereiche lassen sich durch vollständig zu öffnende Wände geradezu als Außenbereich definieren und liegen dennoch unter einem schützenden Dach.

Les murs de verre qui s'ouvrent entièrement dilatent les pièces vers l'extérieur, tout en les maintenant dans l'enveloppe protectrice de la maison.

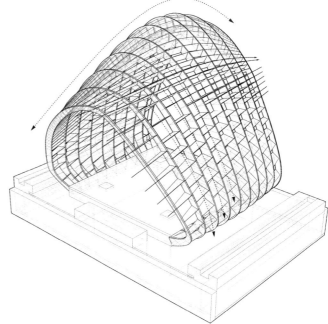

On this page, the wooden detailing of the house is extensive and sometimes takes on organic forms, as in the bedroom screen and ceiling to the left.

Im Haus finden sich auffällig viele Holzarbeiten, oft in organischen Formen wie der Raumteiler und die Decke im Schlafzimmer links.

La présence du bois dans certains détails d'aménagement est très forte. Elle prend parfois une forme organique comme dans la claustra et le plafond de la chambre à gauche.

Interiors echo the contrasting materials employed by the architect outside the house. Large glazed openings offer spectacular views of the natural setting.

Die Innenräume greifen die kontrastierenden Materialien auf, die der Architekt außen verwendete. Große verglaste Öffnungen bieten spektakuläre Ausblicke auf die Natur.

Les espaces intérieurs font écho aux contrastes des matériaux utilisés par l'architecte pour l'extérieur. De larges baies vitrées offrent des vues spectaculaires sur la nature environnante

BERNARDES + JACOBSEN

Bernardes Arquitetura
Rua Corcovado 250
Jardim Botânico
22460–050 Rio de Janeiro, RJ, Brazil

Tel/Fax: +55 21 2512 7743
E-mail: bjrj@bja.com.br
Web: www.bja.com.br

Jacobsen Arquitetura
Rua Pacheco Leão 862
Jardim Botânico
22460–030 Rio de Janeiro, RJ, Brazil

Tel/Fax: +55 21 227 42700
E-mail: contato@jacobsenarquitetura.com
Web: www.jacobsenarquitetura.com

THIAGO BERNARDES was born in Rio de Janeiro in 1974. The office of Bernardes + Jacobsen was created in 1980 by his father, Claudio Bernardes, and Paulo Jacobsen, pioneers of a new type of residential architecture based on an effort to combine contemporary design and Brazilian culture. Thiago Bernardes worked in his father's office from 1991 to 1996, when he left to create his own firm, working on more than 30 residential projects between that date and 2001. With the death of his father, Thiago Bernardes reintegrated the firm and began to work with **PAULO JACOBSEN**, who was born in 1954 in Rio. Jacobsen studied photography in London before graduating from the Bennett Methodist Institute in 1979. **BERNARDO JACOBSEN** was born in 1980 and joined the company in 2007, after graduating from the Federal University of Rio de Janeiro and working in the offices of Christian de Portzamparc and Shigeru Ban. Some of their significant projects include the Gerdau Headquarters (Porto Alegre, 2005); FW House (Guarujá, 2005); and the MPM Agency Main Office (São Paulo, 2006). More recent work includes the JH House (São Paulo, 2008); the JZ House (Bahia, 2008, published here); RW House (Búzios, Rio de Janeiro, 2009); the FN and DB Houses (both in São Paulo, 2009); and the Joá House (Rio de Janeiro, Rio de Janeiro, 2010–11), all in Brazil unless stated otherwise. Finally, they worked together on MAR, Art Museum of Rio (Rio de Janeiro, 2010–13). The office split in 2011, creating Jacobsen Arquitetura (Bernardo and Paulo Jacobsen) and Bernardes Arquitetura.

THIAGO BERNARDES wurde 1974 in Rio de Janeiro geboren. 1980 gründete sein Vater Claudio Bernardes mit Paulo Jacobsen das Büro Bernardes + Jacobsen. Die Partner waren Pioniere einer neuen Wohnbauarchitektur, die zeitgenössische Gestaltung und brasilianische Kultur miteinander vereinte. Von 1991 bis 1996 war Thiago Bernardes im Büro seines Vaters tätig und gründete schließlich sein eigenes Büro, mit dem er zwischen 1996 und 2001 über 30 Wohnbauprojekte realisierte. Nach dem Tod seines Vaters führte Thiago Bernardes die Büros zusammen und arbeitet seither mit **PAULO JACOBSEN**, geboren 1954 in Rio. Jacobsen studierte Fotografie in London, bevor er 1979 sein Studium am Bennett Methodist Institute abschloss. **BERNARDO JACOBSEN** wurde 1980 geboren und ist seit 2007 Miglied der Firma. Zuvor hat er sein Studium an der Bundesuniversität Rio de Janeiro abgeschlossen und in den Büros von Christian de Portzamparc und Shigeru Ban gearbeitet. Ausgewählte Schlüsselprojekte sind u. a. die Gerdau-Zentrale (Porto Alegre, 2005), das Haus FW (Guarujá, 2005) sowie die Hauptniederlassung der Agentur MPM (São Paulo, 2006). Neuere Projekte sind u. a. das Haus JH (São Paulo, 2008), das Haus JZ (Bahia, 2008, hier vorgestellt), das Haus RW (Búzios, Rio de Janeiro, 2009), das Haus FN und das Haus DB (beide in São Paulo, 2009) sowie das Haus Joá (Rio de Janeiro, 2010–11), alle in Brasilien, sofern nicht anders angegeben. Zuletzt arbeiteten sie am Kunstmuseum MAR in Rio (Rio de Janeiro, 2010–13). Das Büro spaltete sich im Jahr 2011 in Jacobsen Arquitetura (Bernardo und Paulo Jacobsen) und Bernardes Arquitetura.

THIAGO BERNARDES est né à Rio de Janeiro en 1974. L'agence Bernardes + Jacobsen a été fondée en 1980 par son père, Claudio Bernardes, et par Paulo Jacobsen, pionniers d'un nouveau type d'architecture résidentielle qui souhaitait associer principes de la conception architecturale contemporaine et culture brésilienne. Thiago Bernardes a travaillé dans l'agence paternelle de 1991 à 1996, puis a créé sa propre structure, réalisant plus de 30 projets résidentiels jusqu'en 2001. Après le décès de son père, il a réintégré l'agence de celui-ci et commencé à collaborer avec **PAULO JACOBSEN**, né en 1954 à Rio de Janeiro. Jacobsen avait étudié la photographie à Londres, avant d'être diplômé de l'Institut méthodiste Bennett de Rio en 1979. **BERNARDO JACOBSEN** est né en 1980 et a rejoint l'agence en 2007, après avoir été diplômé de l'université fédérale de Rio de Janeiro et avoir travaillé dans les agences de Christian de Portzamparc et Shigeru Ban. Parmi leurs réalisations les plus significatives, la plupart au Brésil : le siège de Gerdau (Porto Alegre, 2005) ; la maison FW (Guarujá, 2005) et le siège de l'agence MPM (São Paulo, 2006). Parmi leurs travaux plus récents : la maison JH (São Paulo, 2008) ; la maison JZ (Bahia, 2008, publiée ici) ; la maison RW (Búzios, 2009) ; les maisons FN et DB (São Paulo, 2009) et la maison Joá (Rio de Janeiro, 2010–11). Finalement, ils ont travaillé à MAR, le Musée d'art de Rio (Rio de Janeiro, 2010–13). En 2011, l'agence s'est divisée en Jacobsen Arquitetura (Bernardo et Paulo Jacobsen) et Bernardes Arquitetura.

JZ HOUSE

Camaçari, Bahia, Brazil, 2006–08

Address: not diclosed. Area: 1850 m². Client: not disclosed. Cost: not disclosed
Collaboration: Ricardo C. Branco, Veridiana Ruzzante, Marina Nogaró

The architects deal with the delicate placement of the house on a sand dune by lifting it up in good part on pilotis. Its unusual form is clearly visible in the image below.

Die Architekten reagierten auf die problematische Lage des Hauses auf einer Düne, indem sie es zu einem Großteil auf dünnen Stützen aufständerten. Die ungewöhnliche Form des Hauses ist unten deutlich zu sehen.

Les architectes ont résolu le délicat problème de l'implantation sur une dune en soulevant une grande partie de la maison par des pilotis. La forme très particulière du projet est mise en valeur dans l'image ci-dessous.

Built on a sand dune, this house has a reinforced-concrete base, but is otherwise made entirely of wood. A volume containing bedrooms is lifted on pilotis, creating parking space below. The main part of the house is a "great room" with a view of the ocean and garden. The fact that this volume and much of the house is lifted up on the dune assures ample cross-ventilation from sea winds. This main living space directs the organization of the remaining parts of the house. An effort was made to use local materials, such as eucalyptus trellises and Bahia beige marble for the floors, and also to select tones that blend harmoniously with the sand, for example. A solarium and swimming pool on the beach side complete this undeniably spectacular house.

Das auf einer Düne gelegene Haus hat ein Fundament aus Stahlbeton, besteht ansonsten jedoch ausschließlich aus Holz. Die Schlafzimmer befinden sich im auf dünnen Stützen aufgeständerten Bau, unter dem auf diese Weise Pkw-Stellplätze entstanden. Hauptbereich des Hauses ist ein „großer Raum" mit Blick auf das Meer und den Garten. Dank der Lage dieses Hausbereichs und eines Großteils des Baus auf der Düne werden die Räume ausreichend mit Wind vom Meer durchlüftet. Nach Möglichkeit wurden lokale Baumaterialien genutzt, wie bei den Gittern aus Eukalyptusholz und den cremefarbenen Böden aus Bahia-Marmor. Darüber hinaus wurde darauf geachtet, eine Palette von Farbtönen zu wählen, die mit dem Sand am Strand harmoniert. Eine Sonnenterrasse und ein Pool auf der Strandseite des Gebäudes vervollständigen das zweifellos spektakuläre Haus.

Cette maison entièrement en bois se dresse sur un socle en béton armé au sommet d'une dune de sable. Le volume des chambres est surélevé par des pilotis, libérant un espace de parking au niveau du sol. La partie principale est une « grande pièce » qui donne sur l'océan et le jardin. La surélévation de ce volume et de la plus grande partie de la construction assure une importante ventilation croisée par les vents de la mer. L'espace de séjour principal dicte l'organisation du reste de la résidence. On s'est efforcé d'utiliser des matériaux locaux, comme, par exemple, des treillis en bois d'eucalyptus, du marbre beige de Bahia pour les sols, ou des couleurs harmonisées avec celle du sable. Du côté de la plage, un solarium et une piscine complètent les installations de cette maison spectaculaire.

The house exudes a tropical atmosphere befitting its seaside location. Wood is the most prominent cladding material inside.

Passend zur Lage am Meer vermittelt das Haus eine tropische Atmosphäre. Holz ist das dominierende Material im Innenraum.

L'atmosphère tropicale de l'intérieur de la maison est en accord avec la nature environnante. À l'intérieur, le bois est le matériau d'habillage de prédilection.

Plans and, above all, the image above
show how the residence opens out
toward the beach. From the living
space, both the balcony in the middle
ground and the background ocean
view are part of a carefully designed
and luxurious composition.

Die Grundrisse und vor allem die
Aufnahme oben illustrieren, wie sich
das Haus zum Strand hin öffnet. Vom
Hauptwohnraum aus wirken der
Mittelgrund mit der Empore und der
Meerblick im Hintergrund wie eine
sorgfältig gestaltete, luxuriöse
Komposition.

Les plans, et mieux encore, l'image
ci-dessus, montrent l'ouverture totale
de la maison sur la plage. Vus du
séjour, le balcon intérieur et la vue
sur l'océan font partie d'une composition soignée, placée sous le signe
du luxe.

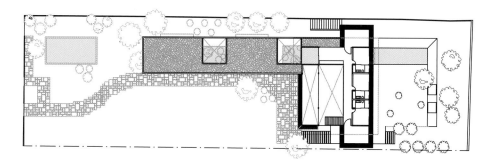

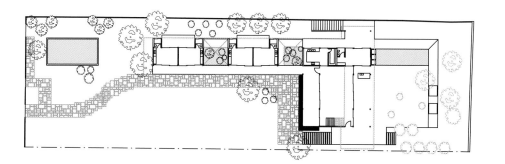

TITUS BERNHARD

Titus Bernhard Architekten
Gögginger Str. 105a
86199 Augsburg
Germany

Tel: +49 821 59 96 05 0
Fax: +49 821 59 96 05 10
E-mail: info@bernhardarchitekten.com
Web: www.bernhardarchitekten.com

TITUS BERNHARD was born in 1963 in Augsburg, Germany. He studied architecture at the Braunschweig Technical University (1983–91) and worked in the office of Richard Meier (New York, 1987), before studying at the Politecnico di Milano under Giorgio Grassi. He created his own office in Augsburg in 1995. His work includes the FCA Stadium (with Bernhard & Kögl Architekten; Augsburg, 2010); House M (Grünwald, 2010); House 11x11 (near Munich, 2010–11, published here); House K (Starnberg, 2012); and House R (Grünwald, 2013), all in Germany.

TITUS BERNHARD wurde 1963 in Augsburg geboren. Er studierte Architektur an der Technischen Universität Braunschweig (1983–91) und arbeitete im Büro von Richard Meier (New York, 1987), bevor er am Politecnico di Milano bei Giorgio Grassi studierte. 1995 gründete er ein Büro in Augsburg. Zu seinen Arbeiten gehören das Stadion des FC Augsburg (mit Bernhard & Kögl Architekten; Augsburg, 2010), Haus M (Grünwald, 2010), Haus 11x11 (bei München, 2010–11, hier vorgestellt), Haus K (Starnberg, 2012) und Haus R (Grünwald, 2013); alle in Deutschland.

TITUS BERNHARD est né en 1963 à Augsbourg, Allemagne. Il a étudié l'architecture à l'Université technique (TU) de Braunschweig (1983–91) et travaillé dans l'agence de Richard Meier (New York, 1987) avant d'étudier à l'École polytechnique de Milan sous la direction de Giorgio Grassi. Il a créé sa propre agence à Augsbourg en 1995. Parmi ses réalisations figurent le FCA Stadium (avec Bernhard & Kögl Architekten ; Augsbourg, 2010) ; la Haus M (Grünwald, 2010) ; la Haus 11x11 (près de Munich, 2010–11, publiée ici) ; la Haus K (Starnberg, 2012) et la Haus R (Grünwald, 2013), toutes en Allemagne.

HOUSE 11x11

near Munich, Germany, 2010–11

Address: not disclosed. Area: 182 m². Client: not disclosed
Cost: not disclosed. Collaboration: Gebrüder Loy (Façade)

The exterior walls and wooden roof of this house were made with prefabricated elements covered with a vertical wood-lamella façade that converges on the roof. Even the wooden window frames are integrated into the pattern, giving an impression of carefully designed forms. The density of the wood pattern varies, reflecting, to some extent, the interior design. The ground floor is an open space, and the plan of the house is a square. The architect states: "The idea behind **HOUSE 11x11** was to design an apparently compact house of homogenous materials, with a low external profile but as large a usable area as possible, a house that serves a family as an inhabitable sculpture and shows its exterior as an image of the inner organization."

Die Außenwände und das Holzdach dieses Hauses bestehen aus vorgefertigten Elementen und sind mit vertikalen, auf dem Dach zusammenlaufenden Holzlamellen versehen. Selbst die hölzernen Fensterrahmen sind in dieses Muster integriert und erwecken den Eindruck sorgsamer Formgebung. Die Dichte des Holzmusters variiert und reflektiert bis zu einem gewissen Grad den inneren Aufbau des Hauses. Das Erdgeschoss ist offen, der Grundriss des Hauses quadratisch. Der Architekt: „Dem **HAUS 11x11** liegt der Gedanke zugrunde, ein in seiner Erscheinung kompaktes und seiner Materialanmutung homogenes Haus mit geringer Hüllfläche bei größtmöglicher Nutzfläche zu entwerfen, ein Haus, das einer Familie als bewohnbare Skulptur dient und sein Äußeres als Abbild der inneren Organisation zeigt."

Les murs extérieurs et la toiture en bois de cette maison sont réalisés en éléments préfabriqués recouverts d'une façade verticale en lamelles de bois qui converge en toiture. Même les châssis en bois des fenêtres sont intégrés dans la trame, ce qui donne l'impression de formes conçues avec un grand soin. La densité de la trame en bois est variable et reflète dans une certaine mesure l'aménagement intérieur. Le rez-de-chaussée se présente sous la forme d'un grand espace, tandis que le plan de la maison définit un carré. L'architecte précise : « L'idée à l'origine de la **HAUS 11x11** consistait à concevoir une maison, apparemment compacte, construite en matériaux homogènes, avec une élévation limitée, mais avec une surface utile aussi vaste que possible, une maison qui sert de sculpture habitable à une famille et dont l'extérieur est une image de l'organisation intérieure. »

The square volume is partially glazed on the ground floor and covered with vertical slats of wood that even include the roof. Right, the interior is bright and essentially white.

Der quaderförmige Baukörper ist im Erdgeschoss teils verglast und bis aufs Dach hinauf mit vertikalen Holz-lamellen verkleidet. Rechts der helle und vornehmlich weiße Innenraum.

Le volume carré est partiellement vitré au rez-de-chaussée et recouvert de lattes verticales de bois qui habillent même la toiture. À droite, l'intérieur est lumineux et majoritai-rement blanc.

Wood is present on the floors and window frames, but otherwise, simple, often angled white walls form the interior spaces.

Fußböden und Fensterrahmen sind aus Holz. Sonst zeichnen sich die Innenräume durch schlichte weiße, teils schräge Wände aus.

Le bois est présent sur les sols et les châssis des fenêtres, tandis que des murs blancs sobres, souvent à angles droits, délimitent les espaces intérieurs.

Above, two floor plans demonstrate how the architect has notched and opened the basic volume, creating such unexpected interior spaces as the one seen above, where a window is angled or bent upward.

Die Grundrisse oben veranschaulichen, wie der Architekt den Baukörper eingeschnitten und geöffnet hat. Überraschende Innenräume entstehen – wie im Bild oben mit einem abgewinkelten Fenster.

Ci-dessus, deux plans de niveau montrent comment l'architecte a entaillé et ouvert le volume de base, créant ainsi des intérieurs aussi inattendus que celui présenté ci-dessus où une fenêtre forme un angle et se plie vers le haut.

BIRK & HEILMEYER

Birk Heilmeyer und Frenzel Gesellschaft von Architekten mbH
Adlerstraße 31
70199 Stuttgart
Germany

Tel: +49 711 664 822 0
Fax: +49 711 664 822 28
E-mail: info@bhundf.com
Web: www.bhundf.de

STEPHAN BIRK was born in 1975 in Stuttgart. He studied architecture at the University of Stuttgart and worked for architects in Stuttgart, Boston, and London before cofounding Birk und Heilmeyer Architekten in Stuttgart in 2005 with his wife. **LIZA HEILMEYER** was born in 1975 in Freiburg im Breisgau, Germany. She studied architecture at the University of Stuttgart, and worked for architects in Stuttgart; Cambridge, Massachusetts; and London before cofounding the studio Birk und Heilmeyer. Their work includes a Glass Tube Bridge (prototype of a glass footbridge, 2003–04); a 500-car parking garage in Coesfeld-Lette (2005–07); Architecture Gallery am Weißenhof (Stuttgart, 2007); the Jübergtower (Hemer, 2010, published here); a modular system of ten new preschools / daycare centers (Frankfurt, 2010–13); and the Robotik and Mechatronic Center (Oberpfaffenhofen, 2011–14), all in Germany.

STEPHAN BIRK wurde 1975 in Stuttgart geboren. Er studierte Architektur an der Universität Stuttgart und arbeitete für verschiedene Architekturbüros in Stuttgart, Boston und London, bevor er 2005 mit seiner Frau das Büro Birk und Heilmeyer Architekten gründete. **LIZA HEILMEYER** wurde 1975 in Freiburg im Breisgau geboren. Sie studierte Architektur an der Universität Stuttgart und arbeitete vor der Gründung von Birk und Heilmeyer Architekten für verschiedene Büros in Stuttgart, Cambridge, Massachusetts und London. Projekte des Teams sind u. a. eine Rohrglasbrücke (Prototyp einer gläsernen Fußgängerbrücke, 2003–04), ein Parkhaus mit 500 Stellplätzen in Coesfeld-Lette (2005–07), die Architekturgalerie am Weißenhof (Stuttgart, 2007), der Jübergturm (Hemer, 2010, hier vorgestellt), ein Baukastensystem für zehn neue Kindertagesstätten (Frankfurt am Main, 2010–13) sowie das Zentrum für Robotik und Mechatronik (Oberpfaffenhofen, 2011–14), alle in Deutschland.

STEPHAN BIRK, né en 1975 à Stuttgart, a étudié l'architecture à l'université de cette ville et travaillé en agence à Stuttgart, Boston et Londres avant de fonder Birk und Heilmeyer Architekten à Stuttgart avec son épouse en 2005. **LIZA HEILMEYER**, née en 1975 à Fribourg-en-Brisgau (Allemagne), a étudié l'architecture à l'université de Stuttgart et travaillé pour des agences à Stuttgart, Cambridge, Massachusetts et Londres avant de fonder leur agence. Parmi leurs réalisations, toutes en Allemagne, figurent : un pont en tubes de verre (prototype d'une passerelle de verre, 2003–04) ; un garage pour 500 voitures à Coesfeld-Lette (2005–07) ; la Galerie d'architecture am Weißenhof (Stuttgart, 2007) ; la tour Jüberg (Hemer, 2010, publiée ici) ; un système modulaire conçu pour dix nouvelles écoles maternelles et jardins d'enfants (Francfort, 2010–13) et le Centre de robotique et mécatronique (Oberpfaffenhofen, 2011–14), tous en Allemagne.

JÜBERGTOWER

Hemer, Germany, 2010

Height: 23.5 meters. Client: Landesgartenschau Hemer 2010. Cost: €500 000
Collaboration: Knippers Helbig Advanced Engineering

This structure is a landmark for the regional garden and flower festival "Landesgartenschau Hemer 2010" in North Rhine–Westphalia. The architects used 240 Siberian larch square glulam beams (8 x 8 centimeters) in a hyperboloid pattern. Steel was used to anchor the tower six meters into the bedrock on which it stands. With its mesh structure expanding toward the top, the tower appears to be progressively lighter and lighter as visitors ascend past the five landing platforms on the way to the observation deck. Built in just six weeks, the structure has a six-meter-diameter base, and a nine-meter-diameter observation deck offering a 360° view.

Der Turm war eine der Landmarken der Landesgartenschau 2010 in Hemer, einer regionalen Blumen- und Gartenschau in Nordrhein-Westfalen. Die Architekten verarbeiteten 240 Brettschichthölzer aus Sibirischer Lärche (8 x 8 cm) zu einem Hyperbolid-Muster. Verankert wurde der Turm mit 6 m langen Stahlstäben im Felsgrund. Die sich nach oben erweiternde Netzstruktur wird lichter und lichter, je höher die Besucher die fünf Treppenabsätze bis zur Aussichtsplattform emporsteigen. Die Basis des in nur sechs Wochen erbauten Turms hat einen Durchmesser von 6 m, die Aussichtsplattform mit 9 m Durchmesser bietet eine 360-Grad-Rundumsicht.

Cette structure a été le centre d'attraction du Festival des jardins et des fleurs « Landesgartenschau Hemer 2010 » en Rhénanie-du-Nord-Westphalie. Les architectes ont utilisé 240 poutres en contrecollé de mélèze de Sibérie (de 8 x 8 cm de section) assemblées selon une forme hyperboloïde. Des ancrages en acier ont été scellés à 6 m de profondeur dans le rocher sur lequel repose la tour. Grâce à sa structure maillée qui s'évase en partie supérieure, celle-ci semble de plus en plus légère et transparente aux visiteurs qui escaladent ses cinq plates-formes intermédiaires avant d'accéder à l'observatoire. Construite en six semaines seulement, la tour possède un diamètre de 6 m à sa base et de 9 m pour la plate-forme du sommet qui offre une vue panoramique à 360°.

The use of larch to form the exterior mesh of the tower makes an interesting contrast between the essentially natural material and the specifically contemporary form of the structure.

Durch den Einsatz von Lärchenholz für das äußere Gitterwerk des Turms entstehen interessante Kontraste zwischen einem natürlichen Material und der dezidiert zeitgenössischen Formensprache des Baus.

Le bois de mélèze de la trame extérieure apporte un contraste intéressant avec la forme spécifiquement contemporaine de cette tour.

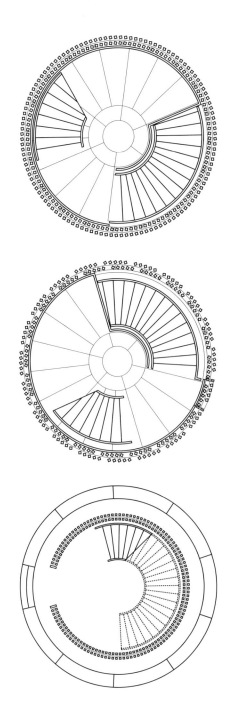

The density of the larch mesh cladding decreases as visitors rise up through the spiral steel staircase of the tower. Floor plans at various levels show the circular design with increasing diameters.

Das Gitternetz der Lärchenverkleidung wird lichter, je weiter die Besucher die stählerne Wendeltreppe im Turm hinaufsteigen. Etagengrundrisse verschiedener Ebenen zeigen den wachsenden Durchmesser der kreisrunden Konstruktion.

Les visiteurs qui empruntent l'escalier en spirale voient la densité de la trame du treillis de mélèze diminuer avec la hauteur. Les plans des niveaux montrent par ailleurs l'augmentation du diamètre des paliers.

BOHLIN CYWINSKI JACKSON

Bohlin Cywinski Jackson
8 West Market Street, Suite 1200
Wilkes-Barre, PA 18701,USA
Tel: +1 570 825 8756 / Fax: +1 570 825 3744
E-mail: bcjwilkesbarre@bcj.com / Web: www.bcj.com

BOHLIN CYWINSKI JACKSON was founded in 1965 by Peter Bohlin and Richard Powell in Wilkes-Barre, Pennsylvania. Peter Bohlin received a B.Arch from Rensselaer Polytechnic Institute (1959), and an M.Arch from Cranbrook Academy of Art (1961). Today the Principals are Peter Bohlin, Bernard Cywinski, Jon Jackson, Dan Haden, Frank Grauman, William Loose, Randy Reid, Karl Backus, Gregory Mottola, Roxanne Sherbeck, and Robert Miller. The firm has additional offices in Pittsburgh, Philadelphia, Seattle, and San Francisco. In 1994, the practice received the Architecture Firm Award from the American Institute of Architects. Significant work includes the Pacific Rim Estate (Medina, Washington, 1997, joint venture with Cutler Anderson Architects); Headquarters for Pixar Animation Studios (Emeryville, California, 2001); and the Liberty Bell Center Independence National Historical Park (Philadelphia, Pennsylvania, 2003). In 2005, they completed the House at the Shawangunks (New Paltz, New York, 2003–05, published here), the Ballard Library and Neighborhood Service Center (Seattle, Washington), listed by the AIA as one of the "Top Ten Green Buildings" for that year, and a couple of years later the Grand Teton Discovery and Visitor Center, Moose Junction (Grand Teton National Park, Wyoming, 2007) and Combs Point Residence (Finger Lakes Region, New York, 2007). Current work includes the Trinity College Master Plan (Hartford, Connecticut, 2008); Williams College Faculty Buildings and Library (Williamstown, Massachusetts, 2008 and 2012); California Institute of Technology Chemistry Building (Pasadena, California, 2010); Peace Arch US Port of Entry (Blaine, Washington, 2012), all in the USA, and retail stores for Apple Inc. in various locations worldwide.

Das Büro **BOHLIN CYWINSKI JACKSON** wurde 1965 von Peter Bohlin und Richard Powell in Wilkes-Barre, Pennsylvania, gegründet. Peter Bohlin machte seinen B. Arch. in Architektur am Rensselaer Polytechnic Institute (1959) und den M. Arch. an der Cranbrook Academy of Art (1961). Die gegenwärtigen Chefs sind Peter Bohlin, Bernard Cywinski, Jon Jackson, Dan Haden, Frank Grauman, William Loose, Randy Reid, Karl Backus, Gregory Mottola, Roxanne Sherbeck und Robert Miller. Die Firma hat weitere Büros in Pittsburgh, Philadelphia, Seattle und San Francisco. 1994 erhielt das Büro den Architecture Firm Award vom American Institute of Architects (AIA). Zu seinen bedeutenden Bauwerken gehören Pacific Rim Estate (Medina, Washington, 1997, als Joint Venture mit Cutler Anderson Architects), die Hauptverwaltung der Pixar Animation Studios (Emeryville, Kalifornien, 2001) sowie das Liberty Bell Center im Independence National Historical Park (Philadelphia, Pennsylvania, 2003). 2005 wurden das House at the Shawangunks (New Paltz, New York, 2003–05, hier veröffentlicht), die Ballard Library und das Neighborhood Service Center (Seattle, Washington) fertiggestellt, die das AIA in die Liste der Top Ten Green Buildings des Jahres aufnahm, und zwei Jahre später das Grand Teton Discovery and Visitor Center, Moose Junction (Grand Teton National Park, Wyoming, 2007) und das Wohnhaus Combs Point (Finger Lakes Region, New York, 2007). Zu den aktuellen Arbeiten des Büros gehören der Masterplan für das Trinity College (Hartford, Connecticut, 2008), Fakultätsbauten und Bibliothek des Williams College (Williamstown, Massachusetts, 2008 und 2012), das Chemistry Building am California Institute of Technology (Pasadena, Kalifornien, 2010), das Monument Peace Arch am US Port of Entry (Blaine, Washington, 2012), alle in den USA, sowie Ladengeschäfte für Apple Computer an verschiedenen Orten weltweit.

L'agence **BOHLIN CYWINSKI JACKSON** a été fondée en 1965 par Peter Bohlin et Richard Powell à Wilkes-Barre (Pennsylvanie). Peter Bohlin est titulaire d'un B.Arch. du Rensselaer Polytechnic Institute (1959) et d'un M.Arch. de la Cranbrook Academy of Art (1961). Les associés actuels sont Peter Bohlin, Bernard Cywinski, Jon Jackson, Dan Haden, Frank Grauman, William Loose, Randy Reid, Karl Backus, Gregory Mottola, Roxanne Sherbeck et Robert Miller. L'agence possède des bureaux à Pittsburgh, Philadelphie, Seattle et San Francisco. En 1994, elle a reçu le prix de l'Agence d'architecture de l'American Institute of Architects. Parmi ses réalisations les plus notables : le Pacific Rim Estate (Medina, Washington, 1997, avec Cutler Anderson Architects) ; le siège des Pixar Animation Studios (Emeryville, Californie, 2001) et le Liberty Bell Center dans l'Independence National Historical Park (Philadelphie, Pennsylvanie, 2003). En 2005, ils ont achevé la House at the Shawangunks (New Paltz, New York, 2003–05, publiée ici), la bibliothèque Ballard et un centre de services de quartier (Seattle, Washington) désigné par l'AIA comme l'une « des dix grandes constructions vertes » de l'année, et deux ans plus tard le centre d'informations des visiteurs de Grand Teton (Moose Junction, Parc national de Grand Teton, Wyoming, 2007) et la résidence Combs Point (Finger Lakes Region, New York, 2007). Plus récemment, ils ont réalisé le plan directeur du Trinity College (Hartford, Connecticut, 2008) ; les bâtiments de la faculté et la bibliothèque du Williams College (Williamstown, Massachusetts, 2008 et 2012) ; le bâtiment de la chimie du California Institute of Technology (Pasadena, Californie, 2010) ; l'arche de la Paix du port d'entrée américain (Blaine, Washington, 2012), toutes aux États-Unis, et plusieurs magasins Apple dans le monde.

HOUSE AT THE SHAWANGUNKS

New Paltz, New York, USA, 2003–05

Address: not diclosed. Floor area: 195 m². Client: not disclosed
Cost: not disclosed. Collaboration: Lee Clark, Julie Scotchie

Taking advantage of the sloping site, the architects angle the roof at approximately the same angle as the natural grade. Red and green surfaces alternate with glazed openings and metal elements.

Im Einklang mit der Hanglage haben die Architekten ein Dach geplant, das nahezu dieselbe Neigung hat wie das Gelände. Rote und grüne Oberflächen wechseln sich mit verglasten Öffnungen und Metallelementen ab.

S'inspirant de la déclivité du terrain, les architectes ont incliné le toit de la maison d'environ le même angle. Des surfaces rouges et vertes alternent avec des baies vitrées et des éléments métalliques.

As the architects say, "The pristine beauty of this steeply sloped, wooded site called for simple geometry and clean, basic materials." The site map to the right shows the location of the house on its slope.

Den Architekten zufolge verlangte „die unverfälschte Schönheit dieses abschüssigen, bewaldeten Geländes eine klare Geometrie und schlichte Ausgangsmaterialien". Der Lageplan rechts verdeutlicht den Standort des Hauses auf dem Abhang.

Pour l'architecte : « La beauté primitive de ce site boisé en forte déclivité appelait une géométrie simple et des matériaux basiques et nets. » À droite, le plan du terrain montre l'implantation de la maison dans la pente.

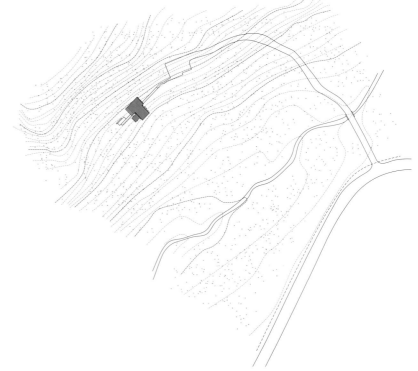

The Shawangunk Ridge is a mountain formation considered to be among the best rock climbing sites in the United States. It is located in New York state, extending from the northernmost point of New Jersey to the Catskill Mountains. New Paltz is in Ulster County, 154 kilometers (90 miles) north of New York City. Built on a steeply sloped, wooded site, "the house's cubic volume projects from the hillside against the backdrop of the Shawangunk Ridge. A diagrammatically proportional rectangular volume rises behind the cube, anchoring it to the sloping landscape. The cube's black-stained concrete foundation forms a strong yet unobtrusive pedestal." Red and green-stained cedar siding marks the exterior of the residence, while a single slope roof rises parallel to the hillside. A glass-walled dining area "appears to float among the trees." The double-height living room with its peeled log corner columns also opens broadly into the natural setting. The clients are artists involved in film, graphic design, and jewelry. Not surprisingly, they are also rock climbers.

Die Shawangunk Ridge gilt als eine der besten Felsformationen zum Klettern in den Vereinigten Staaten. Sie liegt im Staat New York und erstreckt sich vom nördlichsten Punkt New Jerseys bis zu den Catskill Mountains. New Paltz liegt im County Ulster, 154 km nördlich von New York City. Der auf steil abschüssigem, bewaldetem Gelände errichtete „kubische Baukörper des Hauses springt vor dem Hintergrund der Shawangunk Ridge aus dem Hang hervor. Ein quaderförmiger Baukörper erhebt sich hinter dem Kubus und verankert ihn in dem abschüssigen Gelände. Das geschwärzte Betonfundament des Kubus fungiert als solider, gleichwohl unauffälliger Sockel." Rot und grün gebeizte Verschalungen aus Zedernholz kennzeichnen das Äußere des Wohnhauses, während die Neigung des durchgehenden Dachs parallel zum Hang verläuft. Der verglaste Essbereich „scheint zwischen den Bäumen zu schweben". Auch der Wohnraum mit doppelter Geschosshöhe und seinen Eckpfeilern aus entrindeten Baumstämmen öffnet sich weit zur umgebenden Natur. Die Bauherren sind in den Bereichen Film, grafische Gestaltung und Schmuckdesign tätige Künstler; außerdem sind sie natürlich begeisterte Kletterer.

La formation montagneuse de la Shawagunk Ridge est l'un des meilleurs sites d'alpinisme aux États-Unis. Elle se trouve dans l'État de New York entre la pointe nord du New Jersey et les montagnes des Catskill. New Paltz est situé dans le comté d'Ulster, à 154 km de New York. Édifié sur une pente abrupte et boisée, « le volume cubique de la maison se projette du flanc de la colline sur le fond de la Shawagunk Ridge. Un volume sur une base rectangulaire s'élève derrière le cube et l'ancre dans la pente. Les fondations en béton teint en noir forment un socle solide mais discret. » Des bardages en cèdre rouges et verts caractérisent l'extérieur. Une toiture à une pente suit l'inclinaison du terrain. Un espace salle à manger vitré « semble flotter dans les arbres ». Le séjour double hauteur à colonnes d'angles en troncs d'arbre pelés s'ouvre tout aussi largement sur l'environnement naturel. Les clients sont des artistes travaillant respectivement dans le cinéma, la création graphique et la joaillerie. Inutile de préciser que ce sont aussi des alpinistes.

The cedar siding of the house is stained red and green. A single slope roof recalls the slope of the site and rises parallel to the hillside. The dining room projects from the southwest side of the main cubic volume and "appears to float among the trees."

Die Zedernholzverschalung des Hauses ist rot und grün gebeizt. Die geneigte Dachfläche wiederholt das Gefälle des Geländes und steigt parallel zum Abhang an. Das Esszimmer ragt aus der Südwestseite des kubischen Baukörpers hervor und „scheint zwischen den Bäumen zu schweben".

Le bardage de cèdre est teinté en rouge et en vert. Le toit dont le versant unique rappelle la pente du terrain s'élève parallèlement au sol. La salle à manger se projette de la façade sud-ouest du cube principal et « semble flotter dans les arbres ».

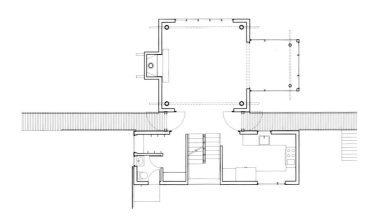
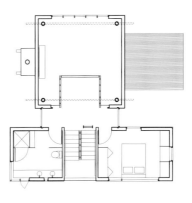
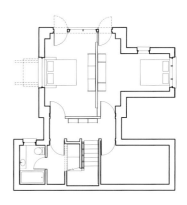

Brightly colored surfaces and light, modern furniture confirm the significance of the cheerful exterior of the house. The presence of the timber roof and log columns is a constant reminder of the presence of the forest, visible through every window of the house.

Leuchtend farbige Oberflächen und leichte, moderne Möbel unterstreichen das freundliche Äußere. Die Präsenz des Holzdachs und der Pfeiler aus unbehandelten Baumstämmen erinnert an die waldreiche Umgebung, die aus jedem Fenster des Hauses zu sehen ist.

Des surfaces de couleurs vives et un mobilier moderne et léger renforcent l'aspect chaleureux de l'extérieur de la maison. Le voligeage en bois et les colonnes en grumes fonctionnent comme un rappel de la présence de la forêt visible de chaque fenêtre de la maison.

BERNARD BÜHLER

Agence Bernard Bühler
5 quai de Bacalan
33300 Bordeaux
France

Tel: +33 5 56 39 27 33
Fax: +33 5 56 69 15 62
E-mail: contact.buhler@gmail.com
Web: www.bernard-buhler.com

BERNARD BÜHLER was born in 1954 in Laparade, France. He grew up in Bordeaux where his practice is based. He received a BEP (a high-school level qualification, 1972) in civil engineering. He worked in a Bordeaux office (Sallier) until 1985 at which time he succeeded in being certified as an architect based on his personal work. He opened his own office the following year and created his present firm in 2000. His work is essentially based on social housing in the area of Bordeaux. As he says, he attempts to offer the residents of low-cost housing "an optimal quality of life," interpreting sustainable development in a way that affords sustainable living conditions. His work includes Arc en Ciel Housing (Bordeaux, 2010); the Hameau de Plantoun (Bayonne, 2008–09, carried out with his daughter Marie Bühler, published here); Les Chais housing (Bordeaux, 2009); Cité Prost housing (Paris, 2007); and the Clos des Sablières housing (Bordeaux, 2009). He has numerous other similar projects underway.

BERNARD BÜHLER wurde 1954 in Laparade, Frankreich, geboren. Er wuchs in Bordeaux auf, wo sich auch sein Büro befindet. 1972 machte er ein Diplom in Ingenieurbau. Er arbeitete in einem Büro in Bordeaux (Salier), bis es ihm 1985 gelang, aufgrund seiner eigenen Arbeiten als Architekt anerkannt zu werden. Im darauffolgenden Jahr eröffnete er sein eigenes Büro, 2000 seine gegenwärtige Firma. Er beschäftigt sich vorwiegend mit sozialem Wohnungsbau in der Umgegend von Bordeaux. Nach eigener Aussage versucht er, den Bewohnern von preiswerten Wohnungen „eine optimale Lebensqualität" zu bieten, und interpretiert nachhaltige Bebauung in einer Weise, die auch nachhaltige Lebensbedingungen garantiert. Zu seinen Projekten zählen die Wohnanlage Arc en Ciel (Bordeaux, 2010), Hameau de Plantoun (Bayonne, 2008–09, ausgeführt zusammen mit seiner Tochter Marie Bühler, hier veröffentlicht), der Wohnungsbau Les Chais (Bordeaux, 2009), die Wohnanlage Cité Prost (Paris, 2007) sowie die Wohnbauten Clos des Sablières (Bordeaux, 2009). Zahlreiche weitere ähnliche Projekte sind in Arbeit.

BERNARD BÜHLER, né en 1954 à Laparade (France), a grandi à Bordeaux où se trouve aujourd'hui son agence. Il a passé un BEP en ingénierie civile en 1972 puis a travaillé dans une agence bordelaise (Sallier) jusqu'en 1985, date à laquelle il est devenu architecte certifié grâce à ses réalisations personnelles. Il a ouvert une agence l'année suivante, puis son agence actuelle en 2000. Il intervient essentiellement dans le secteur du logement social en région bordelaise. Il s'efforce d'offrir aux habitants de ces logements « une qualité de vie optimale » et de mettre la règlementation du développement durable au service de conditions de vie écologiques. Parmi ses réalisations : les logements collectifs Arc en Ciel (Bordeaux, 2010) ; le Hameau de Plantoun (Bayonne, 2008–09, en collaboration avec sa fille Marie Bühler, publié ici) ; les logements collectifs Les Chais (Bordeaux, 2009), ceux de la Cité Prost (Paris, 2007) et du Clos des Sablières (Bordeaux, 2009). De nombreux autres projets de ce type sont en cours.

HAMEAU DE PLANTOUN

Bayonne, France, 2008–09

Address: Avenue Marcel Breuer, Bayonne, France. Area: 3327 m²
Client: OPHLM Bayonne. Cost: €3.804 million. Collaboration: Marie Bühler

This complex is located on Avenue Marcel Breuer, near the Hauts de Sainte-Croix housing (1963–74) designed by Breuer that is currently being renovated. The **HAMEAU DE PLANTOUN** contains 39 residences located in a staggered pattern on either side of a curving path. The architect explains that his choice of wood is related both to cost considerations and to environmental concerns. The light design of the housing, which is set up on wood pilotis and thin metal posts allowed the site to be left relatively intact, while permitting residents parking below the houses. Essentially geometric, the volumes of the houses are variable according to their type, and the overall impression they give is one of unity that emerges from an accumulation of similar forms. The extensive use of plywood is certainly unexpected, as is the resulting overall appearance of the complex. There is a suggestion of temporary housing in the way the Hameau de Plantoun looks, even a certain industrial feeling, and yet the houses themselves are both comfortable and coherent.

Dieser Wohnkomplex liegt an der Avenue Marcel Breuer, nahe der von Breuer geplanten Wohnanlage Hauts de Sainte-Croix (1963–74), die gegenwärtig saniert wird. **HAMEAU DE PLANTOUN** besteht aus 39 Wohnungen in gestaffelter Anordnung zu beiden Seiten eines geschwungenen Wegs. Der Architekt erklärt, dass er sich sowohl aus Kosten- als auch aus Umweltschutzgründen für Holz entschieden habe. Die leichte Gestaltung der Häuser, die auf dünnen Stützen aus Holz und Metall stehen, machte es möglich, das Grundstück relativ unberührt zu belassen, und bietet den Bewohnern Parkmöglichkeiten unter den Gebäuden. Die im Wesentlichen geometrischen Volumen der Häuser variieren entsprechend ihrem Typ und erscheinen in ihrer Gesamtwirkung als einheitliche Zusammenstellung ähnlicher Formen. Die Verwendung von so viel Sperrholz ist zweifellos ungewöhnlich, ebenso das daraus resultierende Erscheinungsbild des gesamten Komplexes. Hameau de Plantoun wirkt ein wenig wie temporäre oder sogar industrielle Bauten; trotzdem sind die Häuser selbst wohnlich und stimmig.

Cet ensemble est situé avenue Marcel Breuer, non loin des logements des Hauts de Sainte-Croix (1963-74) conçus par Breuer et en cours de rénovation. Le **HAMEAU DE PLANTOUN** regroupe 39 résidences selon un plan en zigzag de chaque côté d'une allée en courbes. L'architecte explique que le choix du bois tient à la fois à des considérations de coût et à des préoccupations environnementales. La conception légère de ces logements qui reposent sur des pilotis de bois ou de fins poteaux de métal laisse le site relativement intact tout en permettant aux résidants de garer leurs voitures sous les maisons. Les volumes de géométrie simple sont de dimensions variables, selon leur type. L'impression d'unité naît de l'accumulation de formes similaires. Le recours massif au contreplaqué est assez inattendu, tout comme l'aspect général de l'ensemble. Si l'on ressent une impression de logements temporaires ou même de constructions industrielles, ces maisons semblent néanmoins à la fois confortables et de conception cohérente.

Seen from a distance, the Hameau de Plantoun looks something like a temporary encampment. The natural aging of the wood will make it blend into its wooded background.

Aus der Entfernung sieht Hameau de Plantoun aus wie ein provisorisches Feldlager. Wenn das Holz altert, wird es mit dem bewaldeten Hintergrund verschmelzen.

Vu de loin, le Hameau de Pantoun fait un peu penser à un campement temporaire. La patine progressive du bois favorisera son intégration dans son cadre forestier.

An overall site plan (below) shows the irregular placement of the housing units along the wooded site. Above, the buildings seem very much in harmony with the trees.

Der Gesamtlageplan (unten) zeigt die unregelmäßige Anordnung der Wohneinheiten auf dem bewaldeten Gelände. Oben: Die Bauten wirken inmitten der Bäume sehr harmonisch.

Le plan d'ensemble du site (ci-dessous) montre l'implantation irrégulière des petits immeubles en lisière de la forêt. Ci-dessus, les immeubles semblent très en harmonie avec les arbres.

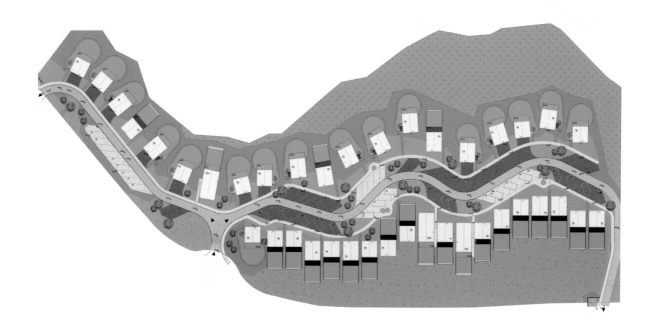

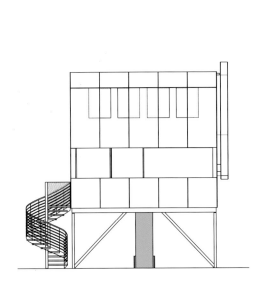
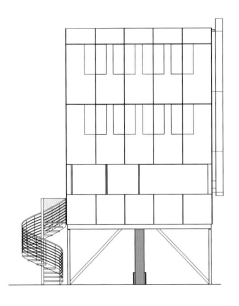
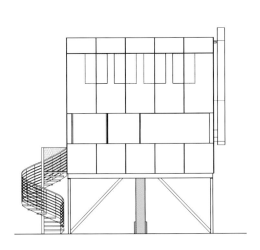

Plans show the flexibility of the
architectural system and the basic,
geometric simplicity of the design.

Die Grundrisse bezeugen die
Flexibilität des architektonischen
Systems und die zugrunde liegende
einfache Geometrie des Entwurfs.

Les plans montrent la souplesse du
système constructif et la simplicité
géométrique du projet.

Lifted up off the ground on metal pilotis, the structures have an even more "temporary" appearance, yet they are designed as permanent residences.

Die auf Metallstützen aufgeständerten Gebäude wirken noch „temporärer"; sie sind jedoch als dauerhafte Wohnbauten geplant.

Rehaussées du sol par des pilotis métalliques, les structures prennent une apparence encore plus « temporaire » bien qu'elles soient conçues pour une résidence permanente.

SANTIAGO CALATRAVA

*Santiago Calatrava SA
Parkring 11 / 8002 Zurich / Switzerland
Tel: +41 1 204 50 00 / Fax: +41 1 204 50 01
E-mail: admin.zurich@calatrava.com
Web: www.calatrava.com*

Born in Valencia, Spain, in 1951, **SANTIAGO CALATRAVA** studied art and architecture at the ETSA of Valencia (1968–73) and engineering at the ETH in Zurich (doctorate in Technical Science, 1981). He opened his own architecture and civil engineering office the same year. Santiago Calatrava received the American Institute of Architects (AIA) 2005 Gold Medal. His built work includes Gallery and Heritage Square, BCE Place (Toronto, Ontario, Canada, 1987); the Torre de Montjuic (Barcelona, Spain, 1989–92); the Kuwait Pavilion at Expo '92, Seville, and the Alamillo Bridge for the same exhibition (Seville, Spain); the Lyon-Saint Exupéry TGV Station (Lyon, France, 1989–94); the Oriente Station in Lisbon (Portugal, 1998); the Valencia City of Science and Planetarium (Valencia, Spain, 1996–2000) and the Valencia Opera in the same city (2004); the Sondica Airport (Bilbao, Spain, 1990–2000); a bridge in Orléans (France, 1996–2000); and Bodegas Ysios (Laguardia, Álava, Spain,1998–2001, published here). Other work includes Tenerife Auditorium (Santa Cruz, Canary Islands, 2003); Milwaukee Art Museum extension (Milwaukee, Wisconsin, USA, 2003); Athens Olympic Sports Complex (Athens, Greece, 2004); Zurich University, Law Faculty (Zurich, Switzerland, 1989–2004, also published here); the Quarto Ponte sul Canal Grande (Fourth Bridge on the Grand Canal, Venice, Italy, 1999–2006); three bridges in Reggio Emilia (Italy, 2002–07); Jerusalem Light Rail Train Bridge (Jerusalem, Israel, 2002–08); and Liège-Guillemins TGV Station (Liège, Belgium, 1996–2009). More recent work includes the Margaret Hunt Hill Bridge (Dallas, Texas, USA, 1998–2012). Current projects include the Transportation Hub for the new World Trade Center site in New York (USA, 2015); Y. Z. Hsu Memorial, Performing Arts Building and Art & Design School Yuan Ze University (Taipei, Taiwan, 2008–15); and the Mons Station (Mons, Belgium, 2004–15).

SANTIAGO CALATRAVA, geboren 1951 Valencia, Spanien, studierte an der dortigen ETSA Kunst und Architektur (1968–73) sowie Bauingenieurwesen an der ETH Zürich, wo er 1981 promoviert wurde. Im selben Jahr gründete er sein Architektur- und Ingenieurbüro. 2005 wurde Calatrava mit der Goldmedaille des American Institute of Architects (AIA) ausgezeichnet. Zu seinen realisierten Bauten gehören der Gallery and Heritage Square, BCE Place in Toronto (1987), die Torre de Montjuïc (Barcelona, 1989–92), der Kuwait-Pavillon und die Alamillo-Brücke für die Expo '92 in Sevilla, der TGV-Bahnhof des Flughafens Lyon-Saint-Exupéry (1989–94), der Oriente-Bahnhof in Lissabon (1998), die Ciudad de las Artes y de las Ciencias (1996–2000) sowie das Opernhaus Palau de les Arts Reina Sofía in Valencia (2004), der Flughafen Sondica in Bilbao (1990–2000), eine Brücke in Orléans (1996–2000) und die Bodegas Ysios (Laguardia, Álava, Spanien,1998–2001, hier vorgestellt). Des Weiteren verwirklichte er das Tenerife Auditorio in Santa Cruz (Teneriffa, 2003), die Erweiterung des Milwaukee Art Museum (Wisconsin, 2003), mehrere Bauten für die Olympia-Sportanlage in Athen (2004), die Juristische Fakultät der Universität Zürich (1989–2004, ebenfalls hier vorgestellt), den Quarto Ponte sul Canal Grande (Venedig, 1999–2006), drei Brückenbauten in Reggio Emilia (2002–07), eine Brücke für die Jerusalemer Stadtbahn (2002–08) und den TGV-Bahnhof Liège-Guillemins (Belgien, 1996–2009). Zu seinen jüngeren Arbeiten zählen die Margaret Hunt Hill Bridge (Dallas, Texas, 1998–2012). Laufende Projekte sind der Verkehrsknotenpunkt des neuen World Trade Center in New York (2015), das Y.-Z.-Hsu-Memorial-Gebäude, das Performing Arts Building und die Hochschule für Kunst und Design der Universität Yuan Ze in Taipeh (Taiwan, 2008–15) sowie der Bahnhof von Mons (Belgien, 2004–15).

Né à Valence (Espagne) en 1951, **SANTIAGO CALATRAVA** a étudié l'art et l'architecture à l'ETSA de Valence (1968–73) et l'ingénierie à l'ETH de Zurich (doctorat en sciences techniques, 1981). Il a ouvert son agence d'architecture et d'ingénierie civile la même année. En 2005, il a reçu la médaille d'or de l'American Institute of Architects (AIA). Parmi ses réalisations : le Gallery and Heritage Square, BCE Place (Toronto, Canada, 1987) ; la tour de Montjuïc (Barcelone, 1989–92) ; le pavillon du Koweit et le pont de l'Alamillo pour Expo '92 (Séville) ; la gare de TGV de l'aéroport de Lyon-Saint Exupéry (Lyon, 1989–94) ; la gare de l'Orient à Lisbonne (1998) ; la Cité des sciences et le planétarium de Valence (1996–2000) ; l'opéra de Valence (2004) ; l'aéroport de Sondica (Bilbao, 1990–2000) ; un pont à Orléans (France, 1996–2000) et les Bodegas Ysios (Laguardia, Álava, Espagne,1998–2001, publié ici). Ses autres réalisations comprennent l'auditorium de Tenerife (Santa Cruz, îles Canaries, 2003) ; l'extension du Milwaukee Art Museum (Milwaukee, 2003) ; le complexe olympique d'Athènes (Athènes, 2004) ; la faculté de droit de l'université de Zurich (Zurich, Suisse, 1989–2004, également publié ici) ; le Quarto Ponte sul Canal Grande (Venise, 1999–2006) ; trois ponts à Reggio Emilia (Italie, 2002–07) ; le pont du train léger de Jérusalem (Israël, 2002–08) et la gare de TGV de Liège-Guillemins (Liège, Belgique, 1996–2009). Ses réalisations plus récentes comprennent le Margaret Hunt Hill Bridge (Dallas, Texas, 1998–2012). Ses projets actuels incluent le nœud ferroviaire du nouveau World Trade Center à New York (2015) ; le mémorial Y. Z. Hsu, le bâtiment des arts du spectacle et de l'école d'art et de design de l'université Yuan Ze (Taipei, Taïwan, 2008–15) et la gare de Mons (Mons, Belgique, 2004–15).

ZURICH UNIVERSITY, LAW FACULTY

Zurich, Switzerland, 1989–2004

Address: Rämistrasse 74/2, 8001 Zurich, Switzerland, +41 44 634 22 33,
www.ius.uzh.ch. Client: Canton of Zurich. Cost: $30 million

The **FACULTY OF LAW OF THE UNIVERSITY OF ZURICH** had been divided into eight different buildings. The facilities for the faculty and the library, including the second largest rare law book collection in Switzerland, were housed in a building designed in 1908 by Hermann Fiertz as a high school and laboratory. Santiago Calatrava was asked in 1989 to study additions to two wings added to this structure in 1930 in order to modernize and enlarge them. Rather than filling in the existing courtyard with floor space, Calatrava proposed to create an atrium in place of the courtyard. A series of seven oval reading levels are hung within the atrium, "staggered on each level so that it is no longer the floor area that increases as they approach the roof but the space they circumscribe." This design allows natural light to penetrate deeper into the heart of the structure and its reading area. As the architect describes the design: "The basic structure of each gallery is formed by a steel torsion tube, from which T-shaped, tapering steel beams cantilever in a regular rhythm. Each gallery is braced by balustrades, which have been designed as load-bearing trusses. By channeling the forces away from the center of the atrium, this design also leaves the basement areas free of obstruction." He goes on to say that "an important aspect of the design is the complete independence of old and new."

Die **JURISTISCHE FAKULTÄT DER UNIVERSITÄT ZÜRICH** war auf acht Standorte verteilt. Die Einrichtungen für die Fakultät und die Bibliothek, darunter die zweitgrößte Sammlung seltener juristischer Bücher in der Schweiz, waren in einem 1908 von Hermann Fiertz als Schule und Labor entworfenen Gebäude untergebracht. Santiago Calatrava wurde 1989 aufgefordert, sich Gedanken über Anbauten an zwei 1930 ergänzte Flügel zu machen, mit dem Ziel, diese Gebäude zu modernisieren und zu vergrößern. Anstatt nun nach Vorstellung der Universität, den vorhandenen Hof zuzubauen, schlug Calatrava vor, ihn in ein Atrium umzuwandeln. Innerhalb des Atriums wurden sieben ovalen Leseebenen aufgehängt, „und zwar nach Ebenen gestaffelt, sodass mit der Annäherung an das Dach nicht mehr die Bodenfläche zunimmt, sondern der von ihnen umschriebene Raum". Dieser Entwurf lässt Tageslicht tiefer in das Gebäudeinnere und die Lesezonen eindringen. Der Architekt beschreibt seinen Entwurf so: „Die grundlegende Konstruktion jeder Empore besteht aus einer Torsionsröhre aus Stahl, von der T-förmige, sich verjüngende Stahlträger in regelmäßigen Abständen vorkragen. Jede Empore wird von Brüstungen versteift, die als tragende Fachwerkbinder konzipiert wurden. Da die Kräfte vom Zentrum des Atriums abgelenkt werden, erlaubt diese Planung ein stützenfreies Untergeschoss." Er führt weiter aus: „Ein wichtiger Aspekt des Entwurfs ist die völlige Autonomie von Alt und Neu."

La **FACULTÉ DE DROIT DE L'UNIVERSITÉ DE ZURICH** répartit ses activités entre huit immeubles. Les installations pour le corps professoral et la bibliothèque, qui contient la seconde plus vaste collection helvétique de livres rares de droit, se trouve dans un bâtiment conçu en 1908 par Hermann Fiertz pour accueillir un collège et des laboratoires. En 1989, Santiago Calatrava reçut commande d'une étude pour agrandir et moderniser deux ailes ajoutées dans les années 1930. Plutôt que de combler la cour existante, il proposa de remplacer celle-ci par un atrium. Sept espaces de lecture de forme ovale sont ainsi suspendus dans l'atrium, « décalés de niveau en niveau, de telle façon que ce n'est plus la surface au sol qui s'accroît au fur et à mesure que l'on monte vers la toiture mais l'espace qu'ils circonscrivent ». Cette disposition permet à la lumière naturelle de mieux pénétrer au cœur même de la structure et des zones de lecture. Comme l'explique l'architecte : « La structure de base de chaque galerie est constituée d'un tube en acier en torsion d'où partent en porte-à-faux, selon un rythme régulier, des poutres d'acier en T effilé. Chaque galerie est entretoisée par des balustrades qui sont en fait des fermes porteuses. En canalisant la charge au-delà du centre de l'atrium, cette conception libère en même temps le rez-de-chaussée de toute obstruction. » Il poursuit : « Un aspect important du projet est la totale indépendance du nouveau par rapport à l'ancien. »

Inserted into an existing courtyard, the new law library, whose central space is visible to the right, shows to what extent the architect is capable of occupying a space and making it his own, even within the relatively tight constraints of this project.

Die in einen vorhandenen Hof eingefügte neue Juristische Bibliothek, deren zentraler Raum rechts zu sehen ist, zeigt, in welchem Maß der Architekt fähig ist, Raum zu besetzen und sich zu eigen zu machen, selbst bei den eher beschränkten Verhältnissen dieses Projekts.

Insérée dans une cour existante, la nouvelle bibliothèque de droit dont le volume central est visible à droite, montre à quel point l'architecte sait occuper un espace et se l'approprier, même dans le cadre des contraintes relativement fortes d'un projet comme celui-ci.

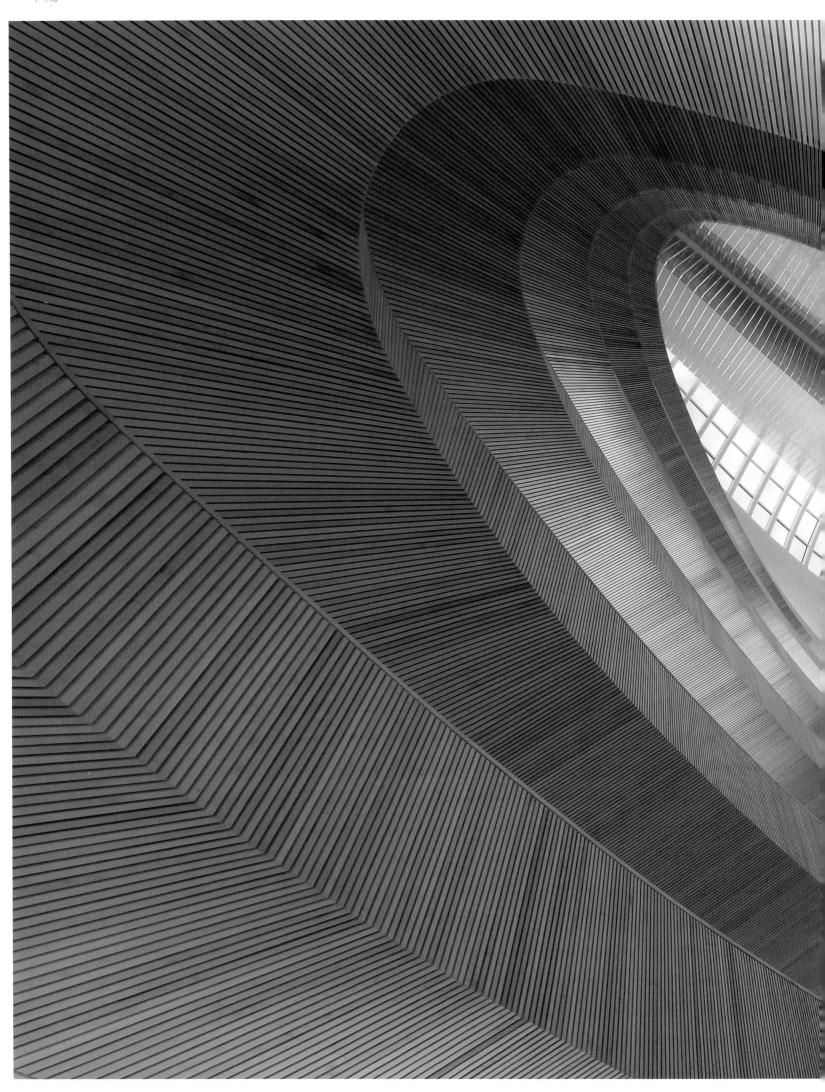

BODEGAS YSIOS

Laguardia, Álava, Spain,1998–2001

Address: Camino de la Hoya, s/n, 01300 Guardia, Álava, Spain, +34 945 60 06 40
Floor area: 8000 m². Client: Bodegas & Bebidas Group. Cost: $10 million

The Bodegas & Bebidas Group wanted a building that would be an icon for its prestigious new Rioja Alavesa wine. They called on architect Santiago Calatrava to design an 8,000-square-meter winery complex, a building that had to be designed to make, store, and sell wine. Vineyards occupy half of the rectangular site. A difference in height of 10 meters from the north to the south of the site complicated the design. The linear program of the winemaking process dictated that the structure should be rectangular and it was set along an east–west axis. Two longitudinal concrete load-bearing walls, separated from each other by 26 meters, trace a 196-meter-long sinusoidal shape in plan and in elevation. These walls are covered with wooden planks, which are mirrored in a reflecting pool and "evoke the image of a row of wine barrels." The roof, composed of a series of laminated wood beams, is designed as a continuation of the façades. The result is a "ruled surface wave," which combines concave and convex surfaces as it evolves along the longitudinal axis. The roof is clad in aluminum, creating a contrast with the warmth of the wooden façades and yet continuing their design. A visitor's center conceived as a "balcony that overlooks the winery and the vineyard" is situated in the center of the structure.

Die Gruppe Bodegas & Bebidas wünschte ein Gebäude, das als Signum für ihren prestigeträchtigen, neuen Rioja-Alavesa-Wein dienen konnte. Sie wandte sich an Santiago Calatrava, der eine 8000 m² große Anlage gestalten sollte, in der Wein hergestellt, gelagert und verkauft werden konnte. Die Hälfte des rechtwinkligen Geländes wird von Rebstöcken eingenommen. Ein zwischen dem nördlichen und südlichen Teil des Geländes bestehender Höhenunterschied von 10 m erschwerte die Aufgabe. Der lineare Ablauf der Weinherstellung gab die Rechtwinkligkeit des Gebäudes vor, das entlang einer Ost-West-Achse errichtet wurde. Zwei längs verlaufende, tragende Betonwände, zwischen denen ein Abstand von 26 m liegt, folgen in Grund- und Aufriss einer Wellenform. Diese Wände sind mit Holzbohlen verschalt, die sich in einem Wasserbecken spiegeln und „das Bild einer Reihe von Weinfässern hervorrufen". Das aus aneinander gereihten Schichtholzbalken bestehende Dach ist als Fortführung der Fassade konzipiert. Entlang der Längsachse entsteht so eine regelmäßig gewellte Oberfläche, bei der konkave und konvexe Flächen kombiniert sind. Das mit Aluminium verkleidete Dach kontrastiert mit der Wärme der Holzfassaden, führt deren Formgebung jedoch weiter. Ein Besucherzentrum, das als „Balkon, der Kellerei und Rebstöcke überschaut," gestaltet ist, befindet sich in der Mitte des Gebäudes.

Le groupe Bodegas & Bebidas souhaitait construire un bâtiment qui symbolisât son prestigieux Rioja Alavesa. Il fit appel à Santiago Calatrava pour ce chai de 8000 m² dédié à l'élaboration, la conservation et la commercialisation de ce nouveau vin. Une dénivellation de 10 m entre la partie nord et la partie sud compliquait l'aménagement de ce terrain rectangulaire occupé pour moitié par des vignes. Le processus linéaire de fabrication du vin exigeait un bâtiment rectangulaire, qui fut implanté est-ouest. Deux murs porteurs en béton, séparés de 26 m, dessinent une forme sinusoïdale de 196 m de long, en plan comme en élévation. Ils sont habillés d'un bardage de bois qui se reflète dans un bassin et « évoquent un alignement de tonneaux de vin ». Le toit, réalisé en poutres de bois lamellé, est dans le prolongement des façades. Il en résulte un effet de « vague » alternant surfaces convexes et concaves tout au long de l'axe longitudinal. L'aluminium qui habille la toiture contraste avec le bois chaleureux des façades. Au centre des installations est implanté le centre d'accueil des visiteurs, conçu comme « un balcon dominant le chai et le vignoble ».

The spectacular undulating roof of the building stands out against its natural setting but nonetheless appears to echo its forms. Right, the main entrance area.

Das spektakuläre, geschwungene Dach des Gebäudes hebt sich von der Landschaft dahinter ab und scheint dennoch ihre Formen widerzuspiegeln; rechts der Haupteingang.

Le spectaculaire toit ondulant du bâtiment se détache nettement de son environnement naturel tout en se faisant l'écho de ses formes. À droite, l'entrée principale.

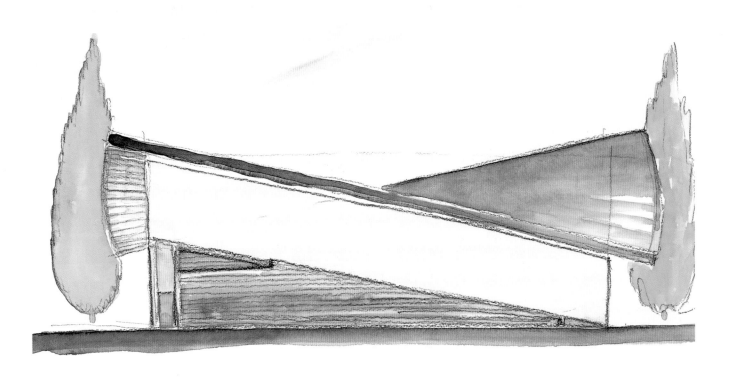

This page, watercolor sketches by the architect show the basic forms of the design. Right, wine barrels under the orchestrated wooden ceilings of Calatrava.

Auf dieser Seite zeigen Aquarelle des Architekten die grundlegenden Formen des Entwurfs; rechts die Weinfässer unter Calatravas Inszenierung der Holzdecke.

Sur cette page, aquarelles de l'architecte montrant les formes élémentaires du projet. À droite, les tonneaux disposés sous les plafonds de bois créés par Calatrava.

CANNON DESIGN

Cannon Design
2170 Whitehaven Road
Grand Island, NY 14072, USA
Tel: +1 716 773 6800 / Fax: +1 716 773 5909
E-mail: info@cannondesign.com
Web: www.cannondesign.com

Founded more than 60 years ago, **CANNON DESIGN** works with a staff of 750 people in the areas of architecture, engineering, and interior design. Robert J. Johnston is a Principal and National Sports Practice Leader for the firm. A captain of the Canadian lacrosse team for the 1978 Commonwealth Games, he received a Master's degree in Environmental Design from the University of Calgary. He was the Project Principal and Lead Planner for the Richmond Olympic Oval (Richmond, British Columbia, Canada, 2005–08, published here). Marion LaRue is a Principal and Operations Leader for Cannon Design. Her work has been concentrated in student life, wellness, sports, and recreational architecture. She received a B.Sc. in both Architecture and Environmental Science from the University of Waterloo. She was the Senior Project Manager for the Richmond Olympic Oval. Larry Podhora has 20 years of experience in the design of recreation centers. He received his M.Arch degree from the Bartlett School of Architecture, the University of London, as well as a B.Arch degree from the University of British Columbia, and was Architect of Record for the Richmond Olympic Oval. Recent projects by Cannon Design include Boston University, John Hancock Student Village (Boston, Massachusetts, 2005); Brigham and Women's Hospital, Shapiro Cardiovascular Center (Boston, Massachusetts, 2008); University of California, San Diego, Price Center East (San Diego, California, 2008); the University Hospitals Seidman Cancer Center (Cleveland, Ohio, 2011); and the Sabancı University Nanotechnology Research and Application Center (SUNUM, Istanbul, Turkey, 2011), all in the USA unless stated otherwise. Ongoing work includes King Faisal Specialist Hospital and Research Center (Riyadh, Saudi Arabia).

CANNON DESIGN, vor über 60 Jahren gegründet, beschäftigt rund 750 Mitarbeiter auf den Gebieten Architektur, Ingenieurwesen und Innenarchitektur. Robert J. Johnston, einer der Direktoren und Landessportchef des Büros, war bei den Commonwealth Games 1978 Kapitän der kanadischen Lacrosse-Mannschaft und schloss sein Studium mit einem Master in umweltverträglicher Planung an der Universität Calgary ab. Er war Projektleiter und Chefplaner beim Richmond Olympic Oval (Richmond, British Columbia, Kanada, 2005–08, hier vorgestellt). Marion LaRue ist Direktorin und Technische Unternehmensleiterin bei Cannon Design. Ihr Projektschwerpunkt sind primär Bildungs-, Wellness-, Sport- und Freizeiteinrichtungen. Sie schloss ihr Studium an der Universität Waterloo mit einem B. Sc. in Architektur und Umwelttechnik ab. Beim Richmond Olympic Oval zeichnete sie als leitende Projektmanagerin verantwortlich. Larry Podhora blickt auf 20 Jahre Erfahrung in der Gestaltung von Freizeiteinrichtungen zurück. Er absolvierte einen M. Arch. an der Bartlett School of Architecture der Universität von London sowie einen B. Arch. an der Universität von British Columbia. Podhora war zuständiger Architekt für das Richmond Olympic Oval. Jüngere Projekte von Cannon Design sind u. a. die John-Hancock-Studentensiedlung der Universität Boston (2005), das Shapiro-Herz-Kreislauf-Zentrum am Brigham and Women's Hospital (Boston, Massachusetts, 2008), das Price Center East an der University of California (San Diego, 2008), das Seidman-Krebszentrum der Universitätsklinik (Cleveland, Ohio, 2011) und das Nanotechnology Research and Application Center der Sabancı-Universität (SUNUM, Istanbul, 2011). Zu den laufenden Projekten zählen zudem die König-Faisal-Fachklinik und -Forschungseinrichtung in Riad (Saudi-Arabien).

Fondée il y a plus de soixante ans, l'agence **CANNON DESIGN** emploie une équipe de 750 personnes dans les domaines de l'architecture, de l'ingénierie et de l'architecture d'intérieur. Robert J. Johnston en est à la fois l'un des directeurs et l'entraîneur de l'équipe sportive de la firme. Capitaine de l'équipe canadienne de crosse aux Jeux du Commonwealth de 1978, il possède un master en architecture bioclimatique de l'université de Calgary. Il était directeur de projet et urbaniste en chef de l'Anneau olympique de Richmond (Richmond, Colombie-Britannique, Canada, 2005–08, publié ici). Marion LaRue est directrice et responsable des opérations pour Cannon Design. Ses activités se sont concentrées sur la vie étudiante, le bien-être, le sport et l'architecture de loisir. Elle est diplômée en architecture et en science environnementale de l'université de Waterloo. Elle était directrice principale du projet de l'Anneau olympique de Richmond. Larry Podhora a vingt ans d'expérience dans le domaine de l'architecture de loisir. Il est titulaire d'un M.Arch. de la Bartlett School de l'université de Londres, ainsi que d'un B.Arch. de l'université de Colombie-Britannique. Il était architecte responsable du projet pour l'Anneau olympique de Richmond. Les récents projets de Cannon Design incluent le complexe John Hancock Student Village à l'université de Boston (Boston, 2005) ; le Brigham and Women's Hospital du Shapiro Cardiovascular Center (Boston, 2008) ; le Price Center East de l'université de Californie (San Diego, 2008) ; le Centre de lutte contre le cancer Seidman des hôpitaux universitaires (Cleveland, 2010) et le Centre universitaire de recherche et d'application en nanotechnologies Sabancı (SUNUM, Istanbul, 2011), tous aux États-Unis, sauf mention contraire. Ses projets en cours incluent le King Faisal Specialist Hospital and Research Center (Riyadh, Arabie saoudite, 2011).

RICHMOND OLYMPIC OVAL

Richmond, British Columbia, Canada, 2005–08

Address: 6111 River Road, Richmond, BC V7C 0A2, Canada, +1 778 296 1400, www.richmondoval.ca
Area: 38 000 m². Client: City of Richmond. Cost: $153.38 million

Completed well in advance of the 2010 Vancouver Winter Olympic Games, the Richmond Olympic Oval is both functional and elegant in its ample use of wood.

Das Richmond Oval, mehr als zeitig vor den Olympischen Winterspielen fertiggestellt, die 2010 in Vancouver ausgetragen wurden, ist sowohl funktional als auch elegant. Holz kommt umfassend zum Einsatz.

Achevé très en avance pour les Jeux d'hiver 2010 de Vancouver, l'Anneau olympique de Richmond, à la fois fonctionnel et élégant, laisse la part belle au bois.

The **RICHMOND OLYMPIC OVAL** was built for the long-track speed-skating events to be held during the 2010 Olympic and Paralympic Winter Games. It is located on a 13-hectare site near the Fraser River and Vancouver International Airport. The Olympic configuration will see the Oval house a 400-meter speed-skating track and seating for about 8000 spectators. The building is also designed for summer indoor sports, such as running or basketball, and includes sport medicine and wellness areas, a fitness center, and a 1393-square-meter anti-doping laboratory for the Winter Games. The basic plan of the building is a straightforward rectangle, underlining its highly functional nature. The Oval is part of a waterfront urban development plan that includes a mixture of residential, commercial, and public facilities. The contribution of Cannon Design to this project assures that a high level of architectural quality is maintained even as the sporting objectives of the facility are fully achieved.

Das **RICHMOND OLYMPIC OVAL** wurde für die Eisschnelllaufwettkämpfe bei den Olympischen und Paralympischen Winterspielen 2010 gebaut. Der Komplex liegt auf einem 13 ha großen Areal unweit des Fraser River und des Flughafens von Vancouver. Für die Olympischen Spiele verfügt das Stadion über eine 400 m lange Eisschnelllaufstrecke und bietet 8000 Besuchern Platz. Dabei ist das Gebäude so angelegt, dass es ebenfalls für Hallensportarten wie Laufen oder Basketball genutzt werden kann. Darüber hinaus gibt es sportmedizinische und Wellnessbereiche, ein Fitnesscenter sowie ein 1393 m² großes Anti-Dopinglabor für die Winterspiele. Der Grundriss des Gebäudes ist ein einfaches Rechteck und betont dessen ausgeprägte Funktionalität. Der Komplex ist Teil einer städtebaulichen Ufererschließung, zu der auch Wohn-, Geschäfts- und öffentliche Bauten gehören. Der Beitrag von Cannon Design für dieses Projekt sorgt für ein hohes architektonisches Niveau und erfüllt zugleich die funktionalen Anforderungen, die an den Sportkomplex gestellt werden.

L'**ANNEAU OLYMPIQUE DE RICHMOND** a été construit pour les courses de patinage de vitesse longue piste des Jeux olympiques et paralympiques d'hiver. Il est implanté sur un site de 13 hectares proche du fleuve Fraser et de l'aéroport international de Vancouver. En configuration olympique, l'Anneau abritera une piste de patinage de vitesse de 400 m et près de 8000 spectateurs. Le bâtiment est naturellement conçu pour des sports d'été en salle, de la course à pied au basket, et comprend des installations de médecine du sport et de bien-être, un centre de culture physique, et un laboratoire antidopage de 1393 m² pour les Jeux d'hiver. Le plan du bâtiment est un simple rectangle, soulignant sa nature hautement fonctionnelle. L'Anneau fait partie d'un plan de développement urbain du bord de l'eau mêlant des équipements résidentiels, commerciaux et publics. La contribution de Cannon Design à ce projet garantit la haute qualité de son architecture tout en remplissant tous les objectifs sportifs de l'installation.

A general interior view showing the broad arch requiring no supporting columns and moveable bleachers in place for pre-Olympic events.

Eine Innenansicht zeigt den breiten Bogen, der keine Stützsäulen benötigt sowie mobile Tribünen, aufgebaut für vorolympische Veranstaltungen.

Vue générale montrant le grand arc sans colonne de soutien et les gradins mobiles mis en place pour les manifestations préolympiques.

The cantilevered canopies of the
building are one of its most interesting architectural elements. To the
right, an overall site plan showing the
roof of the structure.

*Die auskragenden Vordächer zählen
zu den interessantesten architektonischen Elementen des Gebäudes.
Rechts ein Lageplan des Geländes
mit Dachaufsicht.
Les auvents en porte-à-faux du bâtiment constituent un de ses éléments
architecturaux les plus intéressants.
À droite, un plan de situation montre
le toit de la structure.*

ARTHUR CASAS

Studio Arthur Casas SP
Rua Itápolis 818
01245–000 São Paulo, SP
Brazil

Tel: +55 11 2182 7500
Fax: +55 11 3663 6540
E-mail: sp@arthurcasas.com
Web: www.arthurcasas.com

ARTHUR CASAS was born in 1961 and graduated as an architect from the Mackenzie University of São Paulo, Brazil, in 1983. He has concentrated on both interiors and constructions, developing residential and commercial projects with a distinctive vocabulary of forms. He has participated in the Architecture Biennial in São Paulo, in 1997 and 2003, and in the Buenos Aires Biennial, in 2003 and 2005. In 2008, Arthur Casas won the prestigious Red Dot Design Award, in Germany, for developing creative cutlery and dinner-set lines for Riva. His completed commercial projects include the Natura Store (Paris, France, 2005); Alexandre Herchcovitch Store (Tokyo, Japan, 2007); Huis Clos Store (São Paulo, 2008); Cidade Jardim Mall (São Paulo, 2008); Zeferino Store, Oscar Freire Street (São Paulo, 2008); Kosushi Restaurant (São Paulo, 2008); C-View Bar and C-House Restaurant, Affinia Hotel (Chicago, Illinois, USA, 2008); KAA Restaurant (São Paulo, 2008, published here); the Jack Vartanian Store (New York, New York, USA, 2008); and the Quinta da Baroneza (Bragança Paulista, São Paulo, 2009), all in Brazil unless stated otherwise.

ARTHUR CASAS, Jahrgang 1961, schloss sein Architekturstudium 1983 an der Mackenzie-Universität in São Paulo, Brasilien, ab. Seine Schwerpunkte sind sowohl Innengestaltung wie Architektur; seine Wohn- und Geschäftsbauten zeichnen sich durch eine charakteristische Formensprache aus. 1997 und 2003 war Casas auf den Architekturbiennalen in São Paulo vertreten, 2003 und 2005 zudem auf der Biennale in Buenos Aires. 2008 wurde seine kreative Besteck- und Geschirrserie für Riva mit dem renommierten deutschen Red Dot Design Award ausgezeichnet. Zu seinen realisierten Projekten zählen Ladengeschäfte für Natura (Paris, 2005), Alexandre Herchcovitch (Tokio, 2007) und Huis Clos (São Paulo, 2008), das Einkaufszentrum Cidade Jardim (São Paulo, 2008), die Zeferino-Boutique an der Rua Oscar Freire (São Paulo, 2008), das Restaurant Kosushi (São Paulo, 2008), die C-View Bar und das C-House Restaurant im Affinia Hotel (Chicago, Illinois, 2008), das Restaurant KAA (São Paulo, 2008, hier vorgestellt), ein Ladengeschäft für Jack Vartanian (New York, 2008) sowie die Quinta da Baroneza (Bragança Paulista, São Paulo, 2009).

Né en 1961, **ARTHUR CASAS** est diplômé en architecture de l'université Mackenzie à São Paulo (1983). Il se consacre à la fois à l'aménagement intérieur et à l'architecture et met en œuvre dans ses projets résidentiels ou commerciaux un vocabulaire formel personnel. Il a participé à la Biennale d'architecture de São Paulo à deux reprises (1997 et 2003), ainsi qu'à la Biennale de Buenos Aires (2003 et 2005). En 2008, ses lignes de couverts et ses services de table pour Riva ont remporté le prestigieux prix allemand Red Dot Design Award. Parmi ses projets d'architecture commerciale réalisés : le magasin Natura (Paris, France, 2005) ; le magasin Alexandre Herchcovitch (Tokyo, Japon, 2007) ; le magasin Huis Clos (São Paulo, 2008) ; le Cidade Jardim Mall (São Paulo, 2008) ; le magasin Zeferino, rue Oscar Freire (São Paulo, 2008) ; le restaurant Kosushi (São Paulo, 2008) ; le bar C-View et le restaurant C-House de l'Affinia Hotel (Chicago, Illinois, États-Unis, 2008) ; le restaurant KAA (São Paulo, 2008, publié ici) ; le magasin Jack Vartanian (New York, États-Unis, 2008) et la Quinta da Baroneza (Bragança Paulista, São Paulo, 2009), tous au Brésil, sauf mention contraire.

KAA RESTAURANT

São Paulo, São Paulo, Brazil, 2008

*Address: Av. Juscelino Kubitschek 279, Vila Olímpia, 04543–010 São Paulo,
SP, Brazil, +55 11 3045 0043, www.kaarestaurante.com.br
Area: 683 m² (ground floor); 113 m² (mezzanine); 80 m² (kitchen) Client: not disclosed
Cost: not disclosed. Collaboration: Gica Meriara (Landscape Design)*

Built on a long, narrow 797-square-meter site, this new restaurant seeks to offer a refuge from the bustling streets of Brazil's largest city and to bring guests closer to the native environment of the country. A green vertical wall features plants from the Atlantic forest. At its base, a "water mirror" makes reference to the endangered igarapés, or watersheds, of the region. A bar divides the space in two, with its generous shelves mounting up to the ceiling with "indigenous original objects that mimic bottles, cups, and books." The roof of the restaurant is partly made with an automatically opening canvas that allows interior spaces to be transformed into an outdoor urban living room. According to the architect: "The furniture is contemporary and the philosophy of this place is about transporting the urban paulista (i.e., an inhabitant of São Paulo) to a green environment. It is an escape from the chaos."

Dieses neue, auf einem langen, schmalen, 797 m² großen Grundstück errichtete Restaurant will einen Rückzugsort von den hektischen Straßen der größten Stadt Brasiliens bieten und seinen Gästen die ursprüngliche Umgebung des Landes näherbringen. Eine vertikale grüne Wand zeigt Pflanzen aus dem Atlantischen Urwald. An ihrer Basis nimmt ein „Wasserspiegel" Bezug auf den gefährdeten Biotop Igarapés, das Gebiet der Wasserscheide in der Region. Eine Bar, deren hohe Regale bis zur Decke reichen und „originale einheimische Objekte, die Flaschen, Tassen und Bücher nachahmen", enthalten, teilt den Raum. „Ein Teil des Restaurantdachs besteht aus sich automatisch öffnendem Segeltuch, wodurch das Restaurant zu einem Aufenthaltsraum im Freien wird. „Die Möblierung ist zeitgemäß, der Charakter dieses Orts soll den Paulista (den Stadtbewohner von São Paulo) in eine grüne Umgebung versetzen. Es ist ein Rückzugsort aus dem Chaos."

Construit sur un long et étroit terrain de 797 m², ce nouveau restaurant propose en fait à ses clients un havre de paix où se protéger de l'animation des rues de la plus grande ville du Brésil et même de les rapprocher de l'environnement naturel de leur pays. Un grand jardin vertical met en scène des plantes de la forêt atlantique. À sa base, un miroir d'eau fait référence aux *igarapé*, les cours d'eau amazoniens actuellement en danger. Le bar divise l'espace en deux parties. De grandes étagères toute hauteur présentent « des objets indigènes originaux qui imitent des bouteilles, des tasses et des livres ». Le toit est en partie fait d'une toile escamotable télécommandée qui permet de transformer les volumes intérieurs en une sorte de « salle de séjour urbaine en plein air ». « Le mobilier est contemporain et la philosophie du lieu vise à transporter les Paulistes (habitants de São Paulo) dans un environnement de verdure. Une échappée du chaos », précise l'architecte.

In the dining space, the ceiling light is by Rai de Meneres and the tables are designed by Arthur Casas (Taniguchi). The chairs at the bar are by Saarinen (Herança Cultural). The striped chairs are by Ronan & Erwan Bouroullec (Striped Sedia, Magis), while the armchairs below are by Arthur Casas (Casamatriz).

Die Deckenbeleuchtung im Speisesaal stammt von Rai de Meneres, die Tische wurden von Arthur Casas (Taniguchi) entworfen. Die Stühle in der Bar sind von Saarinen (Herança Cultural). Die gestreiften Stühle wurden von Ronan & Erwan Bouroullec entworfen (Striped Sedia, Magis), die Sessel unten stammen von Arthur Casas (Casamatriz).

Dans le restaurant, le luminaire est dû à Rai de Meneres, les tables ont été dessinées par Arthur Casas (Taniguchi) et les fauteuils autour du bar sont de Saarinen (Herança Cultural). Ci-dessous, les chaises à lattes plastiques sont de Ronan & Erwan Bouroullec (Striped Sedia, Magis) et les fauteuils d'Arthur Casas (Casamatriz).

CENTERBROOK

Centerbrook Architects and Planners, LLC
67 Main Street / P.O. Box 955
Centerbrook, CT 06409
USA

Tel: +1 860 767 0175 / Fax: +1 860 767 8719
E-mail: holahan@centerbrook.com
Web: www.centerbrook.com

MARK SIMON, born in 1946 in New York, graduated in 1968 from Brandeis University with a B.A. in Sculpture. He received his M.Arch from Yale University in 1972. He worked in the office of Warren Platner after graduation and then in the office of Charles Moore, beginning in 1974. He became a Partner in Moore Grover Harper, and then helped found Centerbrook in 1975, together with Bill Grover, Jeff Riley, and Chad Floyd, working initially on his own residential green projects. In 2008 Bill Grover became Partner Emeritus. Jim Childress was made a Partner in 1996, and Charles Mueller and Jon Lavy were made Principals of Centerbrook in 2002 and 2010 respectively. Today, Mark Simon is one of four Partners at Centerbrook Architects and Planners in Centerbrook, Connecticut. In addition to Lakewood House (northeast USA, 2004–08, published here), recent and current work of Centerbrook designed by Simon includes the Choate Residence Hall (Wallingford, Connecticut, 2008); Yale University Athletic Campus (New Haven, Connecticut, 2011); the Master Plan for the Yale Peabody Museum (New Haven, Connecticut, 2012); the Math and Science Building for the Berkshire School (Sheffield, Massachusetts, 2012); the Campus Master Plan and Library Addition for Lancaster Historical Society (Lancaster, Pennsylvania, 2012); the Academic and Science Wing for the University School (Hunting Valley, Ohio, 2012); and the Campus Master Plan for University Liggett School (Grosse Pointe Woods, Michigan, 2012), all in the USA.

MARK SIMON, 1946 in New York geboren, schloss sein Studium 1968 an der Brandeis University mit einem B. A. in Bildhauerei ab. 1972 absolvierte er einen M. Arch. an der Yale University. Nach dem Studienabschluss arbeitete er bei Warren Platner, ab 1974 im Büro von Charles Moore. Er wurde Partner bei Moore Grover Harper und gründete 1975 mit Bill Grover, Jeff Riley und Chad Floyd das Büro Centerbrook. Dort arbeitete er zunächst an eigenen grünen Wohnbauprojekten. Seit 2008 ist Bill Grover Partner Emeritus. 1996 wurde Jim Childress Partner, 2002 und 2010 wurden Charles Mueller und Jon Lavy leitende Architekten des Büros. Heute ist Mark Simon einer von vier Partnern bei Centerbrook Architects and Planners in Centerbrook, Connecticut. Neben dem Lakewood House (Nordosten der USA, 2004–08, hier vorgestellt), sind weitere aktuelle Projekte von Mark Simon das Wohnheim Choate (Wallingford, Connecticut, 2008), der Sportcampus der Yale University (New Haven, Connecticut, 2011), der Masterplan für das Yale Peabody Museum (New Haven, Connecticut, 2012), das Gebäude für Mathematik und Naturwissenschaften an der Berkshire School (Sheffield, Massachusetts, 2012), der Masterplan für den Campus und die Bibliothekserweiterung der Lancaster Historical Society (Lancaster, Pennsylvania, 2012), ein akademischer und naturwissenschaftlicher Flügel für die University School (Hunting Valley, Ohio, 2012) sowie der Masterplan für den Campus der University Liggett School (Grosse Pointe Woods, Michigan, 2012), alle in den USA.

MARK SIMON, né en 1946 à New York, a obtenu un B.A. en sculpture à l'université Brandeis en 1968. Il est également titulaire d'un M.Arch. obtenu à Yale en 1972. Après ses études, il a travaillé dans les agences de Warren Platner, puis de Charles Moore à partir de 1974. Il est devenu l'un des partenaires de Moore Grover Harper avant de fonder Centerbrook avec Bill Grover, Jeff Riley et Chad Floyd en 1975, où il a tout d'abord travaillé à ses propres projets résidentiels écologiques. Bill Grover est devenu partenaire émérite en 2008. Jim Childress a rejoint les autres partenaires en 1996, tandis que Charles Mueller et Jon Lavy sont devenus les principaux responsables de Centerbrook en 2002 et 2010. Aujourd'hui, Mark Simon est l'un des quatre partenaires de l'agence Centerbrook Architects and Planners de Centerbrook, Connecticut. En plus de la Lakewood House (Nord-Est des États-Unis, 2004–08, publiée ici), les réalisations récentes et en cours de Centerbrook conçues par Simon comprennent la résidence Choate (Wallingford, Connecticut, 2008) ; le complexe sportif de l'université Yale (New Haven, Connecticut, 2011) ; le plan directeur du musée Peabody de Yale (New Haven, 2012) ; le bâtiment des mathématiques et des sciences de la Berkshire School (Sheffield, Massachusetts, 2012) ; le plan directeur du campus et l'extension de la bibliothèque de la Lancaster Historical Society (Lancaster, Pennsylvanie, 2012) ; l'aile scolaire et scientifique de la University School (Hunting Valley, Ohio, 2012) et le plan directeur du campus de la University Liggett School (Grosse Pointe Woods, Michigan, 2012), toutes aux États-Unis.

LAKEWOOD HOUSE

Northeast USA, 2004–08

Address: not disclosed. Area: 521 m² (main house)
Client: not disclosed. Cost: not disclosed

Located in a pine forest by a lake, the "rustic" aspect of this house is emphasized by the large tree trunks set horizontally on the southern porch walls to filter daylight. The complex includes the main house, a guesthouse, workshop, boathouse, and smaller outbuildings. Sustainable geothermal heating and cooling, abundant insulation, natural and local materials, and passive solar design are all part of the scheme. **LAKEWOOD HOUSE** uses biofuel in a high-efficiency Buderus boiler, allowing electricity consumption for heating and cooling to be half of what it would be in a typical structure built to code. A computerized energy management control system also minimizes energy use. Icynene spray foam insulation up to 30 centimeters thick was used for the ceiling and in a thickness of 25 centimeters for tall walls. Cabinets, floors, and ceilings were made from cherry wood harvested from the property.

Das in einem Kiefernwald an einem See gelegene Haus wirkt besonders „rustikal" durch große Baumstämme, die quer vor Südfassade und -Terrasse gesetzt wurden und das einfallende Licht filtern. Der Komplex umfasst ein Haupthaus, ein Gästehaus, eine Werkstatt, ein Bootshaus sowie kleinere Nebenbauten. Nachhaltige Aspekte des Entwurfs sind eine Erdwärmeheizung- und -kühlung, umfassende Dämmung, der Einsatz natürlicher, lokaler Materialien sowie die passive Nutzung von Sonnenenergie. Im **LAKEWOOD HOUSE** wird Biobrennstoff in einem Hochleistungskessel von Buderus verfeuert; der Stromverbrauch für Heizung und Klimaanlage konnte, im Vergleich zu Bauten nach konventionellen Vorgaben, um die Hälfte reduziert werden. Auch ein elektronisch gesteuertes Energiesparsystem trägt zur Minimierung des Verbrauchs bei. Die Decken erhielten eine bis zu 30 cm starke Schaumdämmung aus Icynene, hohe Wände eine bis zu 25 cm starke Dämmung. Schränke, Böden und Decken wurden aus Kirschholz gefertigt, das auf dem Grundstück geschlagen wurde.

L'apparence « rustique » de cette maison située dans un bois de pins au bord d'un lac est soulignée par les immenses troncs d'arbres posés horizontalement entre les murs du porche sud pour filtrer la lumière du jour. Le complexe compte une résidence principale, une maison d'hôtes, un atelier, un hangar à bateaux et des dépendances plus petites. Le projet comprend le chauffage et la climatisation géothermiques durables, l'isolation renforcée, des matériaux naturels et régionaux et utilise le système solaire passif. La **LAKEWOOD HOUSE** est dotée d'une chaudière Buderus haute efficacité à biocarburant, réduisant de moitié la consommation d'électricité par rapport aux structures conventionnelles. Un système informatisé de contrôle et de gestion de l'énergie permet également de minimiser la consommation. La mousse expansée icynène a été utilisée pour l'isolation du plafond (30 cm d'épaisseur) et des grands murs (25 cm). Placards, sols et plafonds sont en bois de cerisier récolté sur la propriété.

The site plan to the left and the image on the left page show the radiating pavilion-like design of the house. Above, horizontal tree trunks mark the façade of part of the house.

Der Grundstücksplan links und die Aufnahme auf der linken Seite lassen die fächerartig angeordneten Pavillonelemente des Entwurfs erkennen. Die Fassade (oben) zeichnet sich z. T. durch horizontal vorgehängte Baumstämme aus.

Le plan de situation ci-contre et la photo page de gauche montrent la conception rayonnante de type pavillon de la maison. Ci-dessus, des troncs d'arbres posés horizontalement marquent en partie la façade.

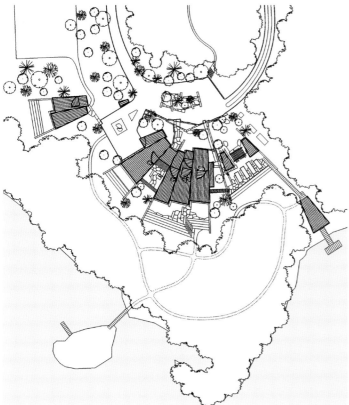

Plans show the ground floor (left) and the first floor (right), confirming the radiating form seen in overall images and the site plan.

Grundrisse von Erdgeschoss (links) und erstem Stock (rechts) bestätigen die Fächerform, die sich auf Gesamtansicht und Lageplan andeutet.

Plans du rez-de-chaussée (à gauche) et du premier étage (à droite) avec, là encore, la forme rayonnante qu'on voit déjà sur les photos et le plan de situation.

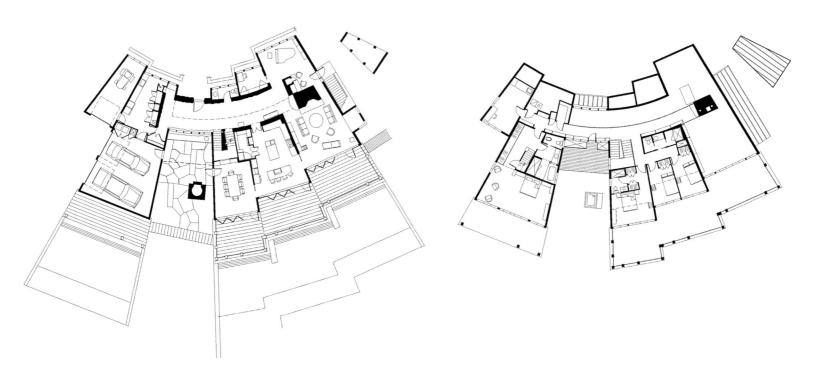

Below and right page, living room and stairway pictures with an emphasis on wood or natural stone relate the residence to its forested environment.

Ansichten von Wohnbereich und Treppe (unten und rechte Seite), die durch den auffälligen Einsatz von Holz und Naturstein den Bezug zwischen Haus und Waldlandschaft schaffen.

Ci-dessous et page de droite, salon et cage d'escalier : l'accent mis sur le bois et la pierre naturels créent un lien entre la maison et la forêt environnante.

Unexpected windows and vertical openings enliven the play of spaces inside the house. Right, the double-height glazing of the master bedroom lights the sloping roof and stepped volumes above the bed.

Überraschende Fenster und vertikale Lichtbänder sorgen für ein leben-diges Zusammenspiel der einzelnen Bereiche im Haus. Rechts die geschosshohe Verglasung des Haupt-schlafzimmers, durch die Licht auf Dachschräge und die Abtreppung über dem Bett fällt.

Des fenêtres à des endroits inatten-dus et des ouvertures verticales égayent les espaces intérieurs. À droite, le vitrage double hauteur de la chambre principale éclaire le plafond incliné et les volumes en escalier au-dessus du lit.

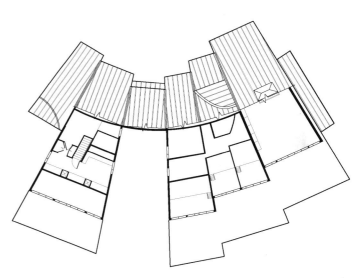

The loft level is seen in the plan above. The double height of the living area is articulated with sloping surfaces.

Der Grundriss oben zeigt das loftar-tige Hauptgeschoss. Die doppelte Geschosshöhe des Wohnbereichs wird durch Schrägen zusätzlich betont.

On voit l'étage loft sur le plan ci-dessus. La double hauteur du salon est articulée par des plans inclinés.

CLAUS + KAAN

Felix Claus Dick van Wageningen Architecten
Krijn Taconiskade 440
1087 HW Amsterdam
The Netherlands

Tel: +31 20 626 03 79
E-mail: info@clausvanwageningen.nl
Web: www.felixclaus.com

KAAN Architecten
Boompjes 55
3011 XB Rotterdam
The Netherlands

Tel: +31 10 206 00 00
E-mail: info@kaanarchitecten.com
Web: www.kaanarchitecten.com

FELIX CLAUS was born in 1956. He founded Claus en Kaan Architecten with Kees Kaan in 1987. Felix Claus has been a Professor at the ETH Zurich and RWTH Aachen. He presently teaches at the ETSA Madrid (since 2006) and EPFL (Lausanne, 2012–). Claus + Kaan specialized in public buildings such as the Dutch Embassy in Maputo (Mozambique, 1998–2004); the Netherlands Forensic Institute (The Hague, 1999–2005); the City Archives (Amsterdam, 2004–07); and the Netherlands Institute of Ecology (NIOO-KNAW, Wageningen, 2009–11, published here). Claus + Kaan also worked on the Supreme Court in Amsterdam (2006–12); the Museum of Fine Arts in Antwerp (Belgium, 2003–14); and the National Military Museum (Soesterberg, 2012–14), all in the Netherlands unless stated otherwise. The firm split in 2014. Kees Kaan then created KAAN Architecten in 2014, together with partners Vincent Panhuysen and Dikkie Scipio, while his former partner now works with his new firm Felix Claus Dick van Wageningen Architecten. KAAN Architecten is currently completing the Center for Molecular Research in Orsay, near Paris (France, 2011–16, started with Claus + Kaan).

FELIX CLAUS wurde 1956 geboren. 1987 gründete er gemeinsam mit Kees Kaan das Büro Claus en Kaan Architecten. Felix Claus war Professor an der ETH Zürich und der RWTH Aachen. Aktuell lehrt er an der ETSA Madrid (seit 2006) und der EPFL (Lausanne, seit 2012). Das Büro spezialisierte sich auf öffentliche Bauten, darunter die Niederländische Botschaft in Maputo (Mosambik, 1998–2004), das Niederländische Institut für Forensik (Den Haag, 1999–2005), das Stadtarchiv in Amsterdam (2004–07) sowie das Niederländische Institut für Ökologie (NIOO-KNAW, Wageningen, 2009–11, hier vorgestellt). Claus + Kaan arbeiteten auch am Obersten Gerichtshof in Amsterdam (2006–12), dem Königlichen Museum für bildende Künste in Antwerpen (Belgien, 2003–14) und dem Landesmilitärmuseum (Soesterberg, Niederlande, 2012–14). Das Büro wurde 2014 aufgelöst. Kees Kaan gründete zusammen mit den Partnern Vincent Panhuysen und Dikkie Scipio im selben Jahr KAAN Architecten, während sein früherer Partner jetzt in seiner neuen Firma Felix Claus Dick van Wageningen Architecten arbeitet. KAAN Architecten stellt gerade das Institut für Molekularforschung in Orsay bei Paris fertig (Institut des sciences moléculaires d'Orsay, 2011–16, begonnen mit Claus + Kaan).

FELIX CLAUS est né en 1956. Il a fondé Claus en Kaan Architecten avec Kees Kaan en 1987. Il a été professeur à l'ETH de Zurich et la RWTH d'Aix-la-Chapelle. Il enseigne actuellement à l'ETSA de Madrid (depuis 2006) et à l'EPFL (Lausanne, 2012–). Claus + Kaan s'est spécialisé dans les bâtiments publics comme l'ambassade des Pays-Bas à Maputo (Mozambique, 1998–2004) ; l'Institut médico-légal des Pays-Bas (La Haye, 1999–2005) ; les archives municipales (Amsterdam, 2004–07) et l'Institut néerlandais de l'écologie (NIOO-KNAW, Wageningen, 2009–11, publié ici). L'agence a aussi travaillé aux projets suivants : la Cour suprême à Amsterdam (2006–12) ; le Musée des beaux-arts d'Anvers (Belgique, 2003–14) et le Musée national militaire (Soesterberg, 2012–14), tous aux Pays-Bas, sauf mention contraire. L'agence s'est séparée en 2014. La même année, Kees Kaan a crée KAAN Architecten avec ses partenaires Vincent Panhuysen et Dikkie Scipio, alors que son ancien associé travaille dans sa nouvelle agence Felix Claus Dick van Wageningen Architecten. KAAN Architecten réalise actuellement l'Institut des sciences moléculaires d'Orsay près de Paris (2011–16, commencé avec Claus + Kaan).

NETHERLANDS INSTITUTE OF ECOLOGY

Wageningen, The Netherlands, 2009–11

Address: Droevendaalsesteeg 10, 6708 PB Wageningen, The Netherlands,
+31 317 473 400, www.nioo.knaw.nl. Area: 11 000 m². Client: Royal Netherlands Academy of Science, Amsterdam
Cost: €17 million. Collaboration: Dick van Wageningen, Katrin Weber

The **NETHERLANDS INSTITUTE OF ECOLOGY** (NIOO) is a research division of the Royal Netherlands Academy of Arts and Sciences (KNAW). This building plot is located near Wageningen University along a street that divides the campus from the rural landscape. The program required offices, conference rooms, laboratories, a restaurant, technical facilities, a series of inside and outside workshops for botanical and zoological research, as well as storage areas and other facilities. Furthermore, the client's goal was to achieve the highest standards of sustainable construction. The client specifically asked the architects and builders to adhere to "Cradle to Cradle" principles in all stages of the design. Claus + Kaan proposed a compact building on the street side to house offices, laboratories, and common spaces. At the back of the site, a series of smaller buildings contain the workshops, greenhouses, birdhouses, and space for storage and technical equipment. These wood-clad buildings are intended to integrate more with the nearby rural environment. In the main building, working areas are located near sources of natural light, including voids pierced through the volume precisely to provide daylight. The project challenged conventional building methods and sought to "borrow from nature" in terms of logic and the multiple use of spaces.

Das **NIEDERLÄNDISCHE INSTITUT FÜR ÖKOLOGIE** (NIOO) ist eine Forschungseinrichtung der Königlich Niederländischen Akademie der Künste und Wissenschaften (KNAW). Das Institutsgelände liegt unweit der Universität Wageningen an einer Straße, die zwischen Campus und Landschaft verläuft. Das Programm forderte Büro- und Konferenzräume, Labors, ein Restaurant, Technikeinrichtungen sowie verschiedene Werkstätten für botanische und zoologische Forschungsprojekte (Innen- und Außenbereiche) sowie Lagerräume und andere Einrichtungen. Dem Bauträger ging es darum, nach höchsten Ansprüchen nachhaltig zu bauen, weshalb er Architekten und Bauunternehmen in sämtlichen Planungs- und Bauphasen auf Ökoeffektivität verpflichtete. Claus + Kaan planten ein zur Straßenseite kompaktes Gebäude, in dem Büros, Labors und Gemeinschaftsflächen liegen. Verschiedene kleinere Bauten an der Rückseite des Grundstücks bieten Raum für Werkstätten, Gewächshäuser, Volièren sowie Lagermöglichkeiten und Raum für technische Geräte. Die holzverschalten Bauten integrieren sich in die ländliche Umgebung. Die Arbeitsbereiche im Hauptgebäude liegen tageslichtnah, Lichtschächte, die durch den Baukörper gezogen sind, sorgen für natürliches Licht. Das Projekt stellt konventionelle Bauprozesse infrage und orientiert sich „an der Natur" – im logischen Aufbau wie auch durch die Multifunktionalität der Räume.

L'**INSTITUT NÉERLANDAIS DE L'ÉCOLOGIE** (NIOO) est un département de recherche de l'Académie royale des arts et sciences des Pays-Bas (KNAW). Le site est situé à proximité de l'université de Wageningen, le long d'une route qui sépare le campus de la campagne. Le programme exigeait des bureaux, des salles de conférences, des laboratoires, un restaurant, des locaux techniques, plusieurs ateliers intérieurs et extérieurs destinés à la recherche botanique et zoologique, ainsi que des espaces de rangement et d'autres équipements. Le client voulait aussi respecter les normes les plus élevées en matière de construction durable. Il a donc demandé expressément aux architectes et constructeurs d'adhérer aux principes « du berceau au berceau » à toutes les étapes de la conception. Claus + Kaan a proposé un bâtiment compact côté rue pour accueillir des bureaux, laboratoires et espaces collectifs. À l'arrière du terrain, une série de constructions plus petites abrite les ateliers, serres, volières et des espaces pour le rangement et les équipements techniques. Revêtues de bois, elles sont conçues pour mieux s'intégrer au milieu rural environnant. Dans le bâtiment principal, les espaces de travail sont placés à proximité De sources lumière naturelle, notamment des orifices percés à cet effet. Le projet remet en question les méthodes traditionnelles de construction et cherche à « emprunter à la nature » en termes de logique et de polyvalence des espaces.

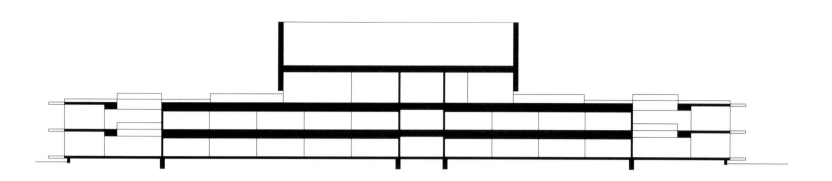

The long glazed base of the building is topped by a wood-clad box that makes it blend with its natural setting while also announcing its ecological function.

Über dem gestreckten und verglasten Sockelgeschoss des Komplexes ruht eine holzverkleidete Box, die mit der Landschaft verschmilzt und die ökologische Funktion anklingen lässt.

La longue base vitrée du bâtiment est surmontée d'un cube revêtu de bois qui lui permet de se fondre dans le décor naturel tout en annonçant sa fonction écologique.

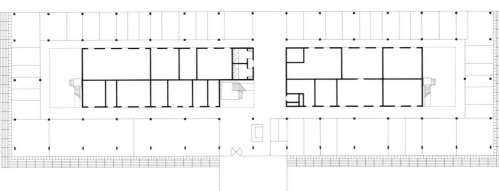

The basic rectangular form of the structure is seen in the plan above. Shades reduce solar gain (above), while natural light and such features as the airy suspended stairway (right) enliven the interiors.

Der Grundriss oben zeigt die rechteckige Grundform des Baus. Sonnenschutzrollos reduzieren den Wärmeeintrag (oben). Tageslicht und Akzente wie die leichte, abgehängte Treppe (rechts) beleben den Innenraum.

La forme de base rectangulaire ressort du plan ci-dessus. Des stores réduisent l'apport solaire (ci-dessus), tandis que la lumière naturelle et certains éléments comme la cage d'escalier suspendue et aérienne (à droite) animent l'intérieur.

The entire design, both inside and out, projects an image of lightness and simplicity which is surely in keeping with its function, but also makes for agreeable working space.

Der Gesamtentwurf gibt sich innen wie außen von einer Leichtigkeit und Einfachheit, die seiner Philosophie entspricht, aber auch ein angenehmes Arbeitsumfeld schafft.

La conception dans son ensemble, à l'intérieur comme à l'extérieur, renvoie une image de légèreté et de simplicité qui correspond à la fonction du bâtiment tout en procurant un espace de travail agréable.

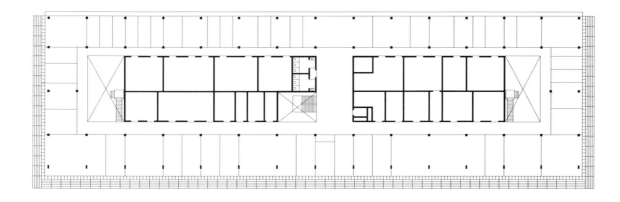

COMUNARQUITECTOS

COMUNarquitectos
Camino el Sauce 22
Santiago 9560000
Chile

Tel: +56 2 855 7031
E-mail: syurjevic@gmail.com / catagcominetti@gmail.com
Web: www.comunarquitectos.cl

SEBASTIAN YURJEVIC ZENTENO obtained his B.Arch from the Universidad Central de Chile (Santiago, 2000). He founded COMUNarquitectos in 2009, and went on to obtain an M.A. in Architectural Design (Waseda University, Tokyo, Japan, 2011), where he is presently a doctoral candidate in Architectural Design. **CATALINA GONZÁLEZ COMINETTI** also obtained her B.Arch degree from the Universidad Central de Chile (Santiago, 2000), and a Master's degree in Global Environmental Studies at Sophia University (Tokyo, Japan, 2012). She cofounded COMUNarquitectos with Sebastian Yurjevic Zenteno in 2009. Their work includes the MA House (Melipilla, 2008); MJ House (Melipilla, 2010–11, published here); and the MG House (Calera de Tango, 2011), all in Chile.

SEBASTIAN YURJEVIC ZENTENO absolvierte einen B. Arch. an der Universidad Central de Chile (Santiago, 2000). Nachdem er 2009 COMUNarquitectos gegründet hatte, erhielt er 2010 einen M. A. im Fach Architekturdesign an der Waseda-Universität in Tokio (2011), wo er derzeit im selben Fach promoviert. **CATALINA GONZÁLEZ COMINETTI** absolvierte ihren B. Arch. ebenfalls an der Universidad Central de Chile (Santiago, 2000) und einen Master im Fach Globale Umweltstudien an der Sophia Universität (Tokio, 2012). 2009 war sie Mitgründerin von COMUNarquitectos. Zu ihren Arbeiten gehören die Casa MA (Melipilla, 2008), Casa MJ (Melipilla, 2010–11, hier vorgestellt) und die Casa MG (Calera de Tango, 2011); alle in Chile.

SEBASTIAN YURJEVIC ZENTENO a obtenu son B.Arch. à l'Université centrale du Chili (Santiago, 2000). Il a fondé COMUNarquitectos en 2009 et obtenu un M.A. en design architectural (université Waseda, Tokyo, Japon, 2011), université où il prépare actuellement un doctorat dans le même domaine. **CATALINA GONZÁLEZ COMINETTI** a également obtenu son B.Arch. à l'Université centrale du Chili (Santiago, 2000) et un master en sciences de l'environnement à l'université Sophia (Tokyo, Japon, 2012). Elle a fondé COMUNarquitectos avec Sebastian Yurjevic Zenteno en 2009. Parmi leurs œuvres figurent la Casa MA (Melipilla, 2008) ; la Casa MJ (Melipilla, 2010–11, publiée ici) et la Casa MG (Calera de Tango, 2011), toutes au Chili.

MJ HOUSE

Melipilla, Chile, 2010–11

Address: not disclosed. Area: 140 m²
Client: Diego Moure, Constanza Jimenez. Cost: $60 000

The architects title their description of this house "The Unpredictability of Wood." It was designed for a young couple working as forestry engineers and their two children. Since both architects were based in Tokyo when they designed this residence, they sought to incorporate some of what they had seen in local traditional and modern architecture. They translated their observations into a design that is closed on the street side and open "inwards," with a dialogue created between the two "conditions" created by an overlap on the roof. "Thus," they write, "the ceiling becomes the pivotal element of the house and its movements and angles correspond to an intention to generate a minimal impact within the existing landscape." To avoid concrete, which they consider to be a "foreign, abstract material," the architects used brick and wood. The natural grain of the wood with its "imperfections and unpredictability" is part of what they wanted, but they also chose to create "straight abstract lines." Local artisans built the house using traditional Chilean construction methods.

Die Architekten nennen ihre Beschreibung dieses Projekts „Die Unberechenbarkeit von Holz". Das Haus wurde für ein junges Forstingenieurspaar mit zwei Kindern entworfen. Da beide Architekten zum Zeitpunkt des Entwurfs in Tokio lebten, sollten Elemente traditioneller und moderner japanischer Architektur einfließen. So entstand ein Haus, das zur Straße hin geschlossen ist und sich zur anderen Seite öffnet. Die sich überschneidende Dachkonstruktion lässt diese beiden „Zustände" in einen Dialog treten. Die Architekten: „Die Decke wird zum zentralen Element des Hauses. Ihre Bewegungen und Winkel korrespondieren mit unserem Wunsch, so wenig wie möglich in die Landschaft einzugreifen." Anstelle von Beton, in den Augen der Architekten ein „fremdartiges, abstraktes Material", kamen Ziegelsteine und Holz zum Einsatz. Zwar war den Architekten an der natürlichen Textur von Holz mit all seinen „Makeln und seiner Unberechenbarkeit" gelegen, trotzdem entschieden sie sich für „gerade abstrakte Linien". Handwerker aus der Region bauten das Haus nach chilenischer Bautradition.

Les architectes parlent de « l'imprévisibilité du bois » pour évoquer leur maison. Elle a été conçue pour un jeune couple d'ingénieurs forestiers et leurs deux enfants. Comme les deux architectes étaient installés à Tokyo lorsqu'ils ont conçu cette résidence, ils ont tenté d'intégrer une partie de ce qu'ils avaient vu dans l'architecture locale traditionnelle et moderne. Ils ont transféré leurs observations dans un projet aveugle côté rue et ouvert « vers l'intérieur » tout en établissant un dialogue entre les deux « conditions » créées par une partie saillante en toiture. « Ainsi, écrivent-ils, le plafond devient l'élément central de la maison ; ses mouvements et ses angles répondent à l'intention de générer un impact minimal sur le paysage existant. » Pour éviter le béton qu'ils considèrent comme un « matériau étranger, abstrait », les architectes ont choisi la brique et le bois. Le grain naturel du bois avec ses « imperfections et son imprévisibilité » fait partie de ce qu'ils voulaient, mais ils ont également choisi de créer « des lignes droites abstraites ». Des artisans locaux ont construit la maison selon des méthodes de construction traditionnelles chiliennes.

A rendering and two photos show the MJ House in its site—where the natural environment seems to prevail as the house itself sits lightly on the land.

Eine Zeichnung und zwei Fotografien zeigen die Casa MJ an ihrem Standort. Das leicht erhöht stehende Gebäude lässt der Natur den Vortritt.

Une vue en perspective et deux photos montrent la Casa MJ dans son site – où l'environnement naturel semble prédominer car la maison repose légèrement sur le terrain.

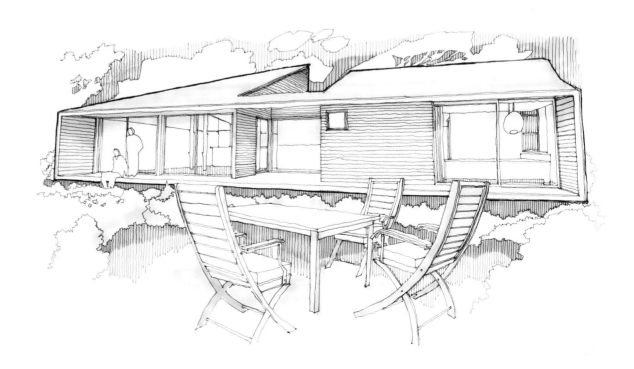

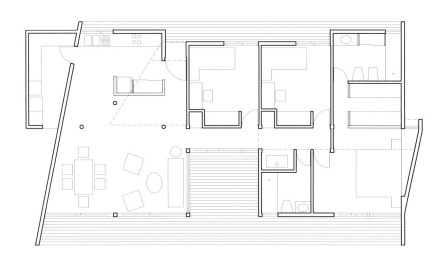

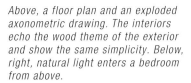

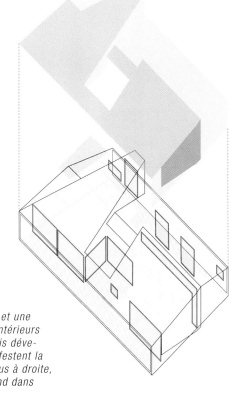

Above, a floor plan and an exploded axonometric drawing. The interiors echo the wood theme of the exterior and show the same simplicity. Below, right, natural light enters a bedroom from above.

Oben ein Grundriss und eine axonometrische Explosionszeichnung. Die Innenräume greifen das im Außenbereich verwendete Holz als Material wieder auf und sind genauso schlicht gehalten. Von oben fällt Tageslicht ins Schlafzimmer (unten rechts).

Ci-dessus un plan d'étage et une axonométrie éclatée. Les intérieurs reprennent le thème du bois développé à l'extérieur et manifestent la même simplicité. Ci-dessous à droite, la lumière naturelle descend dans une chambre à coucher.

Roughly finished solid wood columns
mark the simple interior where full-
height windows offer a generous view
of the surroundings.

Die schlichten Innenräume zeichnen
sich durch grob bearbeitete Massiv-
holzsäulen und raumhohe Fenster
aus, die einen großzügigen Ausblick
auf die Umgebung ermöglichen.

De solides colonnes de bois à la finition brute marquent l'intérieur sobre
où des fenêtres toute hauteur offrent
une vue généreuse sur les environs.

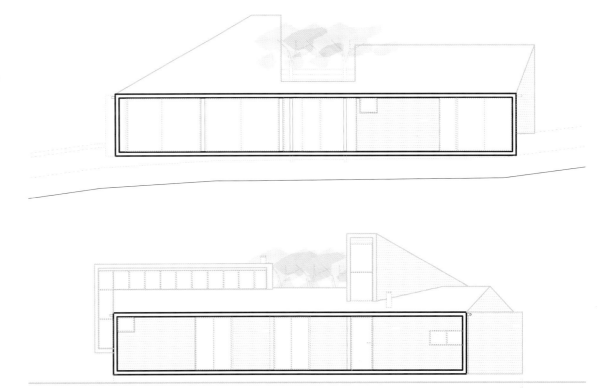

DEKLEVA GREGORIČ

dekleva gregorič arhitekti
Dalmatinova 11
1000 Ljubljana
Slovenia

Tel: +386 1 430 52 70
Fax: +386 1 430 52 71
E-mail: arh@dekleva-gregoric.com
Web: www.dekleva-gregoric.com

ALJOŠA DEKLEVA was born in 1972 in Postojna, Slovenia, and **TINA GREGORIČ** was born in 1974 in Kranj, Slovenia. They created their firm in 2003 in Ljubljana. They both graduated from the Faculty of Architecture of the University of Ljubljana and went on to study at the Architectural Association in London (AA), where they received Master's degrees in Architecture in 2002. At the AA they cofounded an international architectural network called RAMTV. They seek to focus on social, material, and historic contexts in their architectural projects. Their work includes the XXS House (Ljubljana, 2004); a metal recycling plant (Pivka, 2005–07); Pertot Showroom (Trieste, Italy, 2006–08); Housing L (Sežana, 2004–09); the Clifftop House (Maui, Hawaii, USA, 2004–11, published here); and Razgledi Perovo Housing (Kamnik, 2008–11), all in Slovenia unless stated otherwise.

ALJOŠA DEKLEVA wurde 1972 in Postojna, Slowenien, **TINA GREGORIČ** 1974 in Kranj, Slowenien, geboren. Ihr erstes Büro gründeten sie 2003 in Ljubljana. Beide studierten nach ihrem Abschluss an der Architekturfakultät der Universität Ljubljana an der Architectural Association in London (AA), wo sie 2002 ihren M. Arch. absolvierten. An der AA waren sie Mitbegründer des Netzwerks RAMTV. Bei ihren Projekten gilt ihr besonderes Augenmerk sozialen, materiellen und historischen Kontexten. Zu ihren Arbeiten zählen das XXS House (Ljubljana, 2004), eine Metallrecyclinganlage (Pivka, 2005–07), ein Showroom für Pertot (Triest, Italien, 2006–08), Housing L (Sežana, 2004–09), das Clifftop House (Maui, Hawaii, USA, 2004–11, hier vorgestellt) und die Wohnsiedlung Razgledi Perovo (Kamnik, 2008–11), alle in Slowenien, sofern nicht anders angegeben.

ALJOŠA DEKLEVA est né en 1972, à Postojna, en Slovénie, et **TINA GREGORIČ** en 1974 à Kranj, également en Slovénie. Ils ont ouvert leur agence en 2003 à Ljubljana. Ils sont tous les deux diplômés de la faculté d'architecture de l'université de Ljubljana et ont poursuivi leurs études à l'Architectural Association (AA) de Londres où ils ont obtenu un master en architecture en 2002. C'est là également qu'ils ont fondé un réseau international d'architectes appelé RAMTV. Dans leurs projets architecturaux, ils essaient de se concentrer sur les aspects sociaux, matériels et historiques. Leurs réalisations comprennent la maison XXS (Ljubljana, 2004) ; une usine de recyclage de métal (Pivka, 2005–07) ; l'espace d'exposition Pertot (Trieste, Italie, 2006–08) ; le logement L (Sežana, 2004–09) ; la Clifftop House (Maui, Hawaii, États-Unis, 2004–11, publiée ici) et le lotissement Razgledi Perovo (Kamnik, 2008 –11), toutes en Slovénie, sauf mention contraire.

CLIFFTOP HOUSE

Maui, Hawaii, USA, 2004–11

Address: not disclosed. Area: 250 m² (500 m² of covered space)
Client: Robert & Dražena Stroj. Cost: not disclosed
Collaboration: Flavio Coddou, Lea Kovič

This house was designed with a particular emphasis on the site and its perfect ocean view. The architects, admittedly not familiar with such a spectacular natural site, decided to create several "houses" under a common roof that "also serves as a folded wooden deck and integrates the house with the landscape." Because of the very large roof and the nature of the site, cross ventilation eliminates the need for air conditioning. Local wood was used for the floor, terrace, ceilings, and roof, although concrete blocks were used for construction. The owner, an industrial designer, supervised the construction with the architects. The owner writes: "We really wanted to finish construction using natural materials…there are absolutely no paints used anywhere in the house, all walls are covered by custom-made stucco mixed from white concrete, coral sand, dune sand, and lime, all wood is just oiled with pure tang oil, and there is no lacquer or polyurethane used anywhere. All walls are solid concrete (blocks filled with concrete); the timber used on the roof, ceiling, floor, outside deck, glass fascia framing, sliding doors and windows (all fabricated on site), etc. is all Ironwood aka Ipe (chosen for its hardness, natural color, and being able to withstand elements without the use of protective finishes). All vertical panels used to build the kitchen, interior doors, closets, and cabinets are solid bamboo plywood (chosen for its hardness, stability despite changing humidity, as well as its natural grain and color when oiled, contrasting well with the Ironwood)."

Besonderes Augenmerk beim Entwurf dieses Hauses galt dem Grundstück und dem dramatischen Seepanorama. Die Architekten, erklärtermaßen nicht an so spektakuläre Naturgrundstücke gewöhnt, entschieden sich, „mehrere Häuser" unter einem Dach zu konzipieren, „das zugleich als gefaltete Holzterrasse dient und das Haus in die Landschaft integriert". Dank des ungewöhnlich großen Dachs und seiner Lage ist der Bau so gut durchlüftet, dass sich eine Klimaanlage erübrigt. Für Böden, Terrasse, Decken und Dach wurde lokales Holz verbaut, gemauert wurde mit Formsteinen aus Beton. Der Eigentümer, ein Industriedesigner, unterstützte die Architekten bei der Bauleitung. Er schreibt: „Wir wollten den Bau unbedingt mit natürlichen Materialien realisieren … im ganzen Haus wurde konsequent auf den Einsatz von Farben verzichtet, alle Wände wurden mit speziell gefertigtem Putz aus weißem Beton, Korallensand und Kalk verputzt, alle Holzflächen mit reinem Tungöl geölt, auch sonst wurden keinerlei Lacke oder Polyurethane verarbeitet. Die Wände sind aus Beton (ausgegossener Mauerstein), Dach, Decken, Böden, Terrasse, Traufbretter, Schiebetüren und Fenster aus Ipé-Hartholz (unsere Wahl aufgrund von Materialhärte, natürlicher Färbung und seiner Witterungsbeständigkeit ohne weitere Versiegelung). Für Kücheneinbauten, Türen im Innenbereich, Wandschränke und Schränke wurde mit massivem Bambussperrholz gearbeitet (dank seiner Härte und Formstabilität bei variierender Luftfeuchtigkeit sowie der natürlichen Maserung und Farbgebung nach Ölbehandlung ein idealer Kontrast zum Ipé-Hartholz)."

La maison a été conçue en tenant tout particulièrement compte du site et de sa vue imprenable sur l'océan. Les architectes, peu familiers d'un site naturel aussi spectaculaire, ont choisi de créer plusieurs « maisons » sous un même toit qui « forme également une plate-forme plissée en bois et intègre la maison au paysage ». Avec cet immense toit et étant donné la nature du site, la ventilation transversale rend l'air conditionné superflu. Le sol, la terrasse, les plafonds et le toit sont en bois local mais des blocs de béton ont été utilisés pour la construction. Le propriétaire, un designer industriel, a supervisé les travaux avec les architectes. Il écrit : « Nous voulions absolument des matériaux naturels pour les finitions … aucune peinture n'a été utilisée dans toute la maison, les murs sont recouverts d'un stuc fait sur mesure à partir de béton blanc, de sable corallien, de sable de dune et de chaux, le bois est simplement passé à l'huile de tung sans aucun vernis ni polyuréthane. Les murs sont en béton plein (blocs pleins de béton), le bois du toit, des plafonds, du sol, de la terrasse, des encadrements de fenêtres, des portes et baies coulissantes (toutes construites sur place) est de l'ipé ou ironwood (choisi pour sa dureté, sa coloration naturelle et sa résistance aux intempéries qui ne nécessite aucun enduit de protection). Tous les panneaux verticaux qui forment la cuisine, les portes intérieures, les placards et les meubles de rangement sont en contreplaqué de bambou massif (choisi pour sa dureté, sa stabilité aux changements d'humidité, sa veinure naturelle et sa teinte, une fois huilé, qui contraste joliment avec l'ipé). »

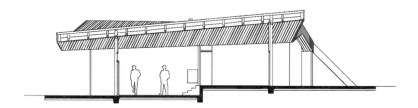

The profile of the house, seen in the section drawings above and in the images, makes it seem to emerge in an organic way from its spectacular natural setting on the island of Maui.

Das Profil des Hauses (Querschnitte oben und Aufnahmen) weckt den Eindruck, der Bau wachse geradezu organisch aus der spektakulären Landschaft der Insel Maui empor.

Le profil de la maison, qu'on voit sur les dessins en coupe ci-dessus et les photos, donne l'impression de la faire émerger presque organiquement du spectaculaire décor naturel de l'île de Maui.

Pictures showing the angled wooden roof of the house and its apparently closed exterior. The plan on this page shows the ocean views and the parking area.

Aufnahmen der Dachschrägen des Hauses und des scheinbar geschlossenen Außenbaus. Der Grundriss illustriert den Meerblick und die Autostellplätze.

Les photos montrent le toit anguleux en bois et son aspect extérieur fermé. Le plan présente le parking et les vues sur l'océan.

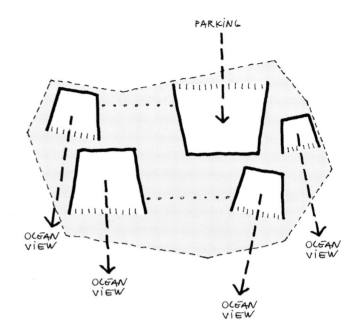

A sheltered wooden terrace offers an unobstructed view of the coastline. Below, a sketch showing the natural ventilation scheme that avoids air conditioning.

Von der geschützten Holzterrasse bietet sich ein unverstellter Ausblick auf die Küste. Die Skizze unten veranschaulicht die Prinzipien natürlicher Durchlüftung, die künstliche Klimatisierung verzichtbar macht.

Une terrasse en bois abritée offre une vue illimitée sur le littoral. Ci-dessous, le croquis montre le principe de ventilation naturelle qui permet d'éviter le recours à l'air conditionné.

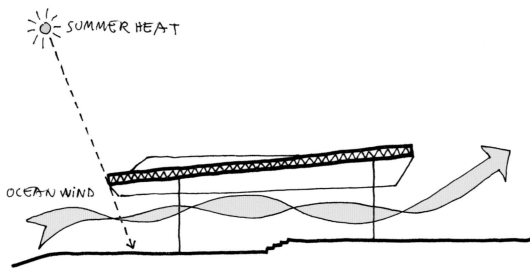

SUMMER HEAT

OCEAN WIND

NO AIRCONDITIONING → NATURAL VENTILATION ONLY

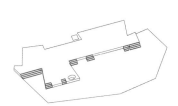
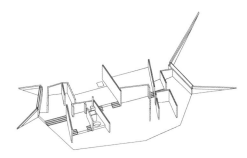
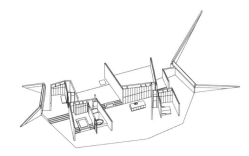

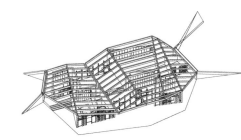

The drawings above show the progressive assembly of the house, including its built-in furniture and enveloping roof deck.

Die Zeichnungen oben visualisieren die verschiedenen Bauphasen des Hauses bis hin zu den Einbauten und dem Terrassendach, das den Bau umschließt.

Les schémas ci-dessus présentent l'assemblage progressif de la maison, y compris ses meubles encastrés et son toit en terrasse enveloppant.

Wooden ceilings and floors continue the extensive presence of this material, that gives a rather dark appearance to the interiors, in contrast to the bright views of the shore.

In den Holzdecken und -böden setzt sich das dominante Materialthema fort, das das Interieur im Kontrast zum hellen Küstenpanorama eher dunkel erscheinen lässt.

Les plafonds et sols en bois rendent encore plus prépondérante la présence de ce matériau qui confère un aspect plutôt sombre à l'intérieur de la maison et contraste avec la clarté des vues sur la côte.

DJURIC+TARDIO

Djuric+Tardio Architectes
17 Rue Ramponeau
75020 Paris
France

Tel: +33 1 40 33 06 41
Fax: +33 1 40 33 93 87
E-mail: contact@djuric-tardio.com
Web: www.djuric-tardio.com

MIRCO TARDIO was born in 1970 in Italy and studied at the Polytechnic Institute of Milan and the Ecole Paris-Belleville. He has lived in France since 1996. Between 2000 and 2009 he worked in the offices of Chaix & Morel and the Ateliers Jean Nouvel. **CAROLINE DJURIC** was born in France in 1974 and studied at the Ecole Paris-Belleville before working in the same offices as Tardio. Winners of the Europan 7 contest in 2004, they created their office in Paris the same year. Their recent work includes 44 apartments in Le Mans (2008–11); a 174-apartment complex in Arcueil (2009–); and "Eco-Neighborhoods" in Le Havre (2010–) and Langoiran-Bordeaux (2010–). They have designed several single-family residences, including the Eco-Sustainable House published here (Antony, 2010–11), all in France. Djuric+Tardio are also working on a number of projects in tandem with Chaix & Morel and Jean Nouvel. Much of their production has been related to research into durable wooden structures.

MIRCO TARDIO, geboren 1970 in Italien, studierte am Polytechnikum Mailand sowie der Ecole Paris-Belleville und lebt seit 1996 in Frankreich. Zwischen 2000 und 2009 war er für Chaix & Morel und Ateliers Jean Nouvel tätig. **CAROLINE DJURIC**, geboren 1974 in Frankreich, studierte an der Ecole Paris-Belleville und arbeitete im Anschluss für dieselben Büros. Nachdem das Team 2004 den Europan-7-Wettbewerb für sich entscheiden konnte, erfolgte im selben Jahr die Bürogründung in Paris. Zu ihren jüngeren Projekten zählen 44 Wohnungen in Le Mans (2008–11), ein Komplex mit 174 Wohnungen in Arcueil (seit 2009) sowie die „Eco-Siedlungen" in Le Havre (seit 2010) und Langoiran-Bordeaux (seit 2010). Das Team plante zahlreiche Einfamilienhäuser, darunter die hier vorgestellte Maison Eco-Durable (Antony, 2010–11), alle in Frankreich. Djuric+Tardio arbeiten darüber hinaus an verschiedenen Projekten mit Chaix & Morel und Jean Nouvel. Ein Großteil ihrer Projekte entwickelte sich aus der intensiven Auseinandersetzung mit nachhaltigen Holzbauweisen.

MIRCO TARDIO est né en 1970 en Italie et a fait ses études à l'Institut polytechnique de Milan et à l'École Paris-Belleville. Il vit en France depuis 1996. Entre 2000 et 2009, il a travaillé dans les agences Chaix & Morel et aux Ateliers Jean Nouvel. **CAROLINE DJURIC** est née en France en 1974 et a fait ses études à l'École Paris-Belleville avant de travailler dans les mêmes agences que Tardio. Vainqueurs du concours Europan 7 en 2004, c'est cette année qu'ils ont ouvert leur agence à Paris. Leurs réalisations récentes comprennent 44 appartements au Mans (2008–11) ; un complexe de 174 appartements à Arcueil (2009–) et des « éco-quartiers » au Havre (2010–) et à Langoiran près de Bordeaux (2010–). Ils ont également conçu plusieurs maisons individuelles, parmi lesquelles la Maison éco-durable publiée ici (Antony, 2010–11), toutes en France. Djuric+Tardio travaillent aussi à plusieurs projets en tandem avec Chaix & Morel et Jean Nouvel. Leurs productions sont pour la plupart liées à la recherche de structures durables en bois.

ECO-SUSTAINABLE HOUSE
Antony, France, 2010–11

Address: not disclosed. Area: 246 m². Client: not disclosed. Cost: not disclosed
Collaboration: Amandine Albertini, Iris Menage, Thomas Panconi

This house was built in just 10 months, including its special concrete foundations. The wooden structure cost €278 000 to build. Low-temperature gas-fired heating is used under the floors, and double-paned argon-filled windows insure appropriate insulation. A "clean" work site, natural ventilation, and the use of rainwater for the garden are some of the other environmental features of the house. The house is intended to "propose a design process and construction system allowing for prefabrication and modular design." Rather than the traditional roof implied by local construction regulations, the architects preferred to open the top of the house with a planted terrace. Kiwis, squash, and grapes are all grown on this terrace. The interior design allows for the easy transformation of volumes according to family needs through such devices as large sliding walls. The Finnish wood panels insulated with wood fiber were completely prefabricated in a workshop and the house was assembled on site in just two weeks.

Das Haus konnte, inklusive seines speziellen Betonfundaments, in nur zehn Monaten erbaut werden. Die Baukosten des Holzbaus beliefen sich auf 278 000 Euro. Eingebaut wurden ein Gasniedertemperaturkessel mit Fußbodenheizung sowie dämmende Isolierglasfenster mit Argonfüllung. Weitere umweltfreundliche Aspekte des Hauses sind eine „saubere" Baustelle, natürliche Durchlüftung und Regenwassernutzung für den Garten. Das Haus dient zugleich als Modellentwurf für „einen Planungsprozess und ein Bausystem, das Vorfertigung und modulare Entwurfsformen erlaubt". Statt eines traditionellen Giebeldachs (nach örtlichen Bauvorgaben vorgesehen) entschieden sich die Architekten für einen offenen Giebel mit begrünter Dachterrasse, auf der Kiwis, Kürbis und Wein wachsen. Im Innern des Baus erlauben großflächige Schiebeelemente das problemlose Umwandeln der Räume je nach den Bedürfnissen der Familie. Das Haus wurde im Werk vollständig aus finnischen Holzfaserdämmplatten vorgefertigt und vor Ort in nur zwei Wochen erbaut.

La maison a été construite en seulement dix mois, y compris les fondations en béton spécial. La structure en bois a coûté 278 000 €. Le chauffage au sol à basse température est alimenté au gaz et les fenêtres en double vitrage à l'argon assurent une isolation adaptée. Un chantier « propre », la ventilation naturelle et l'utilisation de l'eau de pluie pour le jardin ne sont que quelques-uns des autres aspects écologiques de la maison. L'objectif était de « proposer un processus de création et un système de construction permettant la préfabrication et une conception modulaire ». Plutôt que le toit traditionnel préconisé par la réglementation locale en matière de construction, les architectes ont préféré l'ouvrir pour en faire une terrasse où sont cultivés des kiwis, des courges et du raisin. Le découpage intérieur permet la transformation facile des volumes en fonction des besoins de la famille au moyen de dispositifs tels que de grandes cloisons coulissantes. La maison a été entièrement préfabriquée en atelier en panneaux de bois finlandais avec isolant en fibre de bois, et assemblée sur le site en seulement deux semaines.

Surrounded by much more
ordinary suburban houses, the
Eco-Sustainable House stands out
because of its open wood frame
and terraces. Right, a site plan.

Die von ungleich konventionelleren
Bauten gerahmte Maison Eco-Durable
fällt auch durch die offene Holzkonstruktion und die Holzterrassen auf.
Rechts ein Grundstücksplan.

Entourée de maisons de banlieue plus
ordinaires, la Maison éco-durable
s'en distingue par sa charpente
ouverte et ses terrasses. À droite,
un plan de l'ensemble.

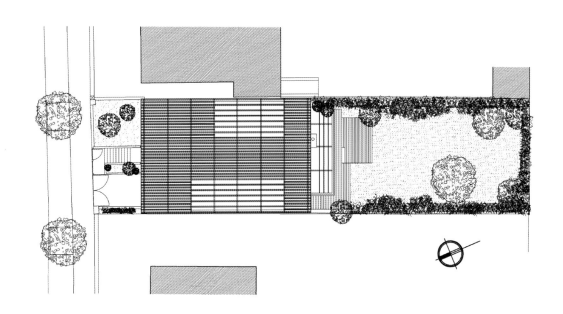

The pitched roof is actually no more than an open wooden frame. Symbolizing the form of the ordinary house, it offers an upper-story wooden terrace.

Das Giebeldach ist im Grunde nichts anderes als eine offene Holzrahmenkonstruktion. Es symbolisiert traditionellere Hausformen und dient zugleich als Dachterrasse in Holz.

Le toit en pente n'est rien d'autre qu'une charpente ouverte en bois. Elle reproduit la forme d'une maison classique et ouvre une terrasse en bois au dernier étage de la maison.

The terrace, to the left, and the rooftop share a sense of protected openness engendered by the light wooden frame.

Die Terrasse links ist ebenso geschützt und zugleich offen wie das Dach, ein Effekt, der sich der leichten Holzrahmenkonstruktion verdankt.

La terrasse de gauche partage avec celle du toit un sentiment d'ouverture protégée engendré par la charpente légère en bois.

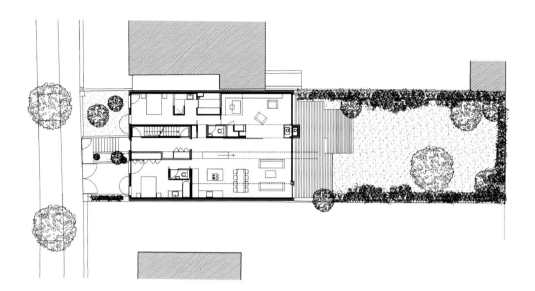

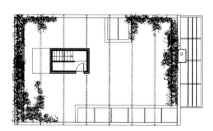

A floor plan and the image below show the rectilinear clarity of the design, which is filled with natural light—and here, very few visible sources of artificial light.

Etagengrundrisse und die Aufnahme unten belegen die geradlinige Klarheit des Entwurfs, der von Tageslicht durchflutet wird – tatsächlich sind hier nur wenige künstliche Lichtquellen erkennbar.

Le plan de niveau et la photo ci-dessous mettent en évidence la clarté rectiligne du design, baigné de lumière naturelle – avec ici de rares sources de lumière artificielle visibles.

Bright interiors are assured by the floor and ceiling color scheme but also by large sliding windows that open into the garden, and a terrace (right).

Die hellen Innenräume profitieren von der Farbwahl bei Böden und Wänden ebenso wie von den großflächigen Schiebefenstern, die sich zu Garten und Terrasse (rechts im Bild) öffnen.

La gamme de couleurs choisie pour le sol et le plafond garantit une grande luminosité à l'intérieur, mais aussi les grandes fenêtres coulissantes qui ouvrent sur le jardin ou une terrasse (à droite).

ESTABLISHED & SONS

Established & Sons
5–7 Wenlock Road
London N1 7SL
UK

Tel: +44 20 76 08 09 90
Fax: +44 20 76 08 01 10
E-mail: info@establishedandsons.com
Web: www.establishedandsons.com

Established & Sons, created in 2005, is a London-based producer of modern and contemporary furniture which is part of the Caparo Industries Group, a manufacturer and supplier of steel and engineering products for the automotive industry. The Chairman of the firm is **ANGAD PAUL**, the Chief Executive of Caparo Group. The cofounder and former CEO of Established & Sons was Alasdhair Willis, the former Publishing Director of the Wallpaper* Group, before he left in 2008. The present CEO is **MAURIZIO MUSSATI**, the former Managing Director of Lighting at Moooi, who joined the firm in 2008. Sebastian Wrong, cofounder and Design Director, was born in 1971 and studied sculpture at Norwich School of Art, before forming his own manufacturing company. Wrong left the firm in 2012. They have worked with such design stars as Zaha Hadid, Konstantin Grcic, the architects Caruso St. John, Jasper Morrison, and Amanda Levete—one of the founding partners of Future Systems, and presented their work at the international furniture fair in Milan, "Established & Sons / Milan 2009," La Pelota (Milan, Italy, 2009, published here).

Established & Sons, gegründet 2005, ist Hersteller moderner und zeitgenössischer Möbel mit Sitz in London. Das Unternehmen ist Teil der Caparo Industries Group, die Stahl- und Maschinenerzeugnisse für die Automobilindustrie produziert. Der Vorsitz der Firma liegt bei **ANGAD PAUL**, Geschäftsführer der Caparo Group. Mitbegründer und ehemaliger Geschäftsführer von Established & Sons war Alasdhair Willis, zuvor Verlagsleiter der Wallpaper* Group. 2008 verließ er das Unternehmen. Geschäftsführer ist seitdem **MAURIZIO MUSSATI**, ehemals Geschäftsführer für den Bereich Leuchten bei Moooi. Sebastian Wrong, ebenfalls Mitbegründer und Design Director, geboren 1971, studierte Skulptur an der Norwich School of Art, ehe er seine eigene Produktionsfirma gründete. Er verließ das Unternehmen 2012. Die Firma kooperierte mit Stardesignern wie Zaha Hadid, Konstantin Grcic, den Architekten Caruso St. John, Jasper Morrison und Amanda Levete, Mitbegründerin von Future Systems, und präsentierte ihr Programm auf der internationalen Möbelmesse in Mailand: „Established & Sons / Milan 2009", La Pelota (Mailand, 2009, hier vorgestellt).

Established & Sons, créé en 2005, est une entreprise londonienne de production et d'édition de mobilier moderne et contemporain qui fait partie du Caparo Industries Group, fabricant et fournisseur de produits en acier et de solutions d'ingénierie pour l'industrie automobile, présidé par **ANGAD PAUL**. Le cofondateur et ancien président-directeur général d'Established & Sons était Alasdhair Willis, ancien directeur de la publication du Wallpaper* Group, avant de le quitter en 2008. L'actuel président-directeur général est **MAURIZIO MUSSATI**, ex-directeur de département « éclairage » de Moooi, qui a rejoint l'entreprise en 2008. Sebastian Wrong, cofondateur et directeur du design, est né en 1971, a étudié la sculpture à l'École d'art de Norwich, avant de créer sa propre société de production. Il a quitté l'entreprise en 2012. Ils ont collaboré avec des stars du design ou de l'architecture comme Zaha Hadid, Konstantin Grcic, Caruso St. John, Jasper Morrison et Amanda Levete, l'une des cofondatrices de Future Systems, et ont présenté leur production au Salon international du meuble de Milan : *Established & Sons / Milan 2009*, La Pelota (Milan, 2009, publié ici).

"ESTABLISHED & SONS / MILAN 2009"

La Pelota, Milan, Italy, 2009

Area: 1750 m². Client: Established & Sons
Cost: not disclosed

The designers created roughly formed enclosures with untreated wood, contrasting markedly with the sophisticated nature of their products.

Die Designer gestalteten grob gezimmerte „Räume" aus unbehandeltem Holz: ein bewusster Kontrast zu den hochwertigen Produkten der Firma.

Les designers ont créé de petits enclos en bois non traité qui contrastent fortement avec la sophistication stylistique de leurs produits.

Another overview of the exhibition space in Milan in 2009, and, below, a detailed plan of the rectangular layout of the area.

Eine weitere Gesamtansicht des Mailänder Messestands 2009. Unten ein detaillierter Grundriss der rechteckigen Ausstellungsfläche.

Autre vue de l'exposition tenue à Milan en 2009 et, ci-dessous, plan détaillé de l'aménagement de l'espace.

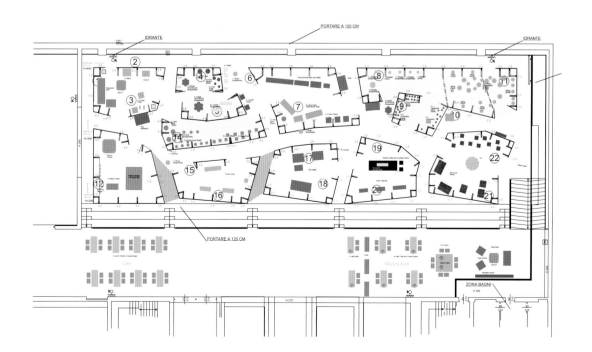

This temporary exhibition was open between April 22 and 26, 2009, during the Milan Salone Internazionale del Mobile. It was held in La Pelota, a former sports arena. Established & Sons launched a total of 16 new designs in Milan in 2009 and began work with Jason Bruges Studio, Mattali Crasset, Front Design, and Ronan and Erwan Bouroullec. The installation spanned the entire floor space of La Pelota with roughly stacked walls ranging from two to four meters in height, making use of 30 tons of untreated American tulipwood. "This year's installation is an intimate, entrenched settlement, an exposed timber flow, raw and basic, formal and frugal and ultimately recycled into product," stated Sebastian Wrong. Thirteen low-lit zones with "trenchlike corridors" were used to "create a sense of density and intensity of space."

Die temporäre Installation war vom 22. bis 26. April 2009 während der Internationalen Mailänder Möbelmesse in La Pelota zu sehen, einem ehemaligen Sportstadion. Established & Sons präsentierte 2009 insgesamt 16 neue Entwürfe in Mailand und kooperierte erstmals mit Jason Bruges Studio, Mattali Crasset, Front Design und Ronan und Erwan Bouroullec. Die Installation belegte mit ihren roh zusammengezimmerten Wänden, die zwischen 2 und 4 m hoch waren und für die 30 t unbehandeltes amerikanisches Tulpenbaumholz verarbeitet wurden, die gesamte Nutzfläche von La Pelota. „Die diesjährige Installation ist eine intime, schützengrabenähnliche Siedlung, ein Fließen aus unverkleidetem Bauholz, rau und simpel, formell und frugal und letztendlich recycelt zu einem Produkt", erklärte Sebastian Wrong. 13 verhalten beleuchtete Zonen mit „schützengrabenähnlichen Korridoren" trugen dazu bei, dass „der Raum dichter und intensiver erlebt" wurde.

Cette exposition temporaire s'est tenue du 22 au 26 avril 2009 pendant le Salon international du meuble de Milan à La Pelota, une ancienne salle de sport. Established & Sons lançait à cette occasion 16 nouveaux produits et commençait à travailler avec le Jason Bruges Studio, Mattali Crasset, Front Design et les frères Ronan et Erwan Bouroullec. L'installation composée de cloisonnements de 2 à 4 m de haut faits d'empilements de pièces de bois (soit 30 tonnes de bois de tulipier américain brut) occupait la totalité du sol de la salle. « L'installation de cette année est un enracinement intime, un flux de bois, brut et basique, elle est formelle et modeste et finira recyclée dans les produits », précisait Sebastian Wrong. Treize zones faiblement éclairées, parcourues de « corridors-tranchées », créaient un « sentiment de densité et d'intensité de l'espace ».

Despite its apparently arbitrary nature, the stacking of the wood reveals
a good deal of sophistication in these
images, again, contrasting with the
objects and furniture presented by
Established & Sons.

*Die vermeintlich willkürlich überein-
ander geschichteten Holzlatten sind,
wie diese Bilder zeigen, tatsächlich
eine ausgeklügelte Konstruktion und
kontrastieren mit den Objekten und
Möbelentwürfen von Established &
Sons.*

*Malgré une implantation apparem-
ment arbitraire, les cloisonnements
de bois font preuve ici d'une certaine
sophistication qui contraste avec les
objets et meubles d'Established &
Sons.*

ESTUDIO NÓMADA

Estudio Nómada
Rua das Hedras 6, Nivel I, Loft E
15895 Santiago de Compostela
Spain

Tel: +34 981 59 59 59
Fax: +34 981 59 59 69
E-mail: nomada@estudionomada.es
Web: www.estudionomada.es

JOSÉ ANTONIO VÁZQUEZ MARTÍN was born in 1972 in Orense, Spain. He received his architecture degree at the ETSA of A Coruña (1997). He worked after that for the apparel company STL for four years, before creating Estudio Nómada with **ENRIQUE DE SANTIAGO**, who was born in San Juan, Puerto Rico, in 1973. De Santiago obtained a BBA degree at Iowa State University in 1996 and an additional degree in Apparel Merchandising, Design, and Production. He then worked as a fashion buyer, before the creation of Nómada. Their work includes the Dominio do Bibei Winery cellar (Manzaneda, Orense, 2006); a house in the Monteprincipe private compound (Boadilla del Monte, Madrid, 2007); Sterling Store (Orense, 2008); the Canteen at the City of Culture of Galicia (Santiago de Compostela, 2010, published here); a house in the Pazo Ramirás private compound (Orense, 2011); and the Fernández-Braso Art Gallery (Madrid, 2011), all in Spain.

JOSÉ ANTONIO VÁZQUEZ MARTÍN wurde 1972 in Orense, Spanien, geboren. Sein Architekturstudium schloss er an der ETSA in A Coruña ab (1997). Im Anschluss daran arbeitete er zunächst vier Jahre für die Bekleidungsfirma STL, ehe er mit **ENRIQUE DE SANTIAGO** das gemeinsame Büro Estudio Nómada gründete. De Santiago, geboren 1973 in San Juan, Puerto Rico, schloss sein Studium mit einem BBA an der Iowa State University (1996) sowie einem weiteren Abschluss in Textilmarketing, -gestaltung und -fertigung ab. Vor der Gründung von Nómada arbeitete er als Einkäufer in der Modebranche. Zu ihren Projekten zählen die Weinkellerei Dominio do Bibei (Manzaneda, Orense, 2006), ein Haus in der privaten Wohnanlage Monteprincipe (Boadilla del Monte, Madrid, 2007), der Sterling Store (Orense, 2008), die Kantine für die Cidade da Cultura de Galicia (Santiago de Compostela, 2010, hier vorgestellt), ein Haus in der privaten Wohnanlage Pazo Ramirás (Orense, 2011) sowie die Galerie Fernández-Braso (Madrid, 2011), alle in Spanien.

JOSÉ ANTONIO VÁZQUEZ MARTÍN est né en 1972 à Orense, Espagne. Il a obtenu son diplôme d'architecture à l'ETSA de La Corogne (1997) et a ensuite travaillé quatre ans dans la société d'habillement STL avant de créer Estudio Nómada avec **ENRIQUE DE SANTIAGO**. Né à San Juan, Porto Rico, en 1973 et titulaire d'un BBA de l'université de l'Iowa en 1996 et d'un diplôme complémentaire en commerce de l'habillement, design et production, ce dernier a travaillé auparavant comme acheteur dans le domaine de la mode. Leurs réalisations comprennent : la cave du domaine Dominio do Bibei (Manzaneda, Orense, 2006) ; une maison dans le complexe privé de Monteprincipe (Boadilla del Monte, Madrid, 2007) ; le magasin Sterling (Orense, 2008) ; la cantine de la Cité de la culture de Galice (Saint-Jacques-de-Compostelle, 2010, publiée ici) ; une maison dans le complexe privé Pazo Ramirás (Orense, 2011) et la galerie d'art Fernández-Braso (Madrid, 2011), toutes en Espagne.

CANTEEN AT THE CITY OF CULTURE OF GALICIA

Santiago de Compostela, Spain, 2010

Address: Rua de San Roque 2, 15704 Santiago de Compostela,
Galicia, Spain, +34 881 99 75 65, www.cidadedacultura.org. Area: 277 m²
Client: Fundacion Cidade da Cultura de Galicia. Cost: not disclosed

This project is situated in two structures next to the Archive of Galicia, part of Peter Eisenman's Galician City of Culture. The architects broke through preexisting walls to link the two spaces of café and shop with one long shared bar, recalling the typology of Galician village canteens. The architects explain: "To begin, we refer to the canteen as a model of traditional establishment in Galicia, a concept that permits reinterpretation through a modern filter. Abstracting this idea, the tables are arranged in parallel, elongated under schematic trees evoking popular festivities…" A "geometric and uninhibited" profusion of color is intended to bring to mind Galician folk art. Both this colorful décor and the trees referred to are abstract presences that fill and animate the space, while allowing the Canteen to remain light and airy.

Das Projekt liegt in zwei Bauten neben dem Galizischen Archiv, einem Teil der Cidade da Cultura de Galicia (Kulturstadt Galiziens) von Peter Eisenman. Mit Durchbrüchen im alten Mauerwerk und einem langen gemeinschaftlichen Tresen, der an die typischen Dorfkantinen Galiziens erinnert, verbanden die Architekten Café und Shop. Die Architekten erklären: „Ausgangspunkt ist die Bezugnahme auf die Kantine als traditionelle, typisch galizische Einrichtung, ein Konzept, das hier durch einen modernen Filter neu interpretiert wird. Abstrahiert wird diese Idee durch längs gestellte, parallele Tischreihen unter stilisierten ‚Bäumen', eine Anspielung auf Dorffeste …" Eine Fülle von Farben, „geometrisch und überbordend", ist Hommage an die galizische Volkskunst. Das farbenfrohe Dekor und die „Bäume" bleiben abstrakt und prägen und beleben den Raum, sodass die Kantine hell und offen bleibt.

Le projet occupe deux bâtiments à proximité des Archives de Galice, dans la Cité de la culture construite par Peter Eisenman. Les architectes ont percé les murs existants pour relier les deux espaces café et boutique par un long bar commun rappelant les cantines des villages galiciens. Ils expliquent : « Pour commencer, nous pensons la cantine comme un modèle d'établissement traditionnel en Galice, ce qui permet sa réinterprétation à travers un filtre moderne. Pour résumer cette idée, les tables sont disposées en lignes parallèles sous des arbres schématisés qui évoquent les fêtes populaires… » Une profusion « géométrique et sans retenue » de couleurs évoque l'art folklorique galicien. Le décor coloré et les références aux arbres constituent des présences abstraites qui emplissent et animent l'espace tout en gardant sa luminosité aérienne à la cantine.

Treelike wooden frames rise above
the tables. Left, in the second room,
tall shelves rise up to the ceiling.

Des arbres schématisés en bois se
dressent au-dessus des tables. À
gauche, dans la seconde pièce, des
étagères montent jusqu'au plafond.

Ein zu Bäumen stilisiertes Holzgerüst
ragt über den Tischen auf. Im zweiten
Raum reichen Regale bis zur Decke
(links).

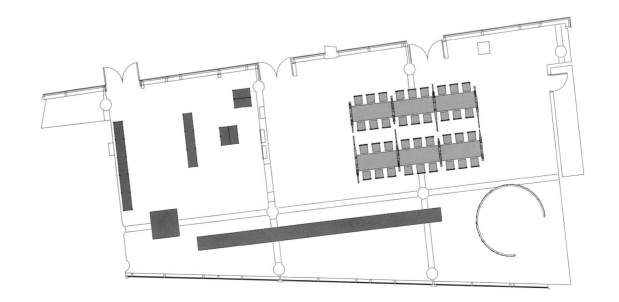

The "colorful décor" referred to by the architects is seen to the right in this otherwise white and tan environment.

Das von den Architekten zitierte farbenfrohe Dekor (rechts) in der ansonsten in Weiß und Naturtönen gehaltenen Umgebung

On aperçoit à droite le « décor coloré » évoqué par les architectes dans l'ensemble sinon blanc et brun clair.

TERUNOBU FUJIMORI

Terunobu Fujimori, Kogakuin University, 1–24–2 Nishi-Shinjuku
Shinjuku-ku, Tokyo 163–8677, Japan
Tel/Fax: +81 3 3340 3574 / E-mail: dt13300@ns.kogakuin.ac.jp

Born in Chino City, Nagano, Japan, in 1946, **TERUNOBU FUJIMORI** attended Tohoku University (1965–71) in Sendai, before receiving his Ph.D. in Architecture from the University of Tokyo (1971–78). He is a Professor Emeritus at the University of Tokyo's Institute of Industrial Science. Although research on Western-style buildings in Japan from the Meiji period onwards remains his main activity, he is also a practicing architect. "I didn't start designing buildings until my 40s, so the condition I set for myself is that I shouldn't just repeat the same things that my colleagues or professors were doing," he has stated. His first built work was the Jinchokan Moriya Historical Museum (Chino City, Nagano, 1990–91), which won mixed praise for the use of local materials over a reinforced-concrete structure. Other completed projects include the Akino Fuku Art Museum (Hamamatsu, Shizuoka, 1995–97); Nira House (Leek House, Machida City, Tokyo, 1995–97); Student Dormitory for Kumamoto Agricultural College (Koshi City, Kumamoto, 1998–2000); Ichiya-tei (One Night Tea House, Ashigarashimo, Kanagawa, 2003); the Takasugi-an (Too-High Tea House, Chino City, Nagano, 2004), set six meters above the ground like a tree house; Chashitsu Tetsu (Tea House Tetsu, Kiyoharu Shirakaba Museum, Nakamaru, Hokuto City, Yamanashi, 2005, published here); and Charred Cedar House (Nagano City, Nagano, 2006–07). He participated in the Sumika Project (Coal House, Utsunomiya, Tochigi, 2008) with Toyo Ito and other well-known architects; and completed Roof House (Omihachiman, Shiga, 2008–09); and Copper House (Kokubunji City, Tokyo, 2009). Recent work includes the "Beetle's House" (Victoria & Albert Museum, London, UK, 2010); the Walking Café (Munich, Germany, 2012); Hamamatsu House (Shizuoka, 2012); and the Stork House (Vienna, Austria, 2013), all in Japan unless stated otherwise.

TERUNOBU FUJIMORI wurde 1946 in Chino in der Präfektur Nagano, Japan, geboren und studierte an der Tohoku Universität in Sendai (1965–71), bevor er an der Universität Tokio in Architektur promovierte (1971–78). Er ist emeritierter Professor des Instituts für Industriewissenschaften an der Universität Tokio. Obwohl er sich hauptsächlich der Erforschung lang vergessener westlicher Bauten in Japan seit der Meiji-Zeit widmet, praktiziert er auch als Architekt. „Mit dem Entwerfen von Bauten habe ich erst angefangen, als ich über 40 war, und so nahm ich mir vor, nicht einfach das zu wiederholen, was meine Kollegen oder Professoren taten", erklärt Fujimori. Sein erster realisierter Bau war das Historische Museum Jinchokan Moriya (Chino, Nagano, 1990–91), das wegen der Verwendung regionaler Materialien über einer Stahlbetonkonstruktion gemischte Reaktionen hervorrief. Weitere gebaute Projekte sind u. a. das Kunstmuseum Akino Fuku (Hamamatsu, Shizuoka, 1995–97), das Nira-Haus (Lauchhaus, Machida, Tokio, 1995–97), ein Studentenwohnheim für die Landwirtschaftliche Hochschule Kumamoto (Koshi, Kumamoto, 1998–2000), das Ichiya-tei (Teehaus für eine Nacht, Ashigarashimo, Kanagawa, 2003), das Chashitsu Tetsu (Teehaus Tetsu, Museum Kiyoharu Shirakaba, Nakamaru, Hokuto, Yamanashi, 2005; hier vorgestellt) sowie das Haus aus verkohltem Zedernholz (Nagano, Nagano, 2006–07). Er nahm mit Toyo Ito und anderen bekannten Architekten am Sumika-Projekt teil (Kohlehaus, Utsunomiya, Tochigi, 2008) und stellte das Dachhaus (Omihachiman, Shiga, 2008–09) und das Kupferhaus fertig (Kokubunji City, Tokio, 2009). Zu seinen neueren Arbeiten zählen das „Beetle's House" (Victoria & Albert Museum, London, 2010), das Walking Café (München, 2012), das Hamamatsu Haus (Shizuoka, 2012) und das Stork-Haus (Wien, 2013).

Né à Chino, Nagano (Japon) en 1946, **TERUNOBU FUJIMORI** a suivi les cours de l'université Tohoku (1965–71) à Sendai avant d'obtenir son doctorat en architecture à l'université de Tokyo (1971–78). Il est aujourd'hui professeur émérite à l'Institut de science industrielle de l'université de Tokyo. Il continue de pratiquer l'architecture, même si la recherche sur les bâtiments de style occidental au Japon à partir de la période Meiji reste son activité principale. « Je n'ai commencé à créer des bâtiments que vers quarante ans, je me suis donc fixé comme condition de ne pas reproduire ce que faisaient mes collègues ou professeurs », déclare-t-il. Son premier projet construit a été le Musée historique Jinchokan Moriya (Chino, Nagano, 1990–91) qui a reçu un accueil mitigé en raison du choix de matériaux locaux sur une structure en béton armé. Ses autres réalisations achevées comprennent le Musée d'art Akino Fuku (Hamamatsu, Shizuoka, 1995–97) ; la maison Nira (Leek House, Machida, Tokyo, 1995–97) ; le dortoir des étudiants du collège agricole de Kumamoto (Koshi, Kumamoto, 1998–2000) ; Ichiya-tei (Maison de thé d'une nuit, Ashigarashimo, Kanagawa, 2003) ; Takasugi-an (Maison de thé trop haute, Chino, 2004), placée à 6 m au-dessus du sol comme une maison dans les arbres ; Chashitsu Tetsu (maison de thé Tetsu, musée Kiyoharu Shirakaba, Nakamaru, Hokuto, Yamanashi, 2005, publiée ici) et la Maison de cèdre brûlé (Nagano, Nagano, 2006–07). Il a également participé au projet Sumika (Maison charbon, Utsunomiya, Tochigi, 2008) avec Toyo Ito et d'autres architectes de renom et a construit la Maison toit (Omihachiman, Shiga, 2008–09) et la Maison de cuivre (Kokubunji, Tokyo, 2009). Parmi ses projets récents : Beetle's House (Victoria & Albert Museum, Londres, 2010) ; le Walking Café (Munich, 2012) ; la maison Hamamatsu (Shizuoka, 2012) et la Maison de la cigogne (Vienne, Autriche, 2013), toutes au Japon, sauf mention contraire.

CHASHITSU TETSU
(TEAHOUSE TETSU)

Kiyoharu Shirakaba Museum, Nakamaru, Hokuto City, Yamanashi, Japan, 2005

Address: 2072 Nagasakacho Nakamaru, Hokuto-shi, Yamanashi 408–0036, Japan,
+81 551 32 4865, www.kiyoharu-art.com/museum Floor area: 6.07 m². Client: Kiyoharu Shirakaba Museum
Cost: not disclosed. Collaboration: Nobumichi Ohshima (Ohshima Atelier)

"The site is famous for cherry blossoms…When I go to see the cherry blossoms at night, it is as if I strayed into a dream world," says Terunobu Fujimori, "I did not intend it this way, but it looks as if it were a house for a gnome from a fairy tale." Approached by the owner of the Yoshii Gallery, Chozo Yoshii, to build a teahouse on the grounds of the Kiyoharu Shirakaba Museum, Fujimori at first proposed a structure that would look down on the cherry trees. This idea was abandoned because of the number of older visitors to the museum, instead this curious wooden structure was set at a height of four meters next to a restaurant designed by Yoshio Taniguchi. Fujimori cut down a cypress on the site and used it as the single support for his unusual wood-frame teahouse. In order to give the design the necessary stability to withstand earthquakes or typhoons, the architect allowed the cypress trunk to extend up into the teahouse, "like a backbone," so that both the support and the house will sway together. Unlike traditional teahouses that are more inward looking, this one was designed to view cherry blossoms, and Fujimori refers to "the gold tearoom that Toyotomi Hideyoshi had Rikyu build for cherry-blossom viewing. [Toyotomi Hideyoshi (1536–98) was a feudal ruler who unified Japan. Rikyu, or Sen no Rikyu (1522–91), is the historical figure who had the most profound influence on the Japanese tea ceremony.] The tearoom was in a tree and had a crawl-in door with a frame embellished all around in gold leaf."

„Dieser Ort ist berühmt für seine Kirschblüte … Wenn ich mir nachts die Kirschblüte ansehe, habe ich das Gefühl, ich verirre mich in eine Traumwelt", sagt Terunobu Fujimori. „Nicht, dass ich es so geplant hätte, aber es sieht aus wie das Haus eines Zwerges aus einem Märchen." Auf Wunsch Chozo Yoshiis, des Besitzers der Galerie Yoshii, ein Teehaus auf dem Gelände des Kiyoharu Shirakaba Museum zu bauen, schlug Fujimori zunächst eine Konstruktion über den Kronen der Kirschbäume vor. Aus Rücksicht auf ältere Museumsbesucher wurde die Idee jedoch wieder aufgegeben und stattdessen diese Holzkonstruktion in 4 m Höhe errichtet, neben einem Restaurant, dessen Entwurf von Yoshio Taniguchi stammt. Dazu ließ Fujimori die Krone einer Zypresse kappen, deren Stamm die einzige Stütze für das Teehaus bildet. Damit die Konstruktion die bei Erdbeben oder Taifunen nötige Stabilität hat, reicht der Baumstamm „wie ein Rückgrat" in das Teehaus hinein, sodass Stütze und Baumhaus gemeinsam schwingen. Im Gegensatz zu traditionellen Teehäusern, die sich eher auf den Innenraum konzentrieren, sollte dieser Entwurf zur Betrachtung der Kirschblüte einladen. Fujimori verweist auf „das goldene Teezimmer, das Toyotomi Hideyoshi sich zum selben Zweck von Rikyu bauen ließ. [Toyotomi Hideyoshi (1536–98) war ein Feudalherr, unter dessen Hand Japan vereinigt wurde. Die historische Figur Rikyu oder Sen no Rikyu (1522–91) hatte maßgeblichen Einfluss auf die japanische Teezeremonie.] Dieses Teezimmer befand sich auf einem Baum und hatte eine kleine Tür, durch die man hineinkriechen musste und deren Rahmen rundherum mit Blattgold geschmückt war."

« Le site est célèbre pour ses cerisiers en fleurs… Lorsque je vais voir les cerisiers la nuit, c'est comme si je me perdais dans un rêve, raconte Terunobu Fujimori, je ne l'ai pas voulu ainsi, mais c'est presque une maison pour un lutin de conte de fée. » Approché par le propriétaire de la galerie Yoshii, Chozo Yoshii, pour construire une maison de thé dans l'enceinte du musée Kiyoharu Shirakaba, Fujimori proposa initialement une structure qui aurait dominé les cerisiers. Cette idée fut abandonnée du fait du grand nombre de visiteurs âgés du musée, mais la construction finale fut néanmoins implantée à une hauteur de 4 m, à proximité d'un restaurant conçu par Yoshio Taniguchi. Fujimori fit couper sur place un cyprès dont il se servit comme support central unique de cette très curieuse maison de thé en bois. Pour assurer la stabilité, la cohésion et la résistance aux tremblements de terre et aux ouragans, l'architecte a fait pénétrer le tronc de l'arbre dans la maison « telle une colonne vertébrale ». À la différence des maisons de thé traditionnelles qui sont davantage tournées sur elles-mêmes, celle-ci a été conçue pour observer les cerisiers en fleurs, et Fujimori se réfère au « salon de thé d'or que Toyotomi Hideyoshi avait fait construire par Rikyu également pour regarder les cerisiers. [Toyotomi Hideyoshi (1536–98) est un souverain féodal qui unifia le Japon. Rikyu ou Sen no Rikyu (1522–91) est la figure historique qui exerça la plus profonde influence sur la cérémonie du thé.] Il était installé dans un arbre et l'on s'y glissait par une porte basse dont le cadre était doré à la feuille d'or ».

Perched on a cypress trunk, four meters off the ground, the tiny structure functions according to the rules of the Japanese tea ceremony.

Das auf einen Zypressenstamm aufgesetzte Häuschen ist so angelegt, dass man in ihm eine japanische Teezeremonie abhalten kann.

Perchée sur un tronc de cyprès, à 4 m du sol, la petite structure fonctionne selon les règles de la cérémonie japonaise du thé.

SOU FUJIMOTO

Sou Fujimoto Architects
6F Ichikawa Seihon Building
10–3 Higashienoki-cho, Shinjuku
Tokyo 162–0807
Japan

Tel: +81 3 3513 5401
Fax: +81 3 3513 5402
E-mail: media@sou-fujimoto.net
Web: www.sou-fujimoto.net

SOU FUJIMOTO was born in 1971. He received a B.Arch degree from the University of Tokyo, Faculty of Engineering, Department of Architecture (1990–94). He established his own firm, Sou Fujimoto Architects, in 2000. He is considered one of the most interesting rising Japanese architects, and his forms usually evade easy classification. His work includes the Industrial Training Facilities for the Mentally Handicapped (Hokkaido, 2003); Environment Art Forum, Annaka (Gunma, 2003–06); Treatment Center for Mentally Disturbed Children (Hokkaido, 2006); House O (Chiba, 2007); N House (Oita Prefecture, 2007–08); and the Final Wooden House (Kumamura, Kumamoto, 2007–08, published here). Other recent work includes his participation in Toyo Ito's Sumika Project (House Before House, Utsunomiya, Tochigi, 2008); Musashino Art University Museum and Library (Tokyo, 2007–09); House H (Tokyo, 2008–09); Tokyo Apartment (Itabashiku, Tokyo, 2009–10); the Uniqlo Store in Shinsaibashi (Osaka, 2010); House NA (Tokyo, 2010); House K (Nishinomiya-shi, Hyogo, 2011–12); and the 2013 Serpentine Summer Pavilion (Kensington Gardens, London, UK, 2013), all in Japan unless stated otherwise.

SOU FUJIMOTO wurde 1971 geboren. Sein Architekturstudium an der Fakultät für Bauingenieurwesen der Universität Tokio schloss er mit einem B. Arch. ab (1990–94). Sein eigenes Büro, Sou Fujimoto Architects, gründete er 2000. Er gilt als einer der interessantesten jungen Architekten Japans, seine Formensprache entzieht sich einfachen Zuordnungen. Zu seinen Projekten zählen Ausbildungsstätten für geistig Behinderte (Hokkaido, 2003), das Environment Art Forum, Annaka (Gunma, 2003 bis 2006), ein Behandlungszentrum für psychisch erkrankte Kinder (Hokkaido, 2006), Haus O (Chiba, 2007), Haus N (Präfektur Oita, 2007–08) und das Final Wooden House in Kumamoto (2007–08, hier vorgestellt). Weitere jüngere Arbeiten sind u. a. seine Beteiligung an Toyo Itos Sumika-Projekt (House Before House, Utsunomiya, Tochigi, 2008), Museum und Bibliothek der Kunsthochschule Musashino (Tokio, 2007–09), das Haus H (Tokio, 2008–09), ein Apartment in Tokio (Itabashiku, 2009–10), der Uniqlo Store in Shinsaibashi (Osaka, 2010), das Haus NA (Tokio, 2010), das Haus K (Nishinomiya-shi, Hyogo, 2011–12) und der Serpentine-Sommer-Pavillon von 2013 (Kensington Gardens, London).

Né en 1971, **SUO FUJIMOTO** a obtenu son diplôme de B.Arch. à l'université de Tokyo (faculté d'ingénierie, département d'Architecture, 1990–94). Il crée sa propre agence, Sou Fujimoto Architects, en 2000. Considéré comme l'un des plus intéressants jeunes architectes japonais du moment, son vocabulaire formel échappe à toute classification aisée. Parmi ses réalisations : des installations de formation pour handicapés mentaux (Hokkaido, 2003) ; l'Environment Art Forum d'Annaka (Gunma, 2003–06) ; un Centre de traitement pour enfants souffrant de troubles mentaux (Hokkaido, 2006) ; la maison O (Chiba, 2007) ; la maison N (préfecture d'Oita, 2007–08) ; la Maison de bois définitive (Kumamura, Kumamoto, 2007–08, publiée ici). Plus récemment, il a participé au projet Sumika de Toyo Ito (Maison d'avant la maison, Utsunomiya, Tochigi, 2008) ; le musée et la bibliothèque de l'Université d'art Musashino (Tokyo, 2007–09); la maison H (Tokyo, 2008–09) ; un appartement à Tokyo (Itabashiku, Tokyo, 2009–10) ; le magasin Uniqlo à Shinsaibashi (Osaka, 2010) ; la maison NA (Tokyo, 2010) ; la maison K (Nishinomiya-shi, Hyogo, 2011–12) et le Pavillon d'été de la Serpentine (Kensington Gardens, Londres, 2013), toutes au Japon, sauf mention contraire.

FINAL WOODEN HOUSE

Kumamura, Kumamoto, Japan, 2007–08

*Address: not disclosed. Area: 22 m². Client: Kumamura Forestry Association
Cost: ¥4.246 million. Collaboration: Hiroshi Kato*

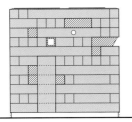 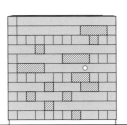 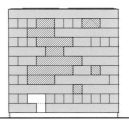 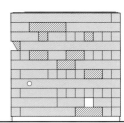

Elevation drawings show how the façades echo the cutout forms of the interior volumes, where openings provide views of the outside where "normal" structures surely would not.

Die Aufrisse zeigen, wie die Fassaden mit den Aussparungen des Innenraums korrespondieren. Die Öffnungen bieten Ausblicke in den Außenraum, wie es „normale" Bauten sicher nicht tun würden.

Les élévations montrent comment la façade est déterminée par la découpe des volumes intérieurs. Les ouvertures offrent des vues sur l'extérieur à des endroits que des constructions « normales » ne permettraient pas.

The Final Wooden House has a sharply delineated cubic form, but the openings in its wooden façades are clearly irregular.

Grundform des Final Wooden House ist ein scharf umrissener Kubus, während die Öffnungen in der Fassade aus Holz deutlich unregelmäßig ausfallen.

La Maison de bois définitive est de forme cubique, mais ses ouvertures forment une composition de nature irrégulière.

As usual, it is the architect himself who most clearly expresses the nature of the project. He engaged in a "mindless" stacking of 35-centimeter square pieces of lumber on a tiny 15-square-meter site. "I envisioned the creation of new spatiality that preserves primitive conditions of a harmonious entity before various functions and roles differentiated," he says. There are no separations, no floors, no real walls or ceilings in this house, allowing visitors to "distribute themselves three-dimensionally in space." Floors become walls or chairs, as he says, causing visitors to rethink the entire idea of a building. "Rather than just a new architecture," Fujimoto concludes, "this is a new origin, a new existence."

Wie üblich ist es der Architekt selbst, der das Wesen seines Projekts am klarsten vermittelt. In diesem Fall entschied er sich, Bauholz mit einem quadratischen Querschnitt von 35 x 35 cm auf einem winzigen, 15 m² großen Grundstück „ohne Sinn und Verstand" übereinanderzuschichten. „Ich hatte die Vision von einem neuartigen Raumerlebnis, das die Urbeschaffenheit einer harmonischen Ganzheit ahnen lässt – bevor man begann, verschiedene Funktionen und Typen zu unterscheiden." Es gibt keine räumliche Gliederung, keine Geschosse, keine echten Wände oder Decken in diesem Haus, was Besuchern erlaubt, „sich dreidimensional im Raum zu verteilen". Böden werden zu Wänden oder Stühlen und regen die Besucher laut Fujimoto an, die Idee, was ein Haus sei, neu zu überdenken. „Es ist mehr als bloß ein neues Stück Architektur," fasst Fujimoto zusammen, „es ist ein neuer Anfang, eine neue Daseinsweise."

Comme souvent, c'est l'architecte lui-même qui exprime le mieux la nature de son projet. Il a entrepris d'empiler « de façon gratuite » des grumes de bois de section carrée de 35 cm de côté sur un petit espace de 15 m². « J'ai envisagé de créer une nouvelle spatialité qui préserve les conditions primitives d'une entité harmonieuse avant que n'interviennent certaines fonctions et rôles différenciés », explique-t-il. Il n'y a ni séparations, ni sols, ni vrais murs, ni plafonds dans cette maison pour permettre aux visiteurs de « se distribuer eux-mêmes en trois dimensions dans cet espace ». Comme il l'explique, les sols deviennent des murs ou des sièges entraînant chacun à repenser l'idée même de maison. « Plutôt que d'être simplement une nouvelle architecture, conclut Fujimoto, c'est une nouvelle origine, une nouvelle existence. »

The unusual stacking method employed by the architect generates spaces that, in a sense, challenge residents (or rather users) to find a place to sit or to make the architecture theirs.

Die ungewöhnliche Stapelmethode, mit der der Architekt hier arbeitet, lässt einen Raum entstehen, der seine Bewohner (oder vielmehr Besucher) herausfordert, einen Sitzplatz zu finden und sich die Architektur zu eigen zu machen.

Le principe d'empilement pratiqué par l'architecte génère des volumes qui incitent les résidants (ou plutôt les usagers) à trouver d'eux-mêmes leur place et à s'approprier l'espace architectural.

GENERAL DESIGN

General Design Co., Ltd.
3–13–3 Jingumae
Shibuya, Tokyo 150–0001
Japan

Tel: +81 3 5775 1298
Fax: +81 3 5775 1299
E-mail: email@general-design.net
Web: www.general-design.net

SHIN OHORI was born in Gifu, Japan, in 1967 and graduated from Musashino Art University (Tokyo) in 1990. He completed his M.Arch at the same institution in 1992. He cofounded Intentionallies in Tokyo in 1995 and General Design in 1999. His work includes a photographer's weekend house (Kujyukuri, Chiba, 2007); Mountain Research (Minamisaku, Nagano, 2007–08, published here); a house in Sakurajyosui (Suginami, Tokyo, 2008); Zucca Aoyama (Minato, Tokyo, 2008); Zucca Paris (Rue Cambon, Paris, France, 2008); Edition Marunouchi (Chiyoda, Tokyo, 2008); T2 Project (Shibuya, Tokyo, 2009); and a house in Sendagaya (Shibuya, Tokyo, 2009), all in Japan unless stated otherwise.

SHIN OHORI wurde 1967 in Gifu, Japan, geboren und studierte bis 1990 an der Musashino Art University (Tokio). 1992 machte er an der gleichen Hochschule den Master in Architektur. Er war 1995 Mitbegründer des Büros Intentionallies in Tokio und 1999 von General Design. Zu seinen Bauten zählen ein Wochenendhaus für einen Fotografen (Kujyukuri, Chiba, 2007), Mountain Research (Minamisaku, Nagano, 2007–08, hier veröffentlicht), ein Wohnhaus in Sakurajyosui (Suginami, Tokio, 2008), Zucca Aoyama (Minato, Tokio, 2008), Zucca Paris (Rue Cambon, Paris, 2008), Edition Marunouchi (Chiyoda, Tokio, 2008), das Projekt T2 (Shibuya, Tokio, 2009) sowie ein Wohnhaus in Sendagaya (Shibuya, Tokio, 2009), alle in Japan, sofern nicht anders angegeben.

SHIN OHORI, né à Gifu (Japon) en 1967, est diplômé de l'Université artistique Musashino (Tokyo, 1990) et a obtenu son M.Arch. de la même institution (1992). Il est l'un des fondateurs de l'agence Intentionallies à Tokyo (1995) et de General Design en 1999. Parmi ses réalisations : une maison de week-end pour un photographe (Kujyukuri, Chiba, 2007) ; une petite structure appelée Mountain Research (Minamisaku, Nagano, 2007–08, publiée ici) ; une maison à Sakurajyosui (Suginami, Tokyo, 2008) ; Zucca Aoyama (Minato, Tokyo, 2008) ; le magasin Zucca Paris (rue Cambon, Paris, 2008) ; Edition Marunouchi (Chiyoda, Tokyo, 2008) ; le T2 Project (Shibuya, Tokyo, 2009) et une maison à Sendagaya (Shibuya, Tokyo, 2009), toutes au Japon, sauf mention contraire.

MOUNTAIN RESEARCH

Minamisaku, Nagano, Japan, 2007–08

Address: not disclosed
Area: 97 m². Client: not disclosed. Cost: not disclosed

A drawing and a photo of the structure on this page show how tents are
supported on the exposed platforms.

Die Zeichnung und das Foto des
Gebäudes auf dieser Seite zeigen,
wie die Zelte auf den offenen Platt-
formen stehen.

Le dessin et la photo de cette page
montrent comment les tentes sont
dressées sur des plates-formes.

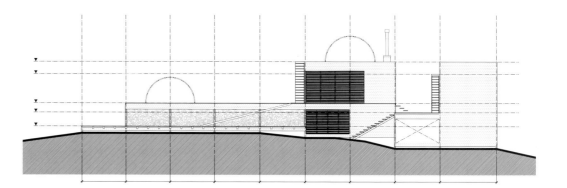

The densely wooded site is visible in the drawing to the right and in the photos published here. The yellow tents sit on top of the wooden structure.

Das dicht bewaldete Grundstück ist auf der Zeichnung rechts und den Fotos zu erkennen. Die gelben Zelte stehen auf der hölzernen Konstruktion.

Le terrain très boisé est visible sur le dessin à droite et sur les photographies. Les tentes jaunes sont posées sur la couverture de la construction en bois.

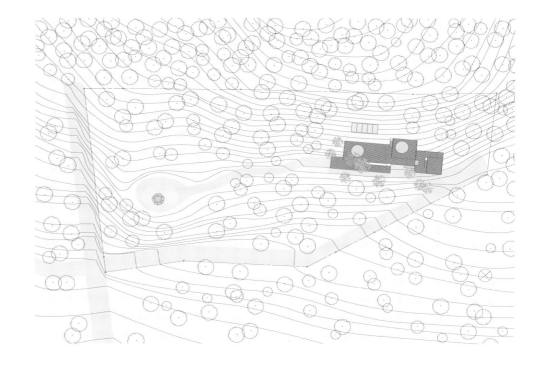

Shin Ohori explains that the client just wanted a place in the woods to set up a tent. The site concerned is a 5300-square-meter area in the mountains of Nagano Prefecture. The architect provided a rough larch deck, kitchen, storage space, bathroom, toilet, shelves for firewood, and a solar panel system, and the client was able to put up his two-meter dome tent. The deck serves as a "living room" while the clients sleep in the tent. "I did not intend to design a regular weekend house," says the architect, "and I didn't want comfortable and protected rooms with beautiful views. I was determined to support his clear and powerful vision of nature, so I eliminated anything that would interfere with his thoughts." It seems in this instance that the desires of the architect met closely with those of his client. "I don't want architecture to be a convenient 'tool' that guarantees safe and ordinary lives," says Shin Ohori. "I hope that architecture will be a place where people discover something new, and make innovations in their lifestyles."

Shin Ohori erklärt, dass der Bauherr nur einen Ort im Wald suchte, um ein Zelt aufzustellen. Das entsprechende Gelände in den Bergen der Präfektur Nagano ist 5300 m² groß. Der Architekt lieferte ein grobes Deck aus Lärchenholz, eine Küche, Abstellraum, Bad, Toilette, Regale für Feuerholz sowie ein System von Solarzellenpaneelen, sodass der Kunde sein 2 m hohes Kuppelzelt aufstellen konnte. Das Deck dient als „Wohnraum", während die Auftraggeber im Zelt schlafen. „Ich hatte nicht die Absicht, ein richtiges Wochenendhaus zu planen", sagt der Architekt, „und auch keine bequemen und geschützten Räume mit schöner Aussicht. Ich war entschlossen, seine klare und kraftvolle Sicht der Natur zu unterstützen, daher ließ ich alles weg, was seiner Auffassung im Weg gestanden hätte." In diesem Fall scheinen die Absichten des Architekten mit denen des Bauherrn übereingestimmt zu haben. „Ich will nicht, dass Architektur ein bequemes ‚Instrument' ist, das ein sicheres und normales Leben garantiert", sagt Shin Ohori. „Ich hoffe, dass die Architektur einen Ort erzeugt, wo Menschen etwas Neues entdecken und ihre Lebensweise erneuern können."

Shin Ohori explique que son client voulait juste pouvoir disposer d'un endroit dans les bois pour planter sa tente. Le terrain de 5300 m² est situé dans les montagnes de la préfecture de Nagano. L'architecte a créé une vaste terrasse de mélèze, une cuisine, un espace de rangement, une salle de bains, des toilettes, des rayonnages pour le bois à brûler et un système de panneaux solaires. Le client a pu y installer ses tentes en forme de dôme de 2 m de diamètre qui font office de chambres. La terrasse sert de « séjour ». « Je ne souhaitais pas dessiner une maison de week-end classique, précise l'architecte, et je ne voulais pas de belles chambres bien protégées ouvrant sur des vues superbes. J'étais déterminé à donner une vision claire et puissante de la nature et j'ai éliminé tout ce qui pouvait s'y opposer. » Il semble qu'ici le désir de l'architecte ait été en phase profonde avec celui de son client. « Je ne veux pas d'une architecture qui devienne un outil pratique au service d'une vie sûre et ordinaire », explique Shin Ohori. « J'espère que cette architecture sera un lieu d'où l'on pourra découvrir quelque chose de nouveau et qui favorisera des changements de style de vie. »

A bathroom opens out onto the main platform area, while chairs are placed in front of a low table, opposite the view.

Das Badezimmer öffnet sich zur großen Plattform; gegenüber sind Stühle vor einem niedrigen Tisch zu sehen.

Une salle de bains grande ouverte sur la terrasse principale. En face, des chaises longues disposées autour d'une table basse.

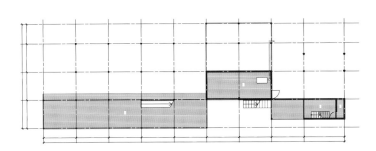

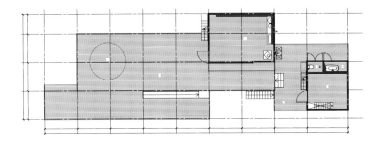

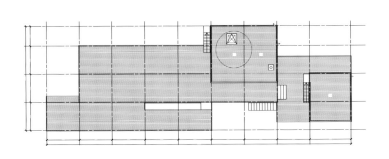

The fairly closed interior spaces are entirely made of wood and provide for some of the basic storage space, and some comforts that are not usually available in tents.

Die geschlosseneren Innenräume sind ganz aus Holz und bieten den notwendigen Stauraum oder sonstige Annehmlichkeiten, die Zelte normalerweise nicht aufweisen.

Les espaces intérieurs assez fermés sont entièrement en bois. Ils offrent divers rangements et un confort que l'on aurait du mal à trouver dans une tente.

SEAN GODSELL

Sean Godsell Architects
2/49 Exhibition Street
Melbourne
Victoria 3000
Australia

Tel: +61 3 9654 2677
Fax: +61 3 9654 3877
E-mail: info@seangodsell.com
Web: www.seangodsell.com

SEAN GODSELL was born in Melbourne, Australia, in 1960. He graduated from the University of Melbourne in 1984 and worked from 1986 to 1988 in London with Sir Denys Lasdun. He created Godsell Associates Pty Ltd. Architects in 1994. After receiving an M.Arch degree from RMIT University (Melbourne, 1999), he was a finalist in the Seppelt Contemporary Art Awards held by the Museum of Contemporary Art in Sydney for his work "Future Shack." In 2000, he won the RAIA Award of Merit for new residential work for the Carter/Tucker House (Breamlea, Victoria, 1999–2000). Further work includes Peninsula House (Victoria, 2001–02); Woodleigh School Science Faculty (Baxter, Victoria, 2002); Lewis House (Dunkeld, Victoria, 2003); Westwood House (Sydney, NSW, 2003); ACN Headquarters (Victoria, 2003); and St Andrews Beach House (Mornington Peninsula, Victoria, 2003–05). Recent work includes the Glenburn House (Glenburn, Victoria, 2007); Kew Studio (Kew, Victoria, 2009–11); Edward Street House (Melbourne, Victoria, 2008–11, published here); the Tanderra House (Victoria, 2005–12); and the RMIT Design Hub (Melbourne, Victoria, 2007–12), all in Australia.

SEAN GODSELL wurde 1960 in Melbourne, Australien, geboren. Er schloss 1984 ein Studium an der University of Melbourne ab und arbeitete von 1986 bis 1988 bei Sir Denys Lasdun in London. 1994 gründete er Godsell Associates Pty Ltd. Architects. Er absolvierte einen M. Arch. an der RMIT University (Melbourne, 1999) und war mit der Arbeit „Future Shack" Finalist bei den Seppelt Contemporary Art Awards des Museum of Contemporary Art in Sydney. Mit seinem Carter/Tucker House (Breamlea, Victoria, 1999–2000) gewann er 2000 den RAIA Award of Merit für Wohnarchitektur. Zu seinen Projekten gehören das Peninsula House (Victoria, 2001–02), ein Anbau für den naturwissenschaftlichen Unterricht an der Woodleigh School (Baxter, Victoria, 2002), Lewis House (Dunkeld, Victoria, 2003), Westwood House (Sydney, 2003), der Hauptsitz für ACN (Victoria, 2003) und das St. Andrews Beach House (Mornington Peninsula, Victoria, 2003–05). Jüngere Arbeiten sind u. a. Glenburn House (Glenburn, Victoria, 2007), Kew Studio (Kew, Victoria, 2009–11), Edward Street House (Melbourne, 2008–11, hier vorgestellt), Tanderra House (Victoria, 2005–12) und das RMIT Design Hub (Melbourne, 2007–12); alle in Australien.

SEAN GODSELL est né à Melbourne, Australie en 1960. Il a été diplômé de l'université de Melbourne en 1984 et a travaillé entre 1986 et 1988 à Londres pour Sir Denys Lasdun. Il a créé l'agence Godsell Associates Pty Ltd. Architects en 1994. Après avoir obtenu son M.Arch. à l'université RMIT (Melbourne, 1999), il a été finaliste du prix Seppelt Contemporary Art décerné par le Musée d'art contemporain de Sydney pour son œuvre « Future Shack ». Le prix du mérite RAIA lui a été décerné en 2000 pour son nouveau projet d'habitation, la Carter/Tucker House (Breamlea, Victoria, 1999–2000). Parmi ses œuvres figurent la Peninsula House (Victoria, 2001–02) ; la faculté des sciences de Woodleigh (Baxter, Victoria, 2002) ; la Lewis House (Dunkeld, Victoria, 2003) ; la Westwood House (Sydney, 2003) ; le siège social d'ACN (Victoria, 2003) et la St Andrews Beach House (Mornington Peninsula, Victoria, 2003–05). Parmi ses réalisations plus récentes figurent la Glenburn House (Glenburn, Victoria, 2007) ; l'atelier Kew (Kew, Victoria, 2009–11) ; l'Edward Street House (Melbourne, Victoria, 2008–11, publiée ici) ; la Tanderra House (Victoria, 2005–12) et le RMIT Design Hub (Melbourne, 2007–12), toutes en Australie.

EDWARD STREET HOUSE
Melbourne, Victoria, Australia, 2008–11

Address: not disclosed. Area: 240 m²
Client: not disclosed. Cost: not disclosed

The architect's description of the area that this house is located in sets the stage: "The **EDWARD STREET HOUSE** is in a tough part of town. It is nestled in the backyard of what was an attached pair of bluestone workers' cottages that date back to the mid-1800s. It backs onto an alleyway where drug dealers and graffiti artists abound. Because of this we wanted the building to present a tough, almost impenetrable steel hide that only invited the world in when the owners chose to operate it." Sean Godsell describes the galvanized steel exterior of the house as a kind of "armor" that also works as a sunscreen. It is by way of contrast that the architect wanted the interior of the house to be "as warm and nurturing as possible." He also calls the inside a "cocoon." Oiled and recycled blackbutt wood (Eucalyptus pilularis) was used for the floor and blackbutt-faced plywood covers the walls and ceilings. Sliding plywood panels are used to subdivide interior space, while most wooden furniture is built-in.

Der Architekt beschreibt die Gegend, in der sich dieses Projekt befindet, folgendermaßen: „Das **EDWARD STREET HOUSE** liegt in einer rauen Nachbarschaft und schmiegt sich in den Hinterhof zweier Arbeiterhäuser aus Schiefer von der Mitte des 19. Jahrhunderts. Rückseitig grenzt es an eine Seitenstraße, in der sich Drogendealer und Graffitikünstler tummeln. Deswegen wollten wir das Haus mit einem nahezu undurchdringlichen Stahlgitter versehen, das nur überwunden werden kann, wenn die Bewohner es öffnen." Godsell bezeichnet das verzinkte, stählerne Äußere als „Schild", der zugleich als Sonnenschutz dient. Im Kontrast dazu sollte das Innere, von Godsell „Kokon" genannt, so „warm und behaglich wie nur möglich" ausfallen. Die Böden bestehen aus geöltem, recyceltem Eukalyptusholz (Eucalyptus pilularis), die Wandverkleidung aus eukalyptusfurnierten Sperrholzplatten. Gleitende Sperrholzplatten unterteilen den Innenraum. Ein Großteil des hölzernen Mobiliars ist eingebaut.

La description par l'architecte de la zone où se situe cette maison fournit une bonne introduction : « L'**EDWARD STREET HOUSE** se trouve dans une partie difficile de la ville. Elle est blottie dans l'arrière-cour de deux anciennes maisons d'ouvriers en bluestone de la moitié du XIXᵉ siècle. Elle donne sur une allée très fréquentée par les dealers et les graffiteurs. C'est pourquoi nous voulions que le bâtiment présente une peau métallique solide, quasiment impénétrable, qui accueillait uniquement lorsque les propriétaires avaient choisi de l'ouvrir. » Sean Godsell décrit la partie extérieure en acier galvanisé de la maison comme une sorte d'« armure » qui joue également le rôle de protection solaire. L'architecte voulait par contraste faire en sorte que l'intérieur de la maison soit « aussi chaleureux et réconfortant que possible ». Il parlait aussi de l'intérieur comme d'un « cocon ». Le sol est réalisé en blackbutt (Eucalyptus pilularis) huilé et recyclé tandis que les murs et les plafonds sont recouverts de contreplaqué à pli extérieur en blackbutt. Des panneaux coulissants en contreplaqué permettent de diviser l'espace, la majorité du mobilier en bois est encastrée.

Despite its urban setting a horizontality is asserted, with wood, metal
grating, and vertical glazed panels
forming most of the house.

Trotz des urbanen Umfelds dominiert
das Horizontale, wobei Holz, Metall-
gitter und vertikale Glaspaneele
Hauptbestandteile des Hauses sind.

En dépit de sa situation urbaine, la
maison est dominée par les horizontales avec des grilles métalliques et
en bois, mais aussi des panneaux
vitrés verticaux qui l'habillent en
grande partie.

Elevation drawings emphasize the horizontality of the house as do photos that show a long top-lit corridor (below).

Ansichtszeichnungen und Fotos des langen, von oben beleuchteten Flurs veranschaulichen die horizontale Linienführung des Hauses (unten).

Les élévations soulignent le caractère horizontal de la maison, de même que les photos qui montrent un long couloir éclairé par le haut (en bas).

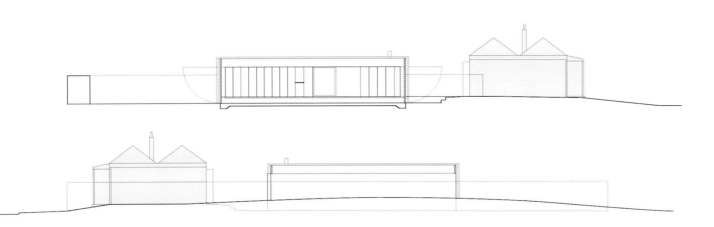

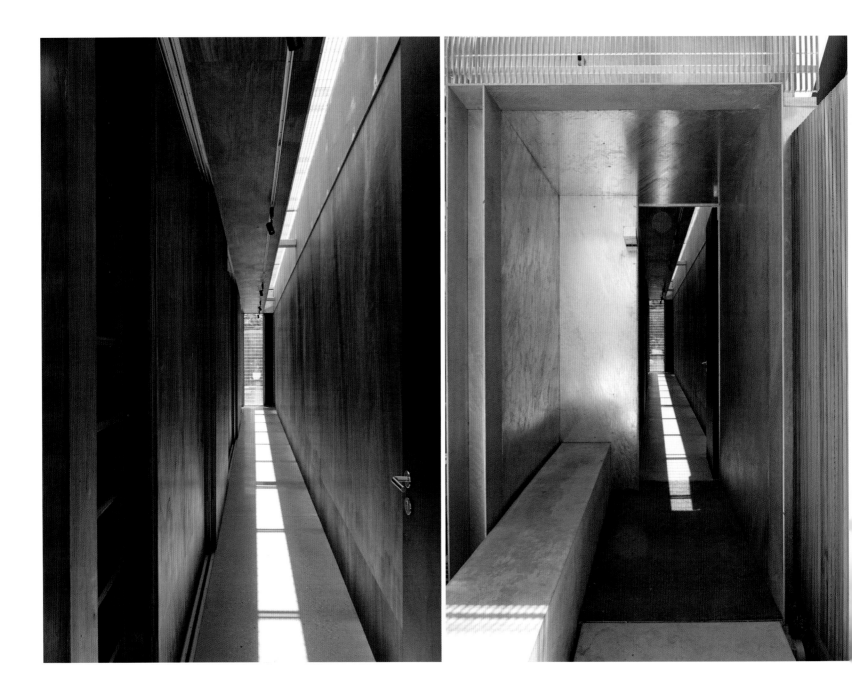

The architect contrasts the external metal grating with warm wood finishing inside—on floors and ceilings, as well as the shelf space seen above.

Der Architekt kontrastiert das Fassadengitter aus Metall mit warmen Holzfußböden, -wänden und Regaleinbauten in den Innenräumen (oben).

L'architecte crée un contraste entre la grille métallique extérieure et le chaleureux aménagement intérieur en bois – aux sols et aux plafonds, ainsi que sur les étagères présentées ci-dessus.

Although windows are partially covered, natural light comes in from above in these warm, wood-clad bathroom views.

Zwar sind die Fenster teilweise verdeckt, von oben fällt jedoch Tageslicht in das warm anmutende, holzverkleidete Badezimmer.

Bien que les fenêtres soient partiellement occultées, de la lumière naturelle arrive d'en haut dans ces chaleureuses salles de bains recouvertes de bois.

Right page, wood is omnipresent inside—as is the case for this built-in desk and shelving.

In den Innenräumen (rechte Seite) ist Holz allgegenwärtig. Das gilt auch für den eingebauten Schreibtisch mit Regalfächern.

Page de droite, le bois est omniprésent à l'intérieur – comme ici avec ce bureau encastré et ses étagères.

The linear nature of the house is emphasized by continuous bands of overhead glazing that bring ample natural light into the wood interiors. Furnishings are simple, with wood and light playing the main role in the design.

Fortlaufende Oberlichter lassen viel natürliches Licht in die Innenräume aus Holz und akzentuieren die lineare Struktur des Hauses. Das Mobiliar ist schlicht, Holz und Licht sind die Hauptakteure der Innenraumgestaltung.

La nature linéaire de la maison est soulignée par des bandes vitrées faîtières en continu qui apportent une généreuse lumière naturelle dans les intérieurs en bois. Le mobilier est sobre, le bois et la lumière jouant un rôle majeur dans la conception.

Right, a floor plan of the house, with the long, narrow corridor projecting to the right. The kitchen (below) is situated on the left of the plan seen here.

Der Grundriss rechts zeigt einen langen Flur, der nach rechts hinausragt. Die unten abgebildete Küche befindet sich links auf dem Plan.

À droite, un plan de la maison avec le long et étroit couloir qui se prolonge vers la droite. La cuisine (ci-dessous) se situe dans la partie gauche du plan ci-contre.

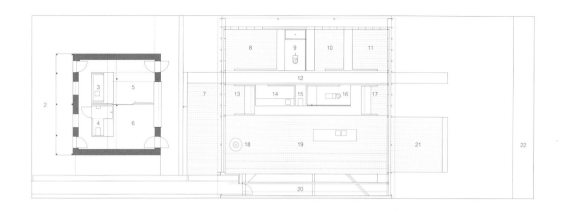

GRAFT

Graft Berlin
Heidestr. 50
10557 Berlin
Germany

Tel: +49 30 30 64 51 03 0 / Fax: +49 30 30 64 51 03 34
E-mail: berlin@graftlab.com / Web: www.graftlab.com

GRAFT was created in Los Angeles in 1998 "as a label for architecture, art, music, and the pursuit of happiness." Lars Krückeberg, Wolfram Putz, Thomas Willemeit, and Gregor Hoheisel are the Partners of Graft, which has about 100 employees worldwide. Graft maintains offices in Los Angeles, Berlin, and Beijing. Lars Krückeberg was educated at the Technical University, Braunschweig, Germany, as an engineer (1988–96) and at SCI-Arc in Los Angeles (1997–98). Wolfram Putz attended the Technical University, Braunschweig (1988–95); the University of Utah, Salt Lake City (1992–93); and SCI-Arc (1996–98). Thomas Willemeit was also educated in Braunschweig, and at the Bauhaus Dessau (1991–92), before working in the office of Daniel Libeskind (1998–2001). Gregor Hoheisel was also educated at the Technical University in Braunschweig (1988–95). They built a studio and house for Brad Pitt in Los Angeles (2000–03) and, working with Brad Pitt and William McDonough + Partners, Graft are the lead architects for the Pink Project and Make It Right initiative in New Orleans (Louisiana, USA, 2007–). They designed the Hotel Q! in Berlin (Germany, 2002–04), as well as restaurants in the Bellagio and Mirage casinos in Las Vegas, such as the Stack Restaurant and Bar, Mirage (Las Vegas, Nevada, USA, 2005, published here) and worked on several luxury resort hotels in the Caribbean. Their most recent work includes the Ginkgo Restaurant (Chengdu, China, 2008); Frankfurt Regionals Store at the International Airport (Frankfurt, Germany, 2009); Wokalicious (Berlin, Germany, 2010–11); and the Russian Jewish Museum of Tolerance (Moscow, Russia, 2007–12).

GRAFT entstand 1998 in Los Angeles als „ein Label für Architektur, Kunst, Musik und das Streben nach Glück". Lars Krückeberg, Wolfram Putz, Thomas Willemeit und Gregor Hoheisel sind Partner bei Graft, beschäftigen weltweit rund 100 Mitarbeiter und unterhalten Büros in Los Angeles, Berlin und Peking. Lars Krückeberg erhielt seine Ausbildung zum Ingenieur an der Technischen Universität Braunschweig (1988–96) und am SCI-Arc in Los Angeles (1997–98). Wolfram Putz besuchte die TU Braunschweig (1988–95), die University of Utah in Salt Lake City (1992–93) sowie das SCI-Arc (1996–98). Auch Thomas Willemeit studierte in Braunschweig sowie anschließend am Bauhaus Dessau (1991–92), ehe er im Büro von Daniel Libeskind arbeitete (1998–2001). Gregor Hoheisel studierte ebenfalls an der TU Braunschweig (1988–95). In Los Angeles bauten sie ein Studio und Haus für Brad Pitt (2000–03). Sie entwarfen das Hotel Q! in Berlin (2002–04) sowie Restaurants in den Kasinos Bellagio und Mirage in Las Vegas, darunter das hier vorgestellte Stack Restaurant and Bar, Mirage (Las Vegas, Nevada, 2005) und arbeiteten an mehreren Luxusresorts in der Karibik. Gemeinsam mit Brad Pitt und William McDonough + Partners sind Graft leitende Architekten des Pink Project und der Make-It-Right-Initiative in New Orleans (seit 2007). Zu ihren jüngsten Projekten zählen das Restaurant Ginkgo (Chengdu, China, 2008), der Frankfurt Regionals Store im Internationalen Flughafen (Frankfurt am Main, 2009), Wokalicious (Berlin, 2010–11) sowie das Russisch-Jüdische Museum der Toleranz (Moskau, 2007–12).

GRAFT a été créé à Los Angeles en 1998 « comme un label en architecture, art, musique et poursuite du bonheur ». Lars Krückeberg, Wolfram Putz, Thomas Willemeit et Gregor Hoheisel sont les partenaires de l'agence qui emploie près de 100 personnes dans le monde entier. Graft possède des bureaux à Los Angeles, Berlin et Pékin. Lars Krückeberg a fait des études d'ingénieur à l'Université technique de Brunswick, Allemagne (1988–96) et au SCI-Arc de Los Angeles (1997–98). Wolfram Putz a fait ses études à l'Université technique de Brunswick (1988–95), l'université de l'Utah à Salt Lake City (1992–93) et l'école SCI-Arc (1996–98). Thomas Willemeit a également été formé à Brunswick et au Bauhaus de Dessau (1991–92) avant de travailler à l'agence de Daniel Libeskind (1998–2001). Gregor Hoheisel sort lui aussi de l'Université technique de Brunswick (1988–95). Ils ont construit un studio et une maison pour Brad Pitt à Los Angeles (2000–03) et ont créé l'hôtel Q! à Berlin (2002–04), ainsi que des restaurants des casinos Bellagio and Mirage de Las Vegas, dont le Stack Restaurant and Bar, Mirage (Las Vegas, 2005, publié ici) et ont collaboré à plusieurs centres hôteliers de luxe dans les Caraïbes. Ils sont les premiers architectes du projet Pink et de l'initiative Make It Right à La Nouvelle-Orléans (Louisiane, 2007–), en collaboration avec Brad Pitt et William McDonough + Partners. Leurs réalisations les plus récentes comprennent : le restaurant Ginkgo (Chengdu, Chine, 2008) ; la boutique régionale à l'aéroport international de Francfort (2009) ; le restaurant Wokalicious (Berlin, 2010–11) et le Musée juif russe de la tolérance (Moscou, 2007–12).

STACK RESTAURANT AND BAR, MIRAGE

Las Vegas, Nevada, USA, 2005

Address: 3400 South Las Vegas Boulevard, Las Vegas, NV 89109, USA, +1 702 693 8300, www.stacklasvegas.com
Floor area: 539 m². Client: The Light Group, MGM Mirage Design Group. Cost: not disclosed
Collaboration: Alejandra Lillo (Project Leader), Sascha Krückeberg, Andrea Schütte, Narineh Mirzaeian

As the architects describe this Las Vegas restaurant, "An enticing canyoning landscape is generated through undulating striations of seating, layered wall and bar, utilizing the generous 5.8-meter height capacity to produce a telescopic effect in depth. The horizontal layers are peeled from one another, creating variation in patterning, cantilevering, and velocity. This effect forms a visible invitation to the space, drawing the visitor in, and gradually frames multiple spatial readings, keeping the guest inside. The canyon wall is embedded with a lighting effect that reveals a random pixilated pattern once one has journeyed inside the restaurant and looks back out. The material for the layered canyon is wood paneling, giving both warmth to the space and translating the canyon feel into a contemporary formal solution." Just as they have in other projects, such as their Q! Hotel in Berlin, Graft seeks here to create an original space in which furniture, lighting, colors, and the very atmosphere become part of an architectural environment. This is certainly a case where the distinction between architecture and design becomes blurred.

Die Architekten beschreiben dieses Restaurant in Las Vegas wie folgt: „Durch die wellenförmigen Streifen der Sitzmöbel, durch die Schichtungen der Wände und Bar, die die großzügige Raumhöhe von 5,8 m nutzen, um eine teleskopische Tiefenwirkung zu erzielen, entsteht eine verlockende ‚Cañonlandschaft'. Die horizontalen Schichten lösen sich voneinander ab, wodurch wechselnde Musterungen, Überstände und Verwirbelungen entstehen. Dieser Effekt wirkt wie eine sichtbare Einladung in den Raum, sie zieht den Besucher förmlich hinein und formuliert peu à peu vielfältige räumliche Lesarten, die den Gast festhalten. Eingebettet in die ‚Cañonwand' ist eine Beleuchtungsanlage, die eine kuriose Zufallsmusterung erkennen lässt, sobald man in das Restaurant vorgedrungen ist und zurückschaut. Der geschichtete Cañon besteht aus einer Holzverschalung, die dem Raum Wärme verleiht und das Gefühl von einer Schlucht in eine formal zeitgemäße Lösung überträgt." Ebenso wie bei anderen Projekten, beispielsweise ihrem Hotel Q!, ist Graft auch hier bestrebt, einen Raum zu schaffen, in dem Möblierung, Beleuchtung, Farben und die Atmosphäre Teil eines architektonischen Environments werden. Hier handelt es sich gewiss um ein Projekt, bei dem die Unterscheidung zwischen Architektur und Design schwerfällt.

Ce projet de restaurant à Las Vegas représente, selon les architectes, « un fascinant paysage de canyon, reconstitué par les stries en ondulations des sièges, des murs stratifiés et du bar, ainsi que par l'utilisation de la généreuse hauteur de plafond de 5,8 m qui génère un effet télescopique de profondeur. Les strates horizontales sont décalées les unes des autres pour créer des variantes de motifs ou de porte-à-faux et un sentiment de vitesse. Ces effets invitent littéralement le visiteur à pénétrer dans cet espace, en lui offrant peu à peu de multiples lectures spatiales qui lui donnent envie de s'installer. Des points lumineux sont incrustés dans le « mur-canyon » et décrivent un motif pixellisé aléatoire qui devient perceptible avec le recul. L'habillage de bois donne de la chaleur à ce volume et change l'impression de se trouver dans un canyon en une expérience formelle plus contemporaine. » De même que dans des projets comme l'Hotel Q ! à Berlin, Graft a cherché ici à créer un espace original dans lequel mobilier, éclairage, couleurs et atmosphère participent à l'environnement architectural. La distinction entre architecture et design est ici difficile à établir.

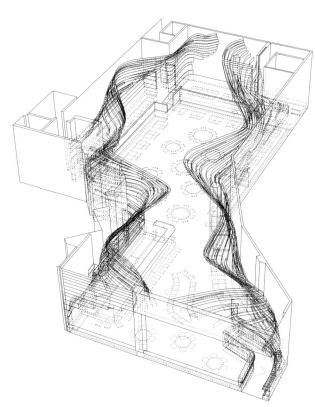

The architects refer to "canyoning" when describing this project. Their use of layers of wood indeed brings to mind topographical maps. The irregular pattern and form of the interior walls is revealed in the drawing of the layout of the restaurant and bar to the right.

Die Architekten sprechen bei diesem Projekt nicht zufällig von Cañons. Die Verwendung von Holzschichten erinnert in der Tat an topografische Karten. Die unregelmäßige Musterung und Form der Innenwände offenbart sich in der Zeichnung der Anlage von Restaurant und Bar rechts.

Les architectes utilisent le terme de « canyon » dans ce projet. Les strates de bois évoquent en effet des cartes géologiques. Les formes et motifs irréguliers des murs intérieurs se révèlent dans le dessin du plan du restaurant et du bar (à droite).

STEVEN HOLL

Steven Holl Architects, P.C.
450 West 31st Street, 11th floor
New York, NY 10001, USA
Tel: +1 212 629 7262 / Fax: +1 212 629 7312
E-mail: nyc@stevenholl.com / Web: www.stevenholl.com

Born in 1947 in Bremerton, Washington, **STEVEN HOLL** obtained his B.Arch degree from the University of Washington (1970). He studied in Rome and at the Architectural Association in London (1976). He began his career in California and opened his own office in New York in 1976. His notable buildings include Void Space / Hinged Space, Housing (Nexus World, Fukuoka, Japan, 1991); Stretto House (Dallas, Texas, USA, 1992); Makuhari Housing (Chiba, Tokyo, Japan, 1997); Chapel of Saint Ignatius, Seattle University (Seattle, Washington, USA, 1997); Kiasma Museum of Contemporary Art (Helsinki, Finland, 1998); an extension to the Cranbrook Institute of Science (Bloomfield Hills, Michigan, USA, 1999); and Y-House (Catskills, New York, USA, 1997–99, published here). Winner of the 1998 Alvar Aalto Medal, Steven Holl, won the competition (2009) for the Glasgow School of Art (Glasgow, UK), and has completed an expansion and renovation of the Nelson-Atkins Museum of Art (Kansas City, Missouri, USA, 1999–2007); Linked Hybrid (Beijing, China, 2005–08); the Knut Hamsun Center (Hamarøy, Norway, 2006–09); HEART: Herning Museum of Contemporary Art (Herning, Denmark, 2007–09); and the Vanke Center / Horizontal Skyscraper (Shenzhen, China, 2008–09), which won the 2011 AIA Honor Award for Architecture. Current and ongoing projects include Cité de l'Océan et du Surf (Biarritz, France, 2005–10, with Solange Fabião); the Nanjing Museum of Art and Architecture (China, 2008–10); Daeyang Gallery and House (Seoul, South Korea, 2010–12); Marina Zaytunay Bay (Beirut, Lebanon, 2013); Glasgow School of Art, Seona Reid Building (Glasgow, UK, 2009–14); and the Visual Arts Building, University Of Iowa (Iowa City, USA, 2010–16).

STEVEN HOLL, geboren 1947 in Bremerton, Washington, absolvierte seinen B. Arch. an der University of Washington (1970) und studierte darüber hinaus in Rom sowie an der Architectural Association in London (1976). Nach beruflichen Anfängen in Kalifornien gründete er 1976 ein Büro in New York. Zu seinen meist beachteten Projekten zählen die Wohnanlage Void Space/Hinged Space (Nexus World, Fukuoka, Japan, 1991), das Stretto House (Dallas, Texas, 1992), die Wohnanlage Makuhari (Chiba, Tokio, 1997), die Sankt-Ignatius-Kapelle, Seattle University (Seattle, Washington, 1997), das Kiasma Museum für zeitgenössische Kunst (Helsinki, 1998), eine Erweiterung des Cranbrook Institute of Science (Bloomfield Hills, Michigan, 1999) sowie das Y-House (Catskills, New York, 1997–99, hier vorgestellt). 1998 wurde Steven Holl mit der Alvar-Aalto-Medaille ausgezeichnet, er konnte den Wettbewerb für die Glasgow School of Art (2009, Glasgow) für sich entscheiden und realisierte die Renovierung und Erweiterung des Nelson-Atkins Museum of Art (Kansas City, Missouri, 1999–2007), das Linked Hybrid (Peking, 2005–08), das Knut-Hamsun-Zentrum (Hamarøy, Norwegen, 2006–09), das Herning Museum für zeitgenössische Kunst (HEART, Herning, Dänemark, 2007–09) sowie das Vanke Center/Horizontal Skyscraper (Shenzhen, China, 2008–09), das 2011 mit dem Ehrenpreis des AIA ausgezeichnet wurde. Aktuelle Projekte sind u. a. die Cité de l'Océan et du Surf (Biarritz, 2005–10, mit Solange Fabião), das Nanjing Museum für Kunst und Architektur (China, 2008–10), ein Haus mit Galerie Daeyang (Seoul, Südkorea, 2010–12), die Marina Zaytunay Bay (Beirut, Libanon, 2013), das Seona Reid Building der Glasgow School of Art (Glasgow, 2009–14) und das Visual Arts Building der Universität von Iowa (Iowa City, 2010–16).

Né en 1947 à Bremerton (État de Washington), **STEVEN HOLL** a obtenu son diplôme de B.Arch. à l'université de Washington (1970). Il a étudié à Rome et à l'Architectureal Association de Londres (1976), a débuté sa carrière en Californie et ouvert son agence à New York la même année. Parmi ses réalisations les plus notables : l'immeuble d'appartements Void Space/Hinged Space (Nexus World, Fukuoka, Japon, 1991) ; la Stretto House (Dallas, Texas, 1992) ; les logements Makuhari (Chiba, Tokyo, 1997) ; la chapelle Saint-Ignace, université de Seattle (Seattle, Washington, 1997) ; le Musée d'art contemporain Kiasma (Helsinki, Finlande, 1998) ; une extension de l'Institut des sciences de Cranbrook (Bloomfield Hills, Michigan, 1999) et la Y-House (Catskills, New York, 1997–99, publiée ici). Il reçoit la médaille Alvar Aalto en 1998 et remporte, en 2009, le concours pour l'École d'art de Glasgow. Il a réalisé l'extension et la rénovation du Musée d'art Nelson Atkins (Kansas City, Missouri, 1999–2007) ; le Linked Hybrid (Pékin, 2005–08) ; le Centre Knut Hamsun (Hamarøy, Norvège, 2006–09) ; le Musée d'art contemporain Herning (HEART, Herning, Danemark, 2007–09) ; le Vanke Center/Gratte-ciel horizontal (Shenzhen, Chine, 2008–09) qui a remporté le prix d'honneur d'architecture de l'AIA en 2011. Parmi ses réalisations actuelles et en cours : la Cité de l'océan et du surf (Biarritz, France, 2005-10, avec Solange Fabião) ; le Musée d'art et d'architecture de Nankin (Chine, 2008–10) ; la galerie et résidence Daeyang (Séoul, Corée-du-Sud, 2010–12) ; la marina de la baie Zaytunay (Beyrouth, Liban, 2013) ; le bâtiment Seona Reid de la Glasgow School of Art (Glasgow, Écosse, 2009–14) et le bâtiment des arts visuels de l'université de l'Iowa (Iowa City, États-Unis, 2010–16).

Y-HOUSE

Catskills, New York, USA, 1997–99

Address: not diclosed. Floor area: 330 m²
Client: not disclosed. Cost: not disclosed

This 330-square-meter house is located in Schoharie County in the Catskill Mountains. The two rectangular volumes of the **Y-HOUSE** split apart to create spaces for two generations of the Austrian family that commissioned the residence. Clad in red painted cedar, the house responds to the topology of the site and not specifically to the red painted wooden barns that are typical of the region, according to the architect. Divided into "day" and "night" zones, the interior spaces flow into each other in an effect that Steven Holl likens to flying. He also notes that this client was the first to accept his initial drawing for a project, allowing him an unprecedented degree of "artistic" freedom in the design. Large, open balconies face from the front of the house toward slightly different views of the countryside.

Das 330 m² große **Y-HOUSE** liegt im Schoharie County in den Catskill Mountains. In den beiden lang gestreckten, im spitzen Winkel zueinander angeordneten Bauteilen befinden sich getrennte Wohnbereiche für zwei Generationen einer österreichischen Familie, die dieses Haus für sich entwerfen ließ. Die Verkleidung aus rot gestrichenem Zedernholz wurde laut Architekt eher von der Topologie des Grundstücks inspiriert als von den für diese Region typischen roten Holzscheunen. Die in „Tag- und Nacht-Zonen" unterteilten Innenräume gehen fließend ineinander über. Steven Holl weist darauf hin, dass seine Auftraggeber bei diesem Projekt erstmalig bereits die erste Entwurfsskizze akzeptierten, was ihm ein bis dahin nicht gekanntes Maß an künstlerischer Freiheit erlaubte. Große, offene Balkone auf der Vorderseite des Hauses bieten leicht variierende Aussichten auf die umgebende Landschaft.

Cette maison de 330 m² est située dans le comté de Schoharie dans les Catskill Mountains. La **Y-HOUSE** se divise en deux volumes rectangulaires que se partagent les propriétaires, deux générations d'Autrichiens. Son bardage de cèdre peint en rouge est une réponse à la topographie locale et non un écho aux granges de cèdre rouge courantes dans la région, a expliqué l'architecte. Divisés en zones de jour et de nuit, les espaces intérieurs s'imbriquent les uns dans les autres, créant un effet que Steven Holl aime comparer à un « envol. » Il fait également remarquer que le client fut le premier a accepter d'emblée son premier projet, lui laissant une liberté artistique sans précédent. De vastes balcons-loggias ouverts sur la façade offrent des vues légèrement différentes sur le paysage agreste environnant.

The architect deals here with the need for distinct housing arrangements within the same residence. His Y-shaped collision of two essentially rectangular forms solves the design problem and adds a spatial richness to the house.

Der Forderung nach getrennten Wohnbereichen innerhalb eines Hauses kam der Architekt durch die Y-förmige Anordnung zweier fast rechteckiger Baukörper nach, die dem Gebäude zudem räumliche Fülle verleiht.

L'architecte était confronté au besoin de distinguer deux zones résidentielles à l'intérieur d'une même maison. La solution retenue – la collision en Y de deux formes à peu près rectangulaires – accroît la spatialité du bâtiment.

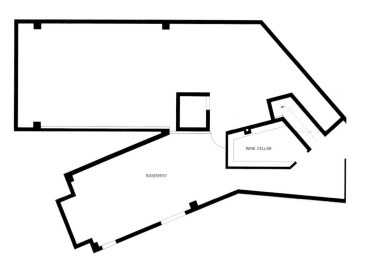

ANTHONY HUDSON

Hudson Architects
9–10 Redwell Street
Norwich NR10 4SN
UK

Tel: +44 16 03 76 62 20
E-mail: info@hudsonarchitects.co.uk
Web: www.hudsonarchitects.co.uk

ANTHONY HUDSON studied engineering (Churchill College, Cambridge, 1972–73) and then architecture (Churchill College, Cambridge School of Architecture, 1973–76) and received his Diploma in Architecture (Part II RIBA) from the University of Westminster (1978–81). He created Anthony Hudson Architects in 1985 and Hudson Architects in 2002. As the architect describes it, his interests include "one-off houses, housing, mixed-use urban and rural regeneration initiatives, art venues, galleries and museums, education and research buildings, cafés and restaurants." His built work includes Norwich OPEN, a renovation of former bank offices to house a new youth venue in Norwich (2009); Salvation Army Citadel (Chelmsford, 2009); Bavent House (Suffolk coast, 2010); the Feering Bury Farm Barn (Essex, 2009–11, published here); and Chantry Barn, the conversion of two timber-framed barns in Suffolk for residential use (2011).

ANTHONY HUDSON studiert zunächst Bauingenieurwesen (Churchill College, Cambridge, 1972–73) und schließlich Architektur (Churchill College, Cambridge School of Architecture, 1973–76) und machte sein Diplom in Architektur (Part II RIBA) an der University of Westminster (1978–81). 1985 gründete er Anthony Hudson Architects, 2002 dann Hudson Architects. Sein Interesse gilt „Hausunikaten, Wohnbauprojekten, Initiativen zur ländlichen und städtebaulichen Erneuerung von Mischgebieten, Kunsteinrichtungen, Galerien und Museen, Bildungs- und Forschungsbauten, Cafés und Restaurants". Zu seinen realisierten Projekten zählen Norwich OPEN, die Sanierung einer ehemaligen Bankverwaltung als Jugendzentrum in Norwich (2009), die Salvation Army Citadel (Chelmsford, 2009), Bavent House (an der Küste von Suffolk, 2010), Scheunenumbau der Feering Bury Farm Barn (Essex, 2009–11, hier vorgestellt) sowie Chantry Barn, der Umbau von zwei Fachwerkscheunen zu Wohnbauten (Suffolk, 2011).

ANTHONY HUDSON a fait des études d'ingénieur (Churchill College, Cambridge, 1972–73), puis d'architecture (Churchill College, Cambridge School of Architecture, 1973–76). Il est diplômé en architecture (RIBA partie II) de l'université de Westminster (1978–81). Il a fondé Anthony Hudson Architects en 1985 et Hudson Architects en 2002. Il détaille ses centres d'intérêt : « Les maisons uniques, le logement, les initiatives de régénération urbaine et rurale à usage mixte, les lieux artistiques, les galeries et musées, les bâtiments destinés à l'éducation et la recherche, les cafés et restaurants. » Ses réalisations déjà construites comprennent : Norwich OPEN, la rénovation des anciens bureaux d'une banque pour accueillir un centre de rencontres pour jeunes à Norwich (2009) ; la Salvation Army Citadel (Chelmsford, 2009) ; la Bavent House (côte du Suffolk, 2010) ; la grange Feering Bury (Essex, 2009–11, publiée ici) et la grange Chantry, reconversion de deux granges à charpente en bois pour un usage résidentiel dans le Suffolk (2011).

FEERING BURY FARM BARN

Feering, Essex, UK, 2009–11

Address: not disclosed. Area: 525 m²
Client: Ben Coode-Adams and Freddie Robins. Cost: £850 000

This project involved the restoration and conversion of a Grade II listed timber barn, located on a working farm with a central structure dating from 1560 and additions from the 18th century, into a large family home and artist studios. Conservation authorities demanded that the industrial aesthetic of the structure be maintained, which made it difficult, for example, to use externally visible roof openings. Reclaimed materials were used throughout the project. The original thatched roof had long since been replaced by corrugated roofing, which was removed by the architect, who installed polycarbonate roof lights covered with expanded steel mesh. The openings are not visible from ground level outside the barn, but they bring daylight into its interior. Existing masonry walls were retained. Black weatherboard replaced the barn's worn and unusable timber cladding. Most of the original timber-framed structure was retained, with only limited use of new wood. Internal 20th-century concrete silos were used to house a staircase, bathrooms, and bedrooms. The owner worked closely with the architects as a design collaborator and project manager.

Bei diesem Projekt ging es um die Sanierung und den Umbau einer denkmalgeschützten Holzscheune mit einem Kern von 1560 und Anbauten aus dem 18. Jahrhundert. Das Gebäude auf einem bewirtschafteten Hof sollte zu einem großzügigen Wohnsitz für eine Familie und Ateliers für Künstler umgebaut werden. Auflagen der Denkmalschutzbehörde erforderten, den Nutzcharakter des Baus zu erhalten, was den Einbau von Fenstern in das Dach erschwerte. Beim gesamten Projekt wurde mit recycelten Baumaterialen gearbeitet. Das ursprünglich mit Reet gedeckte Dach war vor langer Zeit durch Wellblechplatten ersetzt worden, die der Architekt durch Polycarbonatplatten ersetzte, die mit Streckmetall verstärkt wurden und als Oberlichter dienen. Die Fenster sind von unten nicht zu erkennen und lassen Licht ins Innere des Baus. Bestehendes Mauerwerk wurde erhalten. Die verwitterte Holzverkleidung der Scheune wurde durch schwarze Wetterschenkel ersetzt. Ein Großteil der alten Fachwerkkonstruktion wurde erhalten, neues Bauholz kam nur begrenzt zum Einsatz. In den Betonsilos aus dem 20. Jahrhundert im Innern der Scheune wurden Treppen, Bäder und Schlafzimmer untergebracht. Der Bauherr arbeitete beim Entwurf und als Projektmanager eng mit den Architekten zusammen.

Le projet fait intervenir la restauration et la reconversion en un grand logement familial et des ateliers d'artistes d'une grange en bois classée en catégorie II avec une structure centrale de 1560 et des annexes du XVIIIᵉ siècle. Elle appartient à une exploitation agricole en activité. Les autorités chargées de la protection du patrimoine avaient exigé de conserver l'esthétique industrielle de la structure, ce qui avait compliqué la pratique d'ouvertures dans le toit visibles à l'extérieur. Les matériaux de récupération ont été largement utilisés au cours du projet. Le toit de chaume original avait été remplacé depuis longtemps par de la tôle ondulée, puis par des lanterneaux en polycarbonate couverts d'un maillage en acier déployé par l'architecte. De l'extérieur de la grange, les ouvertures ne sont pas visibles d'en bas, mais font entrer la lumière du jour à l'intérieur. Les murs en maçonnerie ont été conservés. Un bardage de clins noirs a remplacé le revêtement en bois usé et inutilisable. La plus grande partie de la structure d'origine et de sa charpente en bois a été conservée et l'emploi de bois neuf réduit. À l'intérieur, des silos en béton du XXᵉ siècle abritent cage d'escalier, salles de bains et chambres à coucher. Les architectes ont travaillé en étroite collaboration avec le propriétaire, qui a contribué à la conception et a géré le projet.

The basic forms of the farm have been preserved. In the view above, perhaps only the large glazed opening in the center makes it apparent that a complete renovation has been undertaken.

Die schlichte Grundform des alten Hofgebäudes wurde erhalten. Auf der Ansicht oben verrät vielleicht nur die große verglaste Toröffnung in der Mitte, dass der Bau grundlegend saniert wurde.

Les formes de base de la ferme ont été conservées. Dans la vue ci-dessus, la vaste ouverture vitrée au centre est peut-être la seule, à témoigner de la rénovation complète qui a été entreprise.

Drawings and a photo show how the transition between a real rural building and a modern conversion has been made. A broad window offers light and access to a rough wood terrace.

Zeichnungen und Fotografie zeigen die Übergänge zwischen dem alten Hofgebäude und den Sanierungsmaßnahmen. Ein großes Fenster lässt Licht in den Bau und bietet Zugang zu einer Terrasse aus unbehandeltem Holz.

Les schémas et cette photo montrent comment la transition a été effectuée entre un bâtiment rural et sa conversion moderne. Une large fenêtre procure de la lumière et donne accès à une terrasse en bois brut.

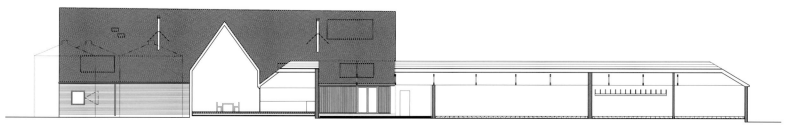

The interior design relies heavily on the timber frame of the barn. Modern amenities are introduced, but in a reasoned way, giving priority to the architecture.

Das Interieur ist stark vom alten Fachwerk der Scheune geprägt. Moderne Haustechnik kam zwar zum Einsatz, jedoch nur zurückhaltend – Vorrang hat eindeutig die Architektur.

Le design intérieur s'appuie fortement sur la charpente en bois de la grange. Les équipements modernes ajoutés l'ont été de manière raisonnée, laissant le premier rôle à l'architecture.

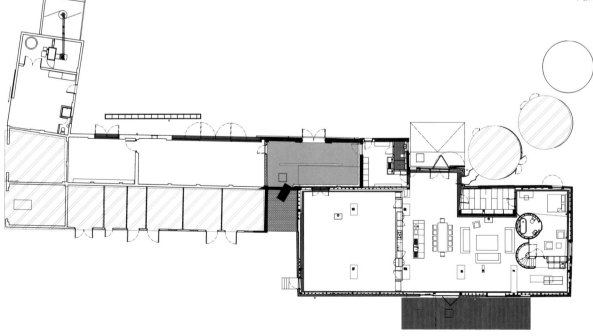

Wood is present everywhere, including in the furniture added by the clients. The interiors are generous and have high ceilings thanks to the orig-inal structure.

Holz ist allgegenwärtig, auch beim Mobiliar, das die Bauherren mitbrachten. Bedingt durch den Altbau sind die Innenräume großzügig, die Decken hoch.

Le bois est omniprésent, y compris dans les meubles apportés par les habitants. La structure originale donne des intérieurs généreux et hauts de plafond.

Natural light enters the structure through windows and doors—one element that might not have been in keeping with the original barn function, but it is done in an elegant way.

Tageslicht fällt durch Fenster und Türen ein – ein Element, das es zwar in der alten Scheune nicht gab, das jedoch elegant ausgeführt wurde.

La lumière naturelle entre par les portes et les fenêtres – un élément qui ne correspond peut-être pas à la fonction première de la grange mais a été réalisé avec élégance.

HWKN

Hollwich Kushner Architecture DPC (HWKN)
1 Whitehall Street, Floor 14
New York, NY 10004
USA

Tel: +1 212 625 2320
E-mail: info@hwkn.com
Web: www.hwkn.com

MATTHIAS HOLLWICH is cofounder and Principal of Hollwich Kushner (HWKN) and cofounder of architizer.com. Before starting his own firms, he worked at OMA (Rotterdam), Eisenman Architects, and Diller+Scofidio (New York). He is currently a Visiting Professor at the University of Pennsylvania, where he was the creator of an international conference on aging and architecture: "New Aging," held in the fall of 2010. **MARC KUSHNER** is a Partner in Hollwich Kushner and CEO of architizer.com. After graduating from Harvard's GSD, he worked with J Mayer H Architects in Berlin and Lewis Tsurumaki Lewis (LTL) in New York. In 2009, Hollwich and his partners founded architizer.com, the "first crowd-sourced database for architecture online." Architizer remains the fastest growing platform for architecture online. Marc Kushner teaches at Columbia University's Graduate School of Architecture, Planning and Preservation, and lectures on the topic of social media and architecture. Their work includes Aging in Africa (Ivory Coast, 2008); Mini Rooftop (New York, New York, 2008); Il laboratorio del gelato (New York, New York, 2010); Uniqlo Cubes (New York, New York, 2011); Wendy (MoMA PS1 Long Island Queens, New York, 2011); and Fire Island Pines Pavilion (Fire Island Pines, New York, 2012–13, published here). Their ongoing work includes 18 Park (Jersey City, New Jersey, 2013–); and the Jerusalem Academy of Music and Dance (Jerusalem, Israel, 2013–), all in the USA unless stated otherwise.

MATTHIAS HOLLWICH ist Mitbegründer und Direktor von Hollwich Kushner (HWKN) sowie Mitbegründer von architizer.com. Bevor er sein eigenes Unternehmen gründete, arbeitete Hollwich bei OMA (Rotterdam), Eisenman Architects sowie Diller+Scofidio (New York). Derzeit ist er Gastprofessor an der University of Pennsylvania, wo er „New Aging" initiierte, eine internationale Konferenz zum Thema Altern und Architektur, die im Herbst 2010 stattfand. **MARC KUSHNER** ist Teilhaber von Hollwich Kushner und Geschäftsführer bei architizer.com. Nach seinem Abschluss an der Harvard Graduate School of Design arbeitete er bei J Mayer H Architects in Berlin sowie bei Lewis Tsurumaki Lewis (LTL) in New York. 2009 rief Hollwich zusammen mit seinen Partnern architizer.com ins Leben, „die erste Crowdsourcing-Onlinedatenbank für Architektur". Architizer ist nach wie vor die am schnellsten wachsende Onlineplattform für Architektur. Marc Kushner unterrichtet an der Graduate School of Architecture, Planning and Preservation der Columbia University und hält Vorträge zum Thema soziale Medien und Architektur. Zu den Arbeiten von HWKN gehören u. a. Aging in Africa (Elfenbeinküste, 2008), Mini Rooftop (New York, 2008), Il laboratorio del gelato (New York, 2010), Uniqlo Cubes (New York, 2011), Wendy (MoMA PS1, Long Island Queens, New York, 2011) und der Fire Island Pines Pavilion (Fire Island Pines, New York, 2012–13, hier vorgestellt). Zu den laufenden Projekten gehören 18 Park (Jersey City, New Jersey, seit 2013) und die Jerusalemer Akademie für Musik und Tanz (Israel, seit 2013).

MATTHIAS HOLLWICH est cofondateur et directeur de Hollwich Kushner (HWKN) et cofondateur d'architizer.com. Avant de lancer ses propres sociétés, il a travaillé dans les agences OMA (Rotterdam), Eisenman Architects et Diller+Scofidio (New York). Il est actuellement professeur invité à l'université de Pennsylvanie où il a organisé une conférence internationale sur le vieillissement et l'architecture : « New Aging », qui s'est tenue à l'automne 2010. **MARC KUSHNER** est partenaire chez Hollwich Kushner et directeur d'architizer.com. Après son diplôme de la Harvard GSD, il a travaillé dans l'agence de J Mayer H Architects à Berlin et chez Lewis Tsurumaki Lewis (LTL) à New York. En 2009, Hollwich et ses partenaires ont créé architizer.com, la « première base de données générée par les utilisateurs pour l'architecture en ligne ». Architizer reste la plate-forme de croissance la plus rapide pour l'architecture en ligne. Marc Kushner enseigne la conception et la conservation à l'école d'architecture de l'université de Columbia et donne des conférences sur le thème des médias sociaux et de l'architecture. Parmi leurs travaux figurent Aging in Africa (Côte d'Ivoire, 2008) ; Mini Rooftop (New York, 2008) ; Il laboratorio del gelato (New York, 2010) ; Uniqlo Cubes (New York, 2011) ; Wendy (MoMA PS1 Long Island Queens, New York, 2011) et le pavillon de Fire Island Pines (Fire Island Pines, New York, 2012–13, publié ici). Parmi leurs travaux en cours figurent 18 Park (Jersey City, New Jersey, 2013–) et l'Académie de musique et de danse de Jérusalem (Jérusalem, Israël, 2013–), tous aux États-Unis, sauf mention contraire.

FIRE ISLAND PINES PAVILION

Fire Island Pines, New York, USA, 2012–13

Address: 36 Fire Island Boulevard, Fire Island, NY 11782, USA,
www.pavilionfireisland.com. Area: 743 m²
Client: Blesso Properties. Cost: not disclosed

The previous **FIRE ISLAND PINES PAVILION**, built in 1985, was destroyed by fire in 2011. The triangular cedar frames employed by the architects are designed to create an open social space. It is intended to visually welcome the 800 000 people who come to the resort area every summer. The Welcome Bar is situated on the ground floor and a dance club is on the upper level, which includes a 223-square-meter dance floor with a retractable roof and a 242-square-meter outdoor terrace. Since it is largely open, the structure requires little air conditioning despite the warm, humid summer nights in the region. Attentive to the recommendations of local residents, the architects made a considerable effort to create a "sustainable" structure, starting with the extensive use of wood, but also, for instance, emphasizing passive cooling and minimizing cladding materials in favor of exposed timber.

Der 1985 errichtete Vorgängerbau des **FIRE ISLAND PINES PAVILION** fiel 2011 einem Feuer zum Opfer. Für das Tragwerk kamen dreieckige Elemente aus Zedernholz zum Einsatz. Der Bau dient als öffentlicher Treffpunkt und soll die 800 000 Besucher, die jeden Sommer in dieses Urlaubsgebiet kommen, visuell in Empfang nehmen. Im Erdgeschoss befindet sich die Welcome Bar, im Obergeschoss ein Tanzklub mit einer 223 m² großen Tanzfläche, die über ein Schiebedach verfügt, sowie eine 242 m² große Terrasse. Das zu großen Teilen offen konstruierte Gebäude kommt weitgehend ohne Klimatisierung aus, trotz der warmen, schwülen Sommernächte in dieser Region. Die Architekten sind den Empfehlungen der Einwohner gefolgt und haben „nachhaltig" gebaut. Außer dem extensiven Einsatz von Holz legten sie beispielsweise Wert auf eine passive Kühlung und minimierten zudem den Einsatz von Materialien zur Fassadenverkleidung zugunsten von Sichtholz.

Le précédent **PAVILLON DE FIRE ISLAND PINES**, construit en 1985, a été détruit au cours d'un incendie en 2011. Les architectes ont eu recours à des éléments triangulaires en cèdre pour créer un espace de loisirs ouvert. Ce bâtiment doit accueillir les quelque 800 000 personnes attendues chaque été sur ce lieu de vacances. Un bar d'accueil se trouve au rez-de-chaussée, et une discothèque – ainsi qu'une piste de danse de 223 m² avec toit rétractable et une terrasse extérieure de 242 m² – au niveau supérieur. Étant largement ouverte, la structure a de faibles besoins en air conditionné malgré les nuits d'été chaudes et humides de la région. Attentifs aux recommandations des riverains, les architectes ont déployé d'importants efforts afin de réaliser une structure « soutenable », à commencer par l'utilisation massive de bois, sans oublier le recours marqué au refroidissement passif et la préférence accordée au bois apparent par rapport aux matériaux de revêtement.

Although the use of wood in contemporary architecture is frequent, it is more unusual to see structures such as this one with an exposed timber frame and essentially open spaces.

Holz kommt in der zeitgenössischen Architektur oft zum Einsatz, offene Holzrahmenkonstruktionen und weitgehend offene Raumsituationen wie hier sind jedoch ungewöhnlich.

Bien que l'usage du bois soit fréquent dans l'architecture contemporaine, il est plus inhabituel de voir de telles structures avec une ossature en bois apparente et des espaces en grande partie ouverts.

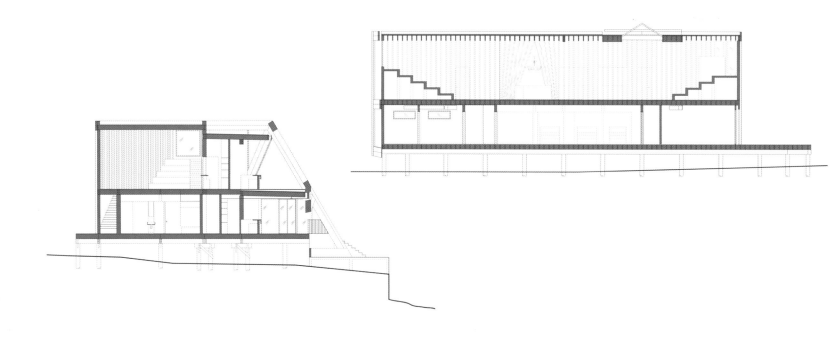

Section drawings show the angled-back main façade and the division of the interior spaces. At nightfall (below), the interior of the building glows from within.

Quer- und Längsschnitt zeigen die schräg abfallende Hauptfassade und die Unterteilung der Innenräume. Bei Dämmerung (unten) leuchtet das Innere des Gebäudes.

Des coupes montrent la façade principale inclinée à l'arrière et l'organisation des espaces intérieurs. À la tombée de la nuit (ci-dessous), l'intérieur du bâtiment rayonne vers l'extérieur.

Above, the dance floor, and below, plans of the ground floor (left) and upper floor (right) reveal that triangular or angled forms are a good part of the basic design of the structure.

Die Tanzfläche (oben) sowie die Grundrisse von Erd- und Obergeschoss (unten links und rechts) zeigen, dass der Entwurf vor allem von dreieckigen und winkligen Formen bestimmt wird.

Ci-dessus, la piste de danse et, ci-dessous, des plans du rez-de-chaussée (à gauche) et de l'étage (à droite) révèlent la part importante accordée aux formes triangulaires ou angulaires dans la conception de base de la structure.

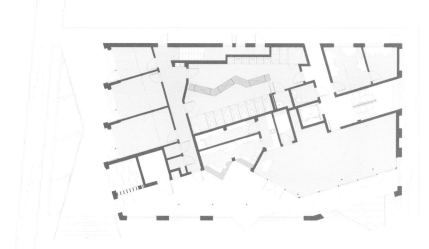

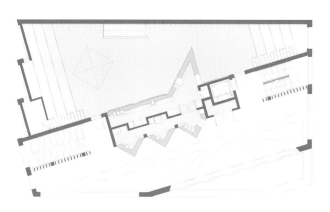

ICD/ITKE

Institute for Computational Design (ICD)
Institute of Building Structures and Structural Design (ITKE)
Universität Stuttgart
Keplerstr. 11
70174 Stuttgart
Germany

Tel: +49 711 68 58 19 20 / +49 711 68 58 32 80
Fax: +49 711 68 58 19 30 / +49 711 68 58 27 56
E-mail: mail@icd.uni-stuttgart.de / info@itke.uni-stuttgart.de
Web: www.icd.uni-stuttgart.de / www.itke.uni-stuttgart.de

The Institute for Computational Design (ICD) and the Institute of Building Structures and Structural Design (ITKE) are part of the Faculty of Architecture and Urban Planning at the University of Stuttgart. According to their own description: "Our goal is to prepare students for the continuing advancement of computational processes in architecture, as they merge the fields of design, engineering, planning, and construction. The interrelation of such topics is exposed as both a technical and intellectual venture of formal, spatial, constructional, and ecological potentials. Through teaching, we establish a practical foundation in the fundamentals of parametric and algorithmic design strategies." Professor **ACHIM MENGES**, born in 1975, is an architect and Director of the ICD. He is a Visiting Professor of Architecture at Harvard University's GSD and Visiting Professor for the Emergent Technologies and Design Graduate Program at the Architectural Association in London. Born in Düsseldorf in 1962, Professor **JAN KNIPPERS** received his Ph.D. in Structural Engineering from the University of Berlin (1983–92). Since 2000, he has been a Professor and Head of the ITKE. Recent works are the ICD/ITKE Research Pavilions (Stuttgart, Germany, 2010, 2011, and 2012, the first of which is published here); and Hygroscope, Meteorosensitive Morphology (Centre Pompidou, Paris, France, 2012, a personal project by Professor Menges).

Das Institut für Computerbasiertes Entwerfen (ICD) und das Institut für Tragkonstruktionen und Konstruktives Entwerfen (ITKE) sind Teil der Fakultät für Architektur und Stadtplanung der Universität Stuttgart: „Ziel des ICD [ist es], die Studierenden auf die zunehmende Ausbreitung computerbasierter Prozesse in der Architektur vorzubereiten, die dazu beitragen, dass die Bereiche Entwerfen, Ingenieurwissenschaften, Planung und Bauen zunehmend verschmelzen. Die Wechselbeziehung dieser Themenfelder wird herausgearbeitet, sowohl als technisches als auch als intellektuelles Unterfangen mit formalen, räumlichen, konstruktiven und ökologischen Potenzialen. Durch sein Lehrangebot schafft das ICD eine praktische Grundlage für die Grundsätze parametrischer und algorithmischer Entwurfsstrategien." Professor **ACHIM MENGES**, geboren 1975, ist Architekt und Direktor des ICD. Darüber hinaus war er Gastprofessor für Architektur an der Harvard Graduate School of Design sowie Gastprofessor für den Studiengang Emergent Technologies and Design an der Architectural Association in London. **JAN KNIPPERS**, 1962 in Düsseldorf geboren, studierte Bauingenieurwesen an der TU Berlin, wo er auch promovierte (1983–92). Seit 2000 ist er Professor und Leiter des ITKE. Zu den jüngsten Projekten gehören die Forschungspavillons von ICD/ITKE (Stuttgart, 2010, 2011 und 2012, der erste wird hier vorgestellt) und Hygroscope, Meteorosensitive Morphology (Centre Pompidou, Paris, 2012, ein persönliches Projekt von Professor Menges).

L'Institut de design assisté par ordinateur (ICD) appartient à l'Institut de construction et de design de structures (ITKE) de la faculté d'architecture et d'urbanisme de l'université de Stuttgart. Selon sa propre description : « Notre objectif est de préparer les étudiants au progrès permanent de l'informatique en architecture, au fur et à mesure qu'elle fait fusionner les domaines du design, du génie, de la conception et de la construction. L'interconnexion de ces différents domaines est présentée comme une entreprise à la fois technique et intellectuelle aux potentiels formels, spatiaux, écologiques et de construction. À travers l'enseignement, nous établissons un fondement pratique pour les principes paramétriques et algorithmiques des stratégies de conception. » Le professeur **ACHIM MENGES**, né en 1975, architecte, est le directeur de l'ICD. Il a également été professeur associé d'architecture à la Harvard GSD et professeur associé du programme de troisième cycle en nouvelles technologies et design à l'Architectural Association de Londres. Né à Dusseldorf en 1962, le professeur **JAN KNIPPERS** est titulaire d'un Ph.D en ingénierie structurelle de l'université de Berlin (1983–92). Depuis 2000, il est professeur et dirige l'ITKE. Leurs réalisations récentes comprennent les pavillons de recherche de l'ICD/ITKE (Stuttgart, 2010, 2011 et 2012, le premier étant publié ici) et Hygroscope, Meteorosensitive Morphology (Centre Pompidou, Paris, France, 2012, un projet personnel du professeur Menges).

ICD/ITKE RESEARCH PAVILION

Stuttgart, Germany, 2010

Address: Keplerstr. 17, University of Stuttgart, Stuttgart, Germany
Area: 85 m². Client: ICD/ITKE. Cost: not disclosed. Collaboration: Andreas Eisenhardt,
Manuel Vollrath, Kristine Wächter

This is the result of a collaboration between two University of Stuttgart entities, the Institute for Computational Design headed by Achim Menges and the Institute of Building Structures and Structural Design headed by Jan Knippers. Designed between October 19, 2009 and June 24, 2010, this pavilion was built between June 24 and July 23, 2010. The structure of the pavilion is based on bent birch plywood strips. According to the ICD: "The strips are robotically manufactured as planar elements, and subsequently connected, so that elastically bent and tensioned regions alternate along their length. The force that is locally stored in each bent region of the strip, and maintained by the corresponding tensioned region of the neighboring strip, greatly increases the structural capacity of the system." The entire structure, with a diameter of more than 10 meters, was built using only 6.5-millimeter-thick birch plywood sheets. The 500 unique pieces necessary were manufactured in the University's robotics plant.

Der Bau entstand als Zusammenarbeit zweier Institute der Universität Stuttgart, des Instituts für Computerbasiertes Entwerfen (ICD), geleitet von Achim Menges, sowie des Instituts für Tragkonstruktionen und Konstruktives Entwerfen (ITKE) unter Leitung von Jan Knippers. Der zwischen dem 19. Oktober 2009 und 24. Juni 2010 entworfene Pavillon wurde zwischen dem 24. Juni 2010 und 23. Juli 2010 realisiert. Die Konstruktion des Pavillons besteht aus gebogenen Birkensperrholzstreifen. Das ICD erklärt: „Die Streifen werden robotisch als plane Elemente gefertigt und schließlich miteinander verkoppelt, sodass sich der Länge nach abwechselnd elastisch gebogene und unter Eigenspannung versetzte Abschnitte ergeben. Die Kraft, die sich in den gebogenen Zonen der Streifen aufbaut und von der entsprechenden unter Eigenspannung gesetzten Region benachbarter Streifen aufgefangen wird, steigert die Tragfähigkeit des Systems erheblich." Die gesamte Konstruktion hat einen Durchmesser von über 10 m und wurde aus nur 6,5 mm starken Birkensperrholzstreifen gebaut. Die 500 individuell geformten Einzelteile wurden in der universitätseigenen robotischen Fertigungsanlage gefräst.

Ce pavillon est l'aboutissement d'une collaboration entre deux instituts de l'université de Stuttgart, l'Institut de design assisté par ordinateur dirigé par Achim Menges et l'Institut de construction et de design de structures dirigé par Jan Knippers. Conçu du 19 octobre 2009 au 24 juin 2010, ce petit bâtiment a été édifié entre le 24 juin et le 23 juillet 2010. De plus de 10 m de diamètre, la structure toute entière est composée de bandes de contreplaqué de bouleau de 6,5 mm d'épaisseur. Selon la présentation de l'ICD : « Ces bandes sont fabriquées par des robots sous forme d'éléments planaires, réunis ensuite entre eux de telle façon que sur toute leur longueur alternent des zones cintrées et en tension. La force qui se concentre localement dans chaque zone cintrée de la bande est maintenue par la zone en tension correspondante de la bande voisine, ce qui accroît de façon importante la capacité structurelle du système. » Les 500 pièces de bois uniques nécessaires ont été fabriquées dans les ateliers robotisés de l'université.

The use of computerized design and manufacturing to create the bent plywood strips that form the pavilion gives it an unexpected appearance, halfway between mathematics and nature.

Mithilfe computerbasierter Entwurfs- und Fertigungsprozesse entstand ein ungewöhnlicher Pavillon aus gebogenen Sperrholzstreifen, ein Zwischending von Natur und Mathematik.

Le recours à des techniques de conception et de fabrication informatisées a permis de créer ces bandeaux de contreplaqué cintré qui donnent au pavillon un aspect surprenant, quelque part entre mathématiques et nature.

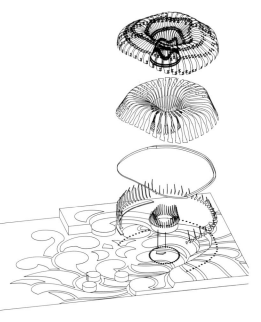

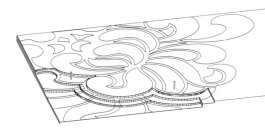

Villa in Hayama

YOSUKE INOUE

Yosuke Inoue Architect & Associates
3F, 2-20-5, Ekoda
Nakano-ku
Tokyo 165–0022
Japan

Tel: +81 3 5913 3525
Fax: +81 3 5913 3526
E-mail: usun@gol.com
Web: www.yosukeinoue.com

YOSUKE INOUE was born in Tokyo, Japan, in 1966. He graduated from the Department of Architecture of Kyoto University in 1991. He worked in the office of Sakakura Associates from 1991 to 2000, when he established his own office, Yosuke Inoue Architect & Associates, in Tokyo. His work includes House in Fuji (Fuji, Shizuoka, 2002); House in Nakanobu (Shinagawa, Tokyo, 2004); House in Setagaya-Sakura (Setagaya, Tokyo, 2004); House in Azamino (Yokohama, Kanagawa, 2005); House in Ichikawa (Ichikawa, Chiba, 2006); Villa in Hayama (Hayama, Kanagawa, 2006–07, published here); House in Den-en-chofu (Ohta, Tokyo, 2007); House in Tsujido (Fujisawa, Kanagawa, 2008); and House in Yotsuya (Shinjuku, Tokyo, 2008). He completed the House in Yoga (Tokyo) and the House in Daita (Tokyo) in 2010, all in Japan.

YOSUKE INOUE wurde 1966 in Tokio geboren und beendete 1991 sein Architekturstudium an der Universität von Kioto. Von 1991 bis 2000 arbeitete er im Büro Sakakura Associates. 2000 gründete er seine eigene Firma, Yosuke Inoue Architect & Associates, in Tokio. Zu seinen ausgeführten Bauten zählen ein Wohnhaus in Fuji (Fuji, Shizuoka, 2002), ein Wohnhaus in Nakanobu (Shinagawa, Tokio, 2004), ein Wohnhaus in Setagaya-Sakura (Setagaya, Tokio, 2004), ein Wohnhaus in Azamino (Yokohama, Kanagawa, 2005), ein Wohnhaus in Ichikawa (Ichikawa, Chiba, 2006), eine Villa in Hayama (Hayama, Kanagawa, 2006–07, hier veröffentlicht), ein Wohnhaus in Den-en-chofu (Ohta, Tokio, 2007), ein Wohnhaus in Tsujido (Fujisawa, Kanagawa, 2008) sowie ein Wohnhaus in Yotsuya (Shinjuku, Tokio, 2008). 2010 fertiggestellt wurden ein Wohnhaus in Yoga (Tokio) und ein Wohnhaus in Daita (Tokio), alle in Japan.

YOSUKE INOUE, né à Tokyo en 1966, est diplômé du département d'architecture de l'université de Kyoto (1991). Il a travaillé dans l'agence Sakakura Associates de 1991 à 2000 avant de fonder sa propre structure, Yosuke Inoue Architect & Associates, à Tokyo. Parmi ses réalisations figurent de nombreuses maisons : à Fuji (Shizuoka, 2002) ; Nakanobu (Shinagawa, Tokyo, 2004) ; Setagaya-Sakura (Setagaya, Tokyo, 2004) ; Azamino (Yokohama, Kanagawa, 2005) ; Ichikawa (Ichikawa, Chiba, 2006) ; Hayama (Kanagawa, 2006–07 publiée ici) ; Den-en-chofu (Ohta, Tokyo, 2007) ; Tsujido (Fujisawa, Kanagawa, 2008) et à Yotsuya (Shinjuku, Tokyo, 2008). Il a achevé une maison à Yoga (Tokyo, 2010) et une à Faita (Tokyo, 2010), toutes au Japon.

VILLA IN HAYAMA

Hayama, Kanagawa, Japan, 2006–07

Address: not disclosed
Area: 157 m². Client: not disclosed. Cost: not disclosed
Collaboration: Keiichi Amano

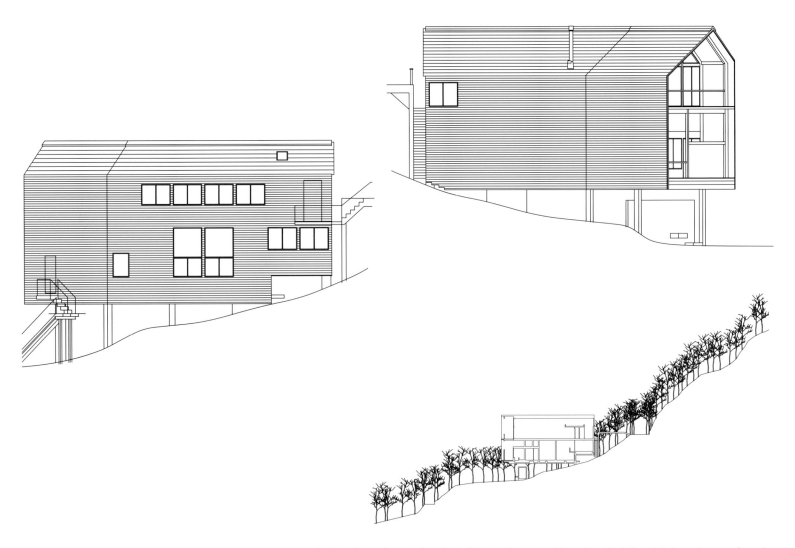

This two-story wooden house is located on a sloping, wooded site facing Sagami Bay. A significant advantage of the site is that Mount Fuji can be seen from the house on a clear day. The residence is set on concrete pilotis that increase in height as the ground slopes down. The entrance to the building, kitchen, and double-height living and dining areas are located on the upper level. The inflected shape of the plan is related to the form of the site and of course to the direction of the views of the ocean and Mount Fuji. Wood is visible everywhere, both in the dark exterior cladding and in the sometimes lighter wood used within the residence.

Dieses zweigeschossige Holzhaus steht auf einem bewaldeten Hanggrundstück mit Blick auf die Bucht von Sagami. Ein beachtlicher Vorzug dieses Geländes ist an klaren Tagen die Sicht auf den Berg Fuji. Das Gebäude steht auf Betonstützen, die es auf dem abfallenden Gelände anheben. Der Eingang, die Küche und der doppelgeschosshohe Wohn- und Essbereich liegen auf der oberen Ebene. Die gebogene Form des Grundrisses folgt dem Verlauf des Grundstücks und natürlich den Blickrichtungen zum Ozean und zum Berg Fuji. Holz tritt überall in Erscheinung, an der dunklen Außenverkleidung sowie teilweise etwas heller innerhalb des Hauses.

Cette villa entièrement en bois de deux niveaux est située sur un terrain en forte pente, face à la baie de Sagami. Une des caractéristiques de ce site est de permettre d'apercevoir le mont Fuji par beau temps. La construction s'appuie sur des pilotis de béton qui compensent la pente du terrain. On accède à la cuisine, le séjour double hauteur et l'espace salle à manger par le niveau supérieur. La forme d'ensemble est déterminée par la déclivité du terrain et l'orientation vers les vues sur l'océan et le mont Fuji. Le bois est omniprésent, aussi bien dans le bardage extérieur de couleur sombre que dans les essences un peu plus claires retenues pour les aménagements intérieurs.

Backed against a steep hillside, as the site drawing above shows, the house has an asymmetric form that is lifted off the ground on the downhill side.

Wie die Zeichnungen oben zeigen, hat das an einen steilen Hang gelehnte Haus eine asymmetrische Form und ist auf der Talseite vom Boden angehoben.

Appuyée contre le flanc d'une colline abrupte, comme le montre le plan de situation ci-dessus, cette maison de plan asymétrique est suspendue du côté de la pente.

The full glazing under the gables of the house allows for a spectacular view of the water and the mountains beyond.

Aus den voll verglasten Giebeln bieten sich spektakuläre Ausblicke zum Wasser und auf die dahinter liegenden Berge.

Le pignon entièrement vitré offre une vue spectaculaire sur l'océan et les montagnes dans le lointain.

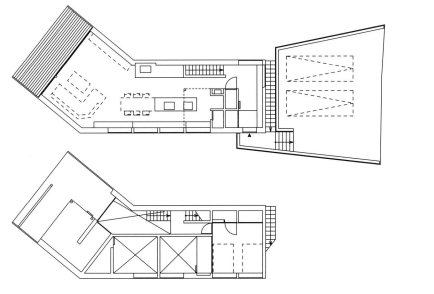

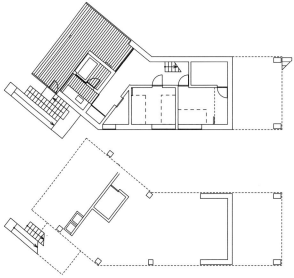

Floor plans show the angled shape of the house, culminating in the framed view seen in the image above.

Die Grundrisse zeigen die eckige Form des Hauses, die in dem gerahmten Ausblick gipfelt, der auf dem oberen Foto zu sehen ist.

Les plans des différents niveaux illustrent la forme en angle de la maison qui aboutit à la vue cadrée ci-dessus.

Wood is present everywhere, including the steeply angled ceilings seen
in the page to the right.

*Holz ist überall präsent, auch an den
steil ansteigenden Decken, wie am
Foto rechts abzulesen.*

*Le bois est omniprésent, y compris
dans les plafonds dont la forte inclinaison suit la toiture (page de droite).*

The same wooden floor continues
from the inside of the house to the
balcony, as seen in the image above.

*Der gleiche hölzerne Boden im Innern
des Hauses wird auf den Balkon wei-
tergeführt, wie das Foto oben zeigt.*

*Le sol en bois de l'intérieur se
prolonge vers le balcon (photo
ci-dessus).*

JENSEN & SKODVIN

Jensen & Skodvin Arkitektkontor AS
Sinsenveien 4D
0572 Oslo
Norway

Tel: +47 22 99 48 99
Fax: +47 22 99 48 88
E-mail: office@jsa.no
Web: www.jsa.no

Jensen & Skodvin was established in 1995 by Olav Jensen and Børre Skodvin. The firm currently has nine architects. Born in 1959, **OLAV JENSEN** received his degree from the Oslo School of Architecture in 1985. He has been a Professor at the Oslo School of Design and Architecture since 2004. He was the Kenzo Tange Visiting Critic at Harvard University (1998), and won a 1998 Aga Khan Award for Architecture for the Lepers Hospital, in Chopda Taluka, India. **BØRRE SKODVIN** was born in 1960 and received his degree from the Oslo School of Architecture in 1988. He has been a teacher at the Oslo School of Design and Architecture since 1998. Their built work includes the Storo Metro Station (Oslo, 2003); headquarters and exhibition space for the Norwegian Design Council (Oslo, 2004); Sinsen Metro Station (Oslo, 2005); a Multipurpose City Block (Trondheim, 2005; collaboration with Team Tre); the plan and designs for a new town in south Oslo (2005; not built); the Tautra Maria Convent (Tautra Island, 2004–06); and a Thermal Bath, Therapy Center, and Hotel (Bad Gleichenberg, Austria, 2005–08, published here). They have worked recently on the Gudbrandsjuvet Tourist project, viewing platforms and bridges (Gudbrandsjuvet, 2008); the Juvet Landscape Hotel (Gudbrandsjuvet, 2007–09); and Giørtz Summer House (Valldal, 2012), all in Norway unless stated otherwise.

Jensen & Skodvin wurde 1995 von Olav Jensen und Børre Skodvin gegründet. Derzeit beschäftigt das Büro neun Architekten. **OLAV JENSEN**, geboren 1959, schloss sein Studium 1985 an der Architektur- und Designhochschule Oslo ab, wo er seit 2004 als Professor tätig ist. Er war Kenzo-Tange-Gastkritiker in Harvard (1998) und wurde 1998 für das Leprakrankenhaus in Chopda Taluka, Indien, mit dem Aga Khan Award for Architecture ausgezeichnet. **BØRRE SKODVIN** wurde 1960 geboren und schloss sein Studium 1988 an der Architektur- und Designhochschule Oslo ab, wo er seit 1998 lehrt. Zu ihren Projekten zählen die Metrostation Storo (Oslo, 2003), die Zentrale und ein Ausstellungsraum für den Norwegischen Designverband (Oslo, 2004), die Metrostation Sinsen (Oslo, 2005), ein Gebäude mit gemischter Nutzung (Trondheim, 2005, mit Team Tre), Planung und Entwurf für ein neues Stadtzentrum in Süd-Oslo (2005, nicht realisiert), das Mariakloster Tautra (Insel Tautra, 2004–06) sowie Therme, Kurhaus und Hotel Bad Gleichenberg (Österreich, 2005–08, hier vorgestellt). In letzter Zeit arbeitete das Büro an Aussichtsplattformen und Brücken für das Gudbrandsjuvet-Tourismusprojekt (Gudbrandsjuvet, 2008), dem Juvet Landscape Hotel (Gudbrandsjuvet, 2007–09) und dem Giørtz-Sommerhaus (Valldal, 2012), alle in Norwegen, sofern nicht anders angegeben.

Jensen & Skodvin a été fondée en 1995 par Olav Jensen et Børre Skodvin. L'agence se compose aujourd'hui de neuf architectes. Né en 1959, **OLAV JENSEN** a obtenu son diplôme à l'École d'architecture d'Oslo en 1985. Il enseigne à l'École de design et architecture d'Oslo depuis 2004. Il a été le critique invité par Kenzo Tange à l'université de Harvard (1998) et a gagné un prix Aga Khan d'architecture en 1998 pour l'hôpital Lepers de Chopda Taluka, en Inde. **BØRRE SKODVIN** est né en 1960 et a obtenu son diplôme à l'École d'architecture d'Oslo en 1988. Il enseigne à l'École de design et architecture d'Oslo depuis 1998. Leurs réalisations comprennent la station de métro Storo (Oslo, 2003) ; le siège et espace d'exposition du Conseil norvégien du design (Oslo, 2004) ; la station de métro Sinsen (Oslo, 2005) ; un complexe urbain polyvalent (Trondheim, 2005, en collaboration avec Team Tre) ; le plan et la conception d'une ville nouvelle dans le Sud d'Oslo (2005, pas construite) ; le couvent Notre-Dame de Tautra (île de Tautra, 2004–06) et une piscine thermale, centre thérapeutique et hôtel (Bad Gleichenberg, Autriche, 2005–08, publié ici). Récemment, ils ont travaillé au projet touristique, plates-formes d'observation et ponts, de Gudbrandsjuvet (Gudbrandsjuvet, 2008) ; à l'hôtel paysager Juvet (Gudbrandsjuvet, 2007–09) et à la résidence estivale Giørtz (Valldal, 2012), tous en Norvège, sauf mention contraire.

THERMAL BATH

Therapy Center, and Hotel, Bad Gleichenberg, Austria, 2005–08

Address: Das Kurhaus, Untere Brunnenstr. 40, 8344 Bad Gleichenberg, Austria,
tel: +43 31 59 22 94 / 40 01, www.lifemedicineresort.com. Area: 17 000 m². Client: HCC/Kappa
Cost: €60 million. Collaboration: Domenig Wallner (Local Architect)

Located in a quiet park, this project includes approximately 50 rooms for medical treatment, a four-star hotel with restaurants and cafés, and a public **THERMAL BATH** for patients and other guests. Waiting areas in the treatment rooms center are arrayed around courtyards allowing in daylight and views of the trees, giving the patients "the impression of waiting in the park itself." One of the main aims of the project, according to the architects, "has been to deinstitutionalize the architecture, making it resemble a hospital in as few ways as possible." An advertising firm designed the interior of the complex. The extensive use of wood cladding, together with the green roof, participates in the sustainable aspects of this design, along with the broad use of natural light.

Der in einem ruhigen Kurpark gelegene Komplex umfasst ein Therapiezentrum mit 50 Behandlungsräumen, ein Vier-Sterne-Hotel mit Restaurants und Cafés sowie ein öffentliches **THERMALBAD** für Patienten und externe Gäste. Die Wartebereiche vor den Behandlungsräumen orientieren sich um Innenhöfe. So fällt Tageslicht in den Bau, der Blick in die Bäume vermittelt den Kurenden „das Gefühl, ihre Wartezeit im Park zu verbringen". Eines der Hauptanliegen des Entwurfs war den Architekten zufolge, „der Architektur ihren institutionellen Charakter zu nehmen und ihr so wenig wie möglich das Gesicht einer Klinik zu geben". Eine Agentur gestaltete die Innenräume des Komplexes. Aspekte, die zur Nachhaltigkeit des Entwurfs beitragen, sind der umfassende Einsatz von Holz ebenso wie das begrünte Dach und die ausgeprägte Tageslichtnutzung.

Situé dans un parc tranquille, le complexe se compose d'une cinquantaine de pièces destinées à des traitements médicaux, d'un hôtel quatre étoiles avec restaurants et cafés et d'une **PISCINE THERMALE** publique ouverte aux patients et aux autres visiteurs. Les salles d'attente du centre médical sont disposées autour de cours qui laissent entrer la lumière du jour avec vue sur des arbres afin de donner aux patients « l'impression d'attendre dans le parc même ». L'un des buts principaux des architectes « était de désinstitutionnaliser l'architecture, afin qu'elle ressemble le moins possible à un hôpital ». Une société publicitaire a conçu l'intérieur. L'usage extensif du bois en revêtement compte, avec le toit végétalisé, parmi les caractéristiques durables du bâtiment, de même que l'exploitation intense de la lumière naturelle.

Wood cladding and the green roof of the complex are visible here. Below a first-floor plan of the complex with its network of courtyard spaces.

Hier im Bild die Holzverschalung sowie die begrünten Dächer des Komplexes. Unten ein Grundriss des Erdgeschosses mit seinem Netzwerk von Innenhöfen.

On voit ici le revêtement de bois et le toit végétalisé du complexe. Ci-dessous, un plan du premier niveau avec son réseau de cours.

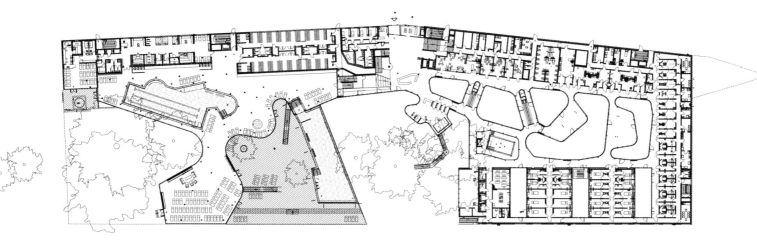

Plans show the relative complexity
of the structure. Below, full-height
glazing and curving walls offer ample
natural life and views through the
complex.

Grundrisse illustrieren die Komplexität der Anlage. Geschosshohe
Verglasung und geschwungene Wände
lassen reichlich Tageslicht in den
Bau einfallen und bieten Durchblicke
durch den gesamten Komplex.

Les plans montrent la relative com-
plexité de l'ensemble. Ci-dessous, le
vitrage pleine hauteur et les courbes
des murs donnent une impression de
grand naturel et permettent de voir à
travers tout le complexe.

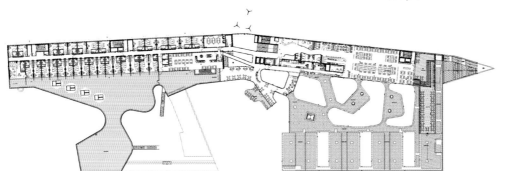

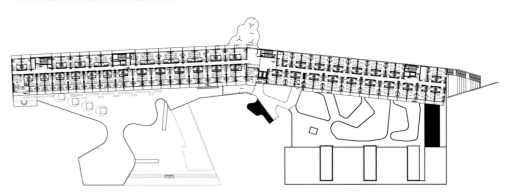

Wood screens are a theme of the building, offering partial views through the space and giving a natural aspect to the whole—confirmed by the wood flooring on the terraces seen here.

Sichtschutzwände aus Holz sind ein Leitmotiv. Durch sie ergeben sich Sichtachsen im Bau, darüber hinaus sorgen sie für natürliche Akzente – unterstrichen wird dieser Eindruck durch die Holzterrassen hier im Bild.

Les panneaux de bois sont repris dans tout le bâtiment, ils permettent des vues partielles de l'espace et confèrent à l'ensemble un effet naturel – souligné par les sols en bois des terrasses que l'on voit ici.

JOHNSEN SCHMALING

Johnsen Schmaling Architects
1699 North Astor Street
Milwaukee, WI 53202
USA

Tel: +1 414 287 9000
Fax: +1 414 287 9025
E-mail: info@johnsenschmaling.com
Web: www.johnsenschmaling.com

BRIAN JOHNSEN received his M.Arch degree from the University of Wisconsin in Milwaukee in 1997. He was a cofounder of Johnsen Schmaling Architects in 2003. **SEBASTIAN SCHMALING** received his M.Arch from the Harvard GSD in 2002. Schmaling, originally from Berlin, had previously attended the University of Wisconsin, where he received another M.Arch degree (1996), and the Technische Universität Berlin, Germany (Vordiplom, Diplom-Ingenieur 1994). He was a cofounder of the firm in 2003 with Brian Johnsen. Their work includes the Storewall corporate headquarters (Milwaukee, 2005); the Camouflage House (Green Lake, 2006); the Blatz Milwaukee, transformation of a former downtown brewery (2006); Celeste 1218, an "urban loft" (Milwaukee, 2007); the Downtown Bar (Milwaukee, 2007–08); and the Ferrous House, a bar and lounge (Spring Prairie, 2007–08, published here). More recently they have worked on the Blur Loft (Milwaukee, 2009); OS House, a sustainable residence (Racine, 2009–10); a studio for a composer (Spring Prairie, 2011); Stacked Cabin (Muscoda, 2011); Topo House (Blue Mounds, 2012), all in Wisconsin; and the Mountain Retreat (Big Sky, Montana, 2013), all in the USA.

BRIAN JOHNSEN absolvierte seinen M. Arch. 1997 an der University of Wisconsin in Milwaukee. 2003 war er Mitbegründer von Johnsen Schmaling Architects. **SEBASTIAN SCHMALING** absolvierte seinen M. Arch. 2002 an der Harvard GSD. Schmaling, ursprünglich aus Berlin, hatte zunächst an der University of Wisconsin studiert, wo er ebenfalls mit einem M. Arch. abschloss (1996), sowie an der Technischen Universität Berlin (Vordiplom, Diplom-Ingenieur 1994). 2003 gründete er mit Brian Johnsen das gemeinsame Büro. Zu ihren Projekten zählen die Firmenzentrale von Storewall (Milwaukee, 2005), das Camouflage House (Green Lake, 2006), Blatz Milwaukee, Umbau einer ehemaligen Brauerei (2006), Celeste 1218, ein „urbanes Loft" (Milwaukee, 2007), die Downtown Bar (Milwaukee, 2007–08) und das Ferrous House, Bar und Lounge (Spring Prairie, 2007–08, hier vorgestellt). In jüngerer Zeit arbeitete das Büro am Blur Loft (Milwaukee, 2009), dem OS House, einem nachhaltigen Einfamilienhaus (Racine, 2009–10), dem Studio für einen Komponisten (Spring Prairie, 2011), der Stacked Cabin (Muscoda, 2011), dem Topo House (Blue Mounds, 2012), alle in Wisconsin, sowie dem Mountain Retreat (Big Sky, Montana, 2013), alle in den USA.

BRIAN JOHNSEN a obtenu son M.Arch. à l'université du Wisconsin de Milwaukee en 1997. Il a été l'un des cofondateurs de Johnsen Schmaling Architects en 2003 avec **SEBASTIAN SCHMALING**. Ce dernier a obtenu son M.Arch. à la Harvard GSD en 2002. Originaire de Berlin, il avait auparavant suivi les cours de l'université du Wisconsin où il a obtenu un autre M.Arch. (1996) et de l'Université technique de Berlin (examen intermédiaire, diplôme d'ingénieur en 1994). Leurs réalisations comprennent le siège de la société Storewall (Milwaukee, 2005) ; la Camouflage House (Green Lake, 2006) ; le Blatz, la transformation d'une ancienne brasserie du centre-ville de Milwaukee (2006) ; Celeste 1218, un « loft urbain » (Milwaukee, 2007) ; le bar Downtown (Milwaukee, 2007–08) et la Ferrous House, un bar et lounge (Spring Prairie, 2007–08, publiée ici). Plus récemment, ils ont travaillé au Blur Loft (Milwaukee, 2009) ; à la OS House, une résidence durable (Racine, 2009–10) ; à un studio pour compositeur (Spring Prairie, 2011) ; à la petite maison Stacked Cabin (Muscoda, 2011) ; à la Topo House (Blue Mounds, 2012), projets tous situés dans le Wisconsin, et à la Mountain Retreat (Big Sky, Montana, 2013), tous aux États-Unis.

FERROUS HOUSE

Spring Prairie, Wisconsin, USA, 2007–08

Address: not disclosed. Area: 121 m²
Client: Eric and J. J. Edstrom. Cost: not disclosed

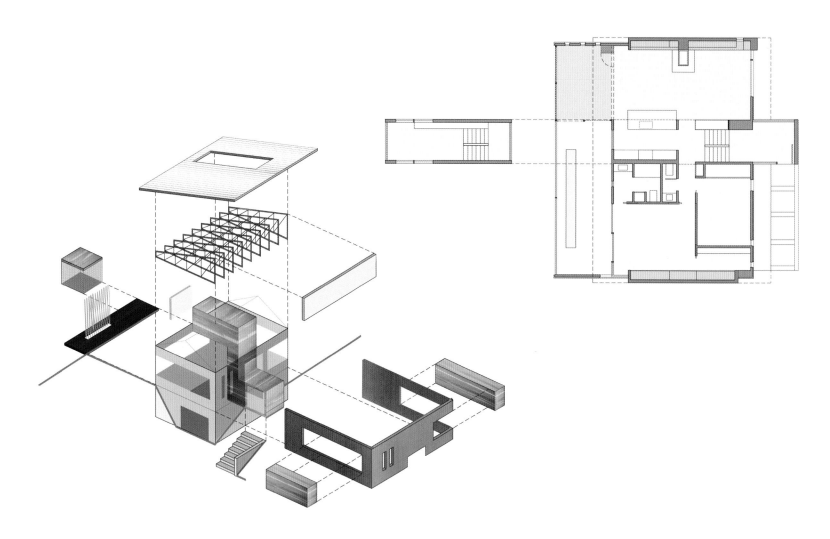

The **FERROUS HOUSE** project involved the "reinvention of a prototypically ill-conceived suburban-production home at the end of its life cycle." Rather than tearing down the old house and rebuilding a new one, the architects took on the task of redesigning it within a limited budget. Foundations, main perimeter walls, and plumbing stacks were reused. The interior was gutted and reorganized to create open, interconnected spaces. Throughout the building, sustainable systems and materials were used, "including low-VOC paints and stains, recycled steel, high-efficiency mechanical systems, Energy Star–rated windows, and locally sourced woods. A high-endurance VaproShield wall membrane and high-efficiency closed-cell expanding foam insulation, sourced from agricultural byproducts to avoid the use of petrochemicals, complement the ventilated perimeter rain screen façade system." Rainwater from the roof is used for natural irrigation of bamboo trees planted near a patio.

Beim **FERROUS HOUSE** ging es darum, „ein geradezu prototypisch schlecht geplantes Vorstadthaus neu zu erfinden, das das Ende seiner Lebensdauer erreicht hatte". Statt den Altbau abzureißen und durch einen Neubau zu ersetzen, stellten sich die Architekten der Herausforderung, das Gebäude in einem knapp gesteckten Budgetrahmen neu zu gestalten. Fundament, Außenwände und Sanitärleitungen wurden beibehalten. Der Bau wurde entkernt und mit ineinandergreifenden Räumen neu organisiert. Im gesamten Haus wurde mit nachhaltigen Systemen und Baustoffen gearbeitet, darunter „schadstoffarmen Farben und Beizen, recyceltem Stahl, Hochleistungshaustechnik, Energiesparfenstern und Holz aus lokaler Forstwirtschaft. Eine hochbeständige Wandmembran (VaproShield) sowie eine hocheffiziente Dämmung aus geschlossenzelligem Dämmschaum aus landwirtschaftlichen Abfallprodukten (um auf petrochemische Produkte verzichten zu können) vervollständigen die vorgehängte hinterlüftete Regenschutzfassade." Regenwasser vom Dach wird zur Bewässerung der Bambuspflanzen an der Terrasse genutzt.

Le projet **FERROUS HOUSE** consistait à « réinventer une maison en fin de vie, produit de banlieue typiquement mal conçu ». Plutôt que de démolir l'ancien bâtiment pour en reconstruire un nouveau, les architectes se sont donné pour tâche de le recomposer avec un budget limité. Les fondations, les principaux murs d'enceinte et les colonnes de plomberie ont été conservés. L'intérieur en revanche a été vidé et réagencé pour créer des espaces ouverts interconnectés. Dans tout le bâtiment, des installations et matériaux durables ont été utilisés, « y compris des peintures et colorants bois à faible teneur en COV, de l'acier recyclé, des systèmes mécaniques haute efficacité, des fenêtres label Energy Star et du bois d'origine locale. Une membrane murale VaproShield très résistante et l'isolation en mousse expansée à cellules fermées haute efficacité, issues de sous-produits agricoles afin d'éviter les produits pétrochimiques, complètent le système périmétrique d'écran pare-pluie ventilé de la façade ». L'eau de pluie qui s'écoule du toit est récupérée pour l'irrigation naturelle de bambous plantés près d'un patio.

Below, before and after views of the house show that the original is quite different from the result. Left page, floor plan and an exploded axonometric drawing show the make-up of the house.

Vorher-/Nachherbilder (unten) belegen, wie stark sich der Vorgängerbau vom Neubau unterscheidet. Grundriss und axonometrische Explosionszeichnung auf der linken Seite veranschaulichen die Anlage des Hauses.

Ci-dessous, vues de la maison avant et après où l'on voit bien que l'original est très différent du résultat. Page de gauche, plan de l'étage et schéma axonométrique éclaté qui montrent l'assemblage de la maison.

Wood on ceilings, some wall surfaces and floors gives a feeling of continuity to the interior, while large windows establish a connection with the exterior.

Der Einsatz von Holz für Decken, einzelne Wandflächen und Böden sorgt für Kontinuität. Die großflächigen Fenster schaffen Verbindungen nach außen.

Le bois des plafonds, de certaines surfaces des murs et des sols donne un sentiment de continuité à l'intérieur, tandis que les grandes fenêtres établissent un lien avec l'extérieur.

TAIJI KAWANO

Taiji Kawano Architects
2–13–11 Takasago
Katsushika
Tokyo 125–0054
Japan

Tel: +81 3 5668 4415
Fax: +81 3 5668 4415
E-mail: info@tk-arc.jp
Web: www.tk-arc.jp

TAIJI KAWANO was born in 1964 in Fukuoka. He received his Bachelor of Engineering degree from Kyushu University in 1988. He worked from 1990 to 2000 in the Kohyama Atelier and established his own firm, Taiji Kawano Architects, in 2001. He has been a Lecturer at the University of Tokyo since 2002. His work includes the I.S.S. Space Museum Project (Inabe, Mie, in collaboration with Yoshito Tomioka, 2001); CoCo Project (Kokonoe, Oita, 2002); J Panel Furniture (2003); Town House in Sendagi, Renovation (Bunkyo-ku, Tokyo, 2005); Town House in Takasago (Katsushika, Tokyo, 2006); Yayoi Auditorium Annex, University of Tokyo (Bunkyo-ku, Tokyo, 2007–08, published here); House at Niiza (Niiza, Saitama, 2008); and Ocha House, Ochanomizu University (Bunkyo-ku, Tokyo, in collaboration with Nobihisa Motooka, 2009), all in Japan. Recent work includes a New Dormitory for Ochanomizu University (Bunkyo-ku, Tokyo, in collaboration with Nobihisa Motooka, 2011).

TAIJI KAWANO wurde 1964 in Fukuoka geboren. Sein Studium an der Universität Kyushu schloss er 1988 mit einem Bachelor in Ingenieurwissenschaften ab. Von 1990 bis 2000 arbeitete er im Atelier Kohyama und gründete 2001 sein eigenes Büro, Taiji Kawano Architects. Seit 2002 ist er Dozent an der Universität Tokio. Zu seinen Projekten zählen das I.S.S. Space Museum Project (Inabe, Mie, in Zusammenarbeit mit Yoshito Tomioka, 2001), das CoCo Project (Kokonoe, Oita, 2002), die Möbelserie „J Panel" (2003), die Sanierung eines Stadthauses in Sendagi (Bunkyo-ku, Tokio, 2005), ein Stadthaus in Takasago (Katsushika, Tokio, 2006), der Anbau an das Yayoi-Auditorium der Universität Tokio (Bunkyo-ku, Tokio, 2007–08, hier vorgestellt), ein Haus in Niiza (Niiza, Saitama, 2008) sowie das Haus Ocha an der Ochanomizu-Universität (Bunkyo-ku, Tokio, in Zusammenarbeit mit Nobihisa Motooka, 2009), alle in Japan. Zu seinen jüngeren Projekten zählt das neue Wohnheim für die Ochanomizu-Universität (Bunkyo-ku, Tokio, in Zusammenarbeit mit Nobihisa Motooka, 2011).

TAIJI KAWANO est né en 1964 à Fukuoka. Il obtient son diplôme d'ingénieur de l'université de Kyushu en 1988. Il travaille de 1990 à 2000 dans l'atelier Kohyama et fonde sa propre agence, Taiji Kawano Architects, en 2001. Il est maître de conférences à l'université de Tokyo depuis 2002. Ses projets réalisés incluent l'I.S.S. Space Museum Project (Inabe, Mie, en collaboration avec Yoshito Tomioka, 2001) ; CoCo Project (Kokonoe, Oita, 2002) ; le mobilier J Panel (2003) ; la rénovation d'un hôtel particulier à Sendagi, (Bunkyo-ku, Tokyo, 2005) ; un hôtel particulier à Takasago (Katsushika, Tokyo, 2006) ; l'annexe de l'auditorium Yayoi de l'université de Tokyo (Bunkyo-ku, Tokyo, 2007–08, publié ici) ; une maison à Niiza (Niiza, Saitama, 2008) et la maison expérimentale Ocha de l'université d'Ochanomizu (Bunkyo-ku, Tokyo, en collaboration avec Nobihisa Motooka, 2009), tous situés au Japon. Un projet récent est une nouvelle résidence universitaire pour l'université d'Ochanomizu (Bunkyo-ku, Tokyo, en collaboration avec Nobihisa Motooka, 2011).

YAYOI AUDITORIUM ANNEX

University of Tokyo, Bunkyo-ku, Tokyo, Japan, 2007–08

Address: 7–3–1 Hongo, Bunkyo-ku, Tokyo 113–8654, Japan
Area: 479 m². Client: University of Tokyo. Cost: not disclosed
Collaboration: Tomoya Nabeno (Staff), Masahiro Inayama (Structural Engineering),
Naoto Ando (Professor of Architecture, University of Tokyo)

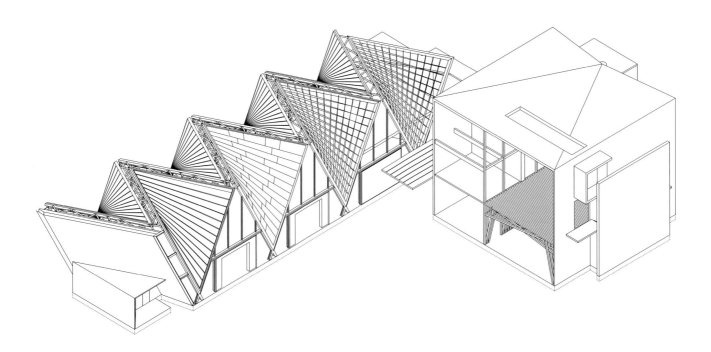

The repetitive folding form of the Annex again contrasts with the more blocky appearance of the earlier building. This is visible in both the drawing above and the photo.

Das repetitive Faltmuster des Anbaus steht im Kontrast zur eher kubischen Erscheinungsform des vorhandenem Gebäudes. Zeichnung (oben) und Foto zeigen dies deutlich.

La forme plissée répétitive de l'annexe contraste avec l'aspect plus cubique du bâtiment existant, comme on peut le voir sur le dessin ci-dessus et sur la photo.

This new Auditorium Annex is situated in a green zone of the University of Tokyo, on the north side of the front gate, near Hongo Street. The structure was situated to avoid cutting mature trees. The architect and client decided on a wood building, based on a hyperbolic paraboloid shell. Models in half scale and then on a full scale were made of the shell to find the appropriate ways to fix the plywood without causing it to twist. Exterior cladding is in sheet copper, ThermoWood (Japanese cedar), and plaster (FMX). Floors on the ground level are in polished concrete, while Japanese cedar is used on the upper level. Red cedar is used on walls and ceilings and, for other wall areas, Randomized Strand Board (Japanese cypress). The architect places a great deal of emphasis on the green, shaded surroundings. "If a lot of people experience the place as they would the shade of a tree in the forest that filters natural light, in the center of the city, that is great."

Der Hörsaalanbau liegt in einem Grünbereich der Universität Tokio, nördlich des Haupttors, unweit der Hongostraße. Die Lage des Baus wurde so gewählt, dass kein alter Baum gefällt werden musste. Architekt und Auftraggeber verständigten sich auf einen Holzbau aus einer hyperbolischen Parabolschale. Modelle in halber und schließlich in voller Größe wurden vorab gefertigt, um zu ermitteln, wie sich das Sperrholz fixieren lässt, ohne sich zu verdrehen. Die äußere Verschalung besteht aus Kupferplatten, ThermoWood (japanische Zeder) und Putz (FMX). Die Böden im Erdgeschoss sind aus poliertem Beton, im Obergeschoss kam japanische Zeder zum Einsatz. Für Wände und Decken wurde Rotzeder verwendet, für weitere Wandflächen RSB (japanische Zypresse). Besonderen Wert legte der Architekt auf das grüne, schattige Umfeld: „Es wäre schön, wenn viele Menschen diesen Ort wie den Schatten eines Baums im Wald erleben würden, der natürliches Licht filtert – und das mitten in der Stadt."

Cette nouvelle annexe de l'auditorium est implantée dans une zone verte de l'université de Tokyo, du côté nord du portail, près de la rue Hongo. Le bâtiment a été placé de manière à éviter de couper les arbres adultes. L'architecte et le client ont décidé d'un bâtiment en bois, basé sur le principe d'une coque en forme de paraboloïde hyperbolique. Des maquettes à demi-échelle, puis à l'échelle, ont été construites pour trouver la manière appropriée de fixer le contreplaqué sans le fausser. Les revêtements externes utilisent du cuivre en feuilles, du ThermoWood (cèdre du Japon), et de l'enduit (FMX). Les sols du rez-de-chaussée sont en béton poli, tandis que le cèdre du Japon est utilisé à l'étage. On a utilisé du cèdre rouge pour les murs et les plafonds, et pour d'autres surfaces de mur, des panneaux de particules à orientation aléatoire (cyprès du Japon). L'architecte attache beaucoup d'importance à l'environnement végétal ombragé. «Que beaucoup de gens puissent ressentir ce lieu au cœur de la ville comme la sensation procurée par l'ombre d'un arbre dans une forêt filtrant la lumière naturelle, en pleine ville, c'est formidable ! »

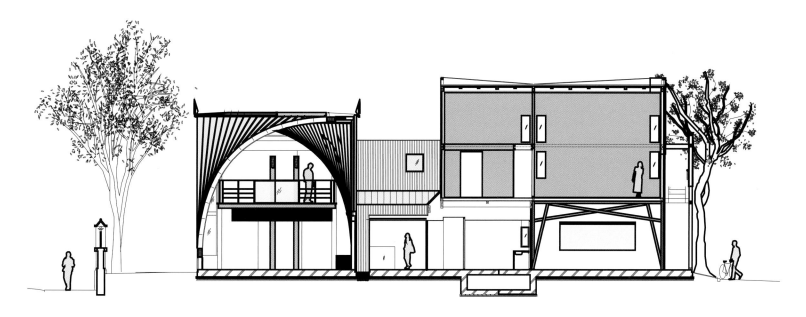

A section drawing above shows the relation of the Annex (left) to the original structure.

Der Querschnitt oben illustriert das Verhältnis zwischen Anbau (links) und vorhandenem Gebäude.

Une coupe, ci-dessus, montre la relation de l'annexe (à gauche) avec le bâtiment d'origine.

The structures have a light design with wood as the dominant material. Trees nearby contribute to the airiness of the overall site.

Die Bauten wirken leicht, Holz ist das prägende Material. Auch die Bäume tragen zum luftigen Eindruck der Gesamtanlage bei.

Les structures légères sont construites essentiellement en bois. La proximité des arbres contribue à l'aspect aéré de l'ensemble du site.

The arching roof forms descend to floor level, leaving full-height glazed openings between each roof sequence. Right, the Annex is visible at the top of this site drawing.

Die gewölbeartigen Dachsegmente reichen bis auf den Boden herab. Zwischen den einzelnen Sequenzen sind raumhohe Glasfronten eingefügt. Auf dem Lageplan rechts ist der Anbau im oberen Bereich zu erkennen.

Les voussures du toit descendent jusqu'au niveau du sol, avec des baies vitrées occupant toute la hauteur comprise entre les éléments de toiture consécutifs. À droite, l'annexe est visible en haut du plan de situation.

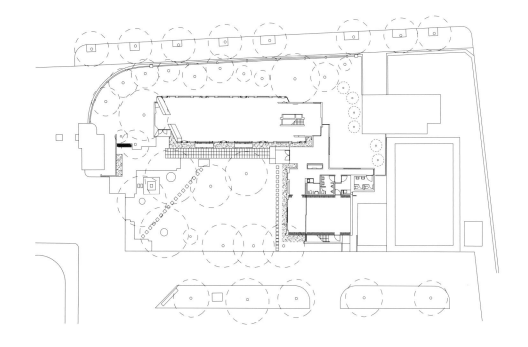

BENJAMIN KRAMPULZ

bkarch / Benjamin Krampulz
Avenue de Gilamont 46
1800 Vevey
Switzerland

Tel: +41 21 921 67 89
Fax: +41 21 921 59 89
E-mail: bonjour@bkar.ch
Web: www.bkar.ch

BENJAMIN KRAMPULZ was born in Alba Iulia, Romania, in 1980. He completed an apprenticeship in carpentry in Germany (2002), before studying architecture at the University of Stuttgart (2002) and at the EPFL (Lausanne, 2005–06). He worked in the office of Bonnard Woeffrey (Monthey, 2006/2008–10) before and after obtaining his M.Arch (University of Stuttgart, 2008). He created his firm, bkarch, in Vevey, Switzerland, in 2011. Recent work includes the Transformation of a Barn (Gluringen, Valais, 2011, published here); a competition for the cafeteria of the Château de Chillon (with Laurent Fesselet, Veytaux, 2013); another competition for a primary school (with Laurent Fesselet, Les Collines, Sion, 2013); the transformation of a villa (Clarens, 2013); and an ongoing apartment building project (Monthey, 2013), all in Switzerland.

BENJAMIN KRAMPULZ wurde 1980 im rumänischen Alba Iulia geboren. Er absolvierte in Deutschland eine Ausbildung zum Tischler (2002), bevor er an der Universität Stuttgart (2002) und an der EPFL (Lausanne, 2005–06) Architektur studierte. Bevor er seinen Master in Architektur erwarb (Universität Stuttgart, 2008) und danach, arbeitete Krampulz im Büro von Bonnard Woeffrey (Monthey, 2006, 2008–10). Seine Firma bkarch gründete er 2011 im schweizerischen Vevey. Zu seinen jüngeren Projekten zählen u. a. transformation stall (Gluringen, Wallis, 2011, hier vorgestellt), ein Wettbewerb für die Cafeteria des Château de Chillon (mit Laurent Fesselet, Veytaux, 2013), ein weiterer Wettbewerb für eine Grundschule (mit Laurent Fesselet, Les Collines, Sion, 2013), der Umbau einer Villa (Clarens, 2013) sowie ein Apartmentgebäude (Monthey, 2013); alle in der Schweiz.

BENJAMIN KRAMPULZ est né à Alba Iulia, Roumanie, en 1980. Il a suivi un apprentissage de menuiserie en Allemagne (2002) avant d'étudier l'architecture à l'université de Stuttgart (2002) et à l'EPFL (Lausanne, 2005–06). Il a travaillé dans l'agence de Bonnard Woeffrey (Monthey, 2006/2008–10) avant et après l'obtention de son master en architecture (université de Stuttgart, 2008). Il a créé sa propre agence, bkarch, à Vevey, Suisse en 2011. Parmi ses œuvres récentes figurent la reconversion d'une grange (Gluringen, Valais, 2011, publié ici) ; un concours pour la cafétéria du château de Chillon (avec Laurent Fesselet, Veytaux, 2013) ; un autre concours d'école primaire (avec Laurent Fesselet, Les Collines, Sion, 2013) ; la transformation d'une villa (Clarens, 2013) et un projet d'appartement en cours (Monthey, 2013), tous en Suisse.

TRANSFORMATION OF A BARN

Gluringen, Valais, Switzerland, 2011

Address: Dorfstrasse, Parzelle 1312, Gluringen, Valais, Switzerland
Area: 80 m². Client: not disclosed. Cost: €320 000

This project involved the transformation of an existing barn into a holiday residence in the German-speaking part of the Canton of Valais. Set at an altitude of 1400 meters, the larch-wood barn was built in 1932. Fire regulations required that the barn be displaced and the architect took advantage of the change to increase ceiling heights, introduce insulation, and allow for more natural light and views of the mountains. Benjamin Krampulz sought to maintain the appearance of the original barn as much as possible. Divided into three levels, the residence includes a bedroom, technical and storage areas, and a bathroom on the ground floor, a living area on the upper floor, and a suspended gallery above with space for an extra bed.

Für dieses Projekt im deutschsprachigen Teil des Kantons Wallis wurde eine Scheune aus Lärchenholz, errichtet 1932 auf 1400 m Höhe, zu einem Ferienhaus umgebaut. Da die Scheune wegen der Feuerschutzbestimmungen versetzt werden musste, ergriff der Architekt die Gelegenheit, die Deckenhöhe zu vergrößern, Dämmmaterialien einzubringen und für mehr Licht und freie Sicht auf das Bergpanorama zu sorgen. Benjamin Krampulz lag daran, so viel vom Erscheinungsbild der Scheune zu erhalten wie möglich. Das über drei Ebenen verfügende Ferienhaus hat im Erdgeschoss ein Schlafzimmer, Versorgungs- und Abstellräume sowie ein Badezimmer, im Obergeschoss einen Wohnbereich sowie eine abgehängte Galerie mit Platz für ein Extrabett.

Ce projet consiste en la reconversion d'une grange en maison de vacances dans la partie germanophone du canton du Valais. Située à une altitude de 1400 m, la grange en mélèze a été construite en 1932. Tirant profit de la réglementation sur l'incendie qui imposait le remplacement de la grange, l'architecte a augmenté les hauteurs sous plafond, ajouté une isolation thermique et augmenté l'éclairage naturel ainsi que le nombre de vues sur les montagnes. Benjamin Krampulz s'est efforcé de conserver l'apparence de la grange d'origine autant que possible. Répartie sur trois niveaux, la résidence comprend une chambre à coucher, des locaux techniques et de stockage et une salle de bains au rez-de-chaussée, une salle de séjour à l'étage et une galerie suspendue au-dessus pouvant accueillir un lit supplémentaire.

The exterior of the barn is typical of structures seen in the Valais area of Switzerland, where the original wood is blackened by the passage of time. Interiors are bright and airy, as seen to the left.

Das Äußere der Scheune mit ihrer im Lauf der Zeit dunkler gewordenen Holzfassade ist typisch für das schweizerische Wallis. Der Innenraum links mutet hell und luftig an.

L'extérieur de la grange est typique des structures de la région du Valais suisse où le bois d'origine noircit au fil du temps. Les intérieurs sont lumineux et aérés, comme vu sur la gauche.

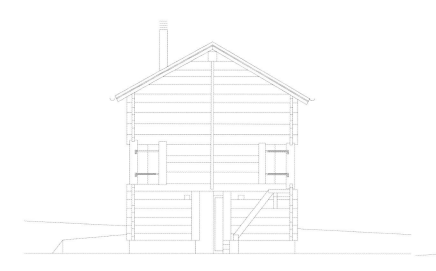
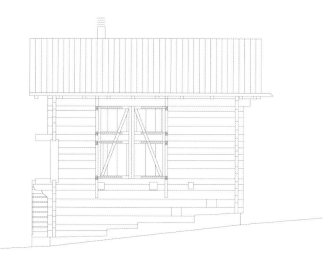

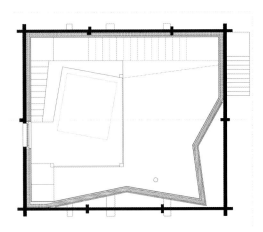
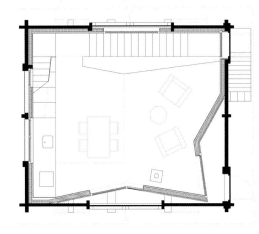
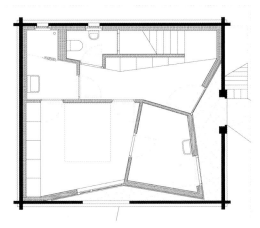

Plans show the angled walls that have been added to the rectangular space. Light-colored wood is complemented by the use of brightly painted surfaces that reflect their color in the daylight.

Auf den Plänen sind die in den rechteckigen Raum eingesetzten schrägen Wände zu erkennen. Leuchtend gestrichene Oberflächen ergänzen das helle Holz, das bei Tageslicht deren Farbe reflektiert.

Les plans montrent les murs formant des angles qui ont été ajoutés à l'espace rectangulaire. Le bois clair est complété par quelques surfaces vivement colorées qui reflètent leur couleur dans la lumière du jour.

KENGO KUMA

Kengo Kuma & Associates
2–24–8 Minamiaoyama
Minato-ku, Tokyo 107–0062
Japan

Tel: +81 3 3401 7721 / Fax: +81 3 3401 7778
E-mail: kuma@ba2.so-net.ne.jp / Web: www.kkaa.co.jp

Born in 1954 in Kanagawa, Japan, **KENGO KUMA** graduated in 1979 from the University of Tokyo with an M.Arch degree. In 1985–86 he received an Asian Cultural Council Fellowship Grant and was a Visiting Scholar at Columbia University. In 1987 he established the Spatial Design Studio, and in 1991 he created Kengo Kuma & Associates. His work includes the Karuizawa Resort Hotel (Karuizawa, 1993); Kiro-san Observatory (Ehime, 1994); Atami Guesthouse, for Bandai Corp (Atami, 1992–95); the Japanese Pavilion for the Venice Biennale (Venice, Italy, 1995); Tomioka Lakewood Golf Club House (Tomioka, 1993–96); and Toyoma Noh-Theater (Miyagi, 1995–96). He has also completed the Great (Bamboo) Wall Guesthouse (Beijing, China, 2002); One Omotesando (Tokyo, 2003); LVMH Osaka (Osaka, 2004); the Nagasaki Prefectural Art Museum (Nagasaki, 2005); and the Zhongtai Box, Z58 building (Shanghai, China, 2003–06). Recent work includes the Steel House (Bunkyo-ku, Tokyo, 2005–07); Sakenohana (London, UK, 2007); Tiffany Ginza (Tokyo, 2008); Jugetsudo (Paris, France, 2008, published here); Nezu Museum (Tokyo, 2007–09); Museum of Kanayama (Ota City, Gunma, 2009); Glass Wood House (New Canaan, Connecticut, USA, 2007–10); Yusuhara Marche (Yusuhara, Kochi, 2009–10); the GC Prostho Museum Research Center (Torii Matsu Machi, Aichi, 2009–10, also published here); the Yusuhara Wooden Bridge Museum (Yusuhara-cho, Takaoka-gun, Kochi, 2010); Café Kureon (Toyama, 2010–11); and Starbucks, Dazaifu Omotesando (Dazaifu, Fukuoka, 2011), all in Japan unless stated otherwise.

KENGO KUMA, geboren 1954 in Kanagawa, Japan, schloss sein Studium 1979 an der Universität Tokyo mit einem M.Arch. ab. 1985/86 hatte er ein Stipendium des Asian Cultural Council und war Gastdozent an der Columbia University. 1987 gründete er zunächst sein Spatial Design Studio, 1991 dann Kengo Kuma & Associates. Zu seinen Projekten zählen die Hotelanlage Karuizawa (Karuizawa, 1993), das Observatorium Kiro-san (Ehime, 1994), ein Gästehaus für die Bandai Corp (Atami, 1992 bis 1995), der Japanische Pavillon für die Biennale in Venedig (Italien, 1995), ein Klubhaus für den Tomioka Lakewood Golfclub (Tomioka, 1993–96) und das No-Theater in Toyoma (Miyagi, 1995–96). Darüber hinaus realisierte er das Gästehaus Great (Bamboo) Wall (Peking, 2002), One Omotesando (Tokio, 2003), LVMH Osaka (Osaka, 2004), das Kunstmuseum der Präfektur Nagasaki (Nagasaki, 2005) sowie die Zhongtai Box, Z58 (Schanghai, 2003–06). Jüngere Projekte sind u. a. das Steel House (Bunkyo-ku, Tokio, 2005–07), Sakenohana (London, 2007), Tiffany Ginza (Tokio, 2008), das Jugetsudo (Paris, 2008, hier vorgestellt), das Nezu-Museum (Tokio, 2007–09), das Museum der Burgruine von Kanayama (Ota, Gunma, 2009), das Glass Wood House (New Canaan, Connecticut, 2007–10), Yusuhara Marché (Yusuhara, Kochi, 2009–10), das Forschungszentrum am GC Prostho Museum (Torii Matsu Machi, Aichi, 2009–10, ebenfalls hier vorgestellt), das Yusuhara Wooden Bridge Museum (Yusuhara-cho, Takaoka-gun, Kochi, 2010), Café Kureon (Toyama, 2010–11) und Starbucks, Dazaifu Omotesando (Dazaifu, Fukuoka, 2011), alle in Japan, sofern nicht anders angegeben.

Né en 1954 à Kanagawa (Japon), **KENGO KUMA** est diplômé (M.Arch.) de l'université de Tokyo (1979). En 1985–86, il bénéficie d'une bourse de l'Asian Cultural Council et devient chercheur invité à l'université Columbia. En 1987, il crée le Spatial Design Studio et, en 1991, Kengo Kuma & Associates. Parmi ses réalisations : l'hôtel de vacances Karuizawa (Karuizawa, 1993) ; l'observatoire Kiro-san (Ehime, 1994) ; la maison d'hôtes d'Atami pour Bandai Corp (Atami, 1992–95) ; le Pavillon japonais pour la Biennale de Venise (1995) ; le club-house du golf du lac de Tomioka (Tomioka, 1993–96) et le théâtre de nô Toyoma (Miyagi, 1995–96). Il a également réalisé la maison d'hôtes de la Grande Muraille (de bambou) (Pékin, 2002) ; l'immeuble One Omotesando (Tokyo, 2003) ; l'immeuble LVMH Osaka (2004) ; le Musée d'art de la préfecture de Nagasaki (Nagasaki, 2005) et l'immeuble Zhongtai Box, Z58 (Shanghai, 2003–06). Plus récemment, il a construit la Steel House (Bunkyo-ku, Tokyo, 2005–07) ; le restaurant Sakenohana (Londres, 2007) ; l'immeuble Tiffany Ginza (Tokyo, 2008) ; le salon de thé Jugetsudo (Paris, 2008, publié ici) ; le musée Nezu (Tokyo, 2007–09) ; le musée de Kanayama (Ota, Gunma ; 2009) ; la Glass Wood House (New Canaan, Connecticut, 2007–10) ; le marché de Yusuhara (Yusuhara, Kochi, 2009–10) ; le centre de recherches du musée GC Prostho (Torii Matsu Machi, Aichi, 2009–10, également publié ici) ; le musée du Pont de bois de Yusuhara (Yusuhara-cho, Takaoka-gun, Kochi, 2010) ; le café Kureon (Toyama, 2010–11) et le Starbucks de Dazaifu Omotesando (Dazaifu, Fukuoka, 2011), tous au Japon, sauf mention contraire.

GC PROSTHO MUSEUM RESEARCH CENTER

Torii Matsu Machi, Aichi, Japan, 2009–10

Address: 2–294 Torii Matsu Machi, Kasugai-shi, Aichi, Japan
Area: 626 m². Client: GC Corporation
Cost: not disclosed. Collaboration: Shin Ohba, Sayaka Mizuno

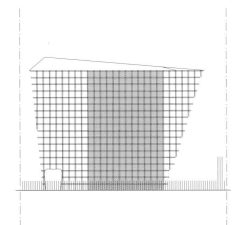
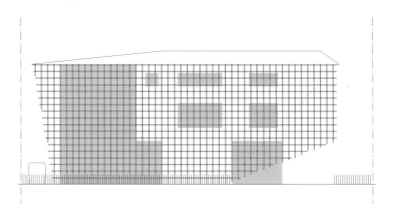

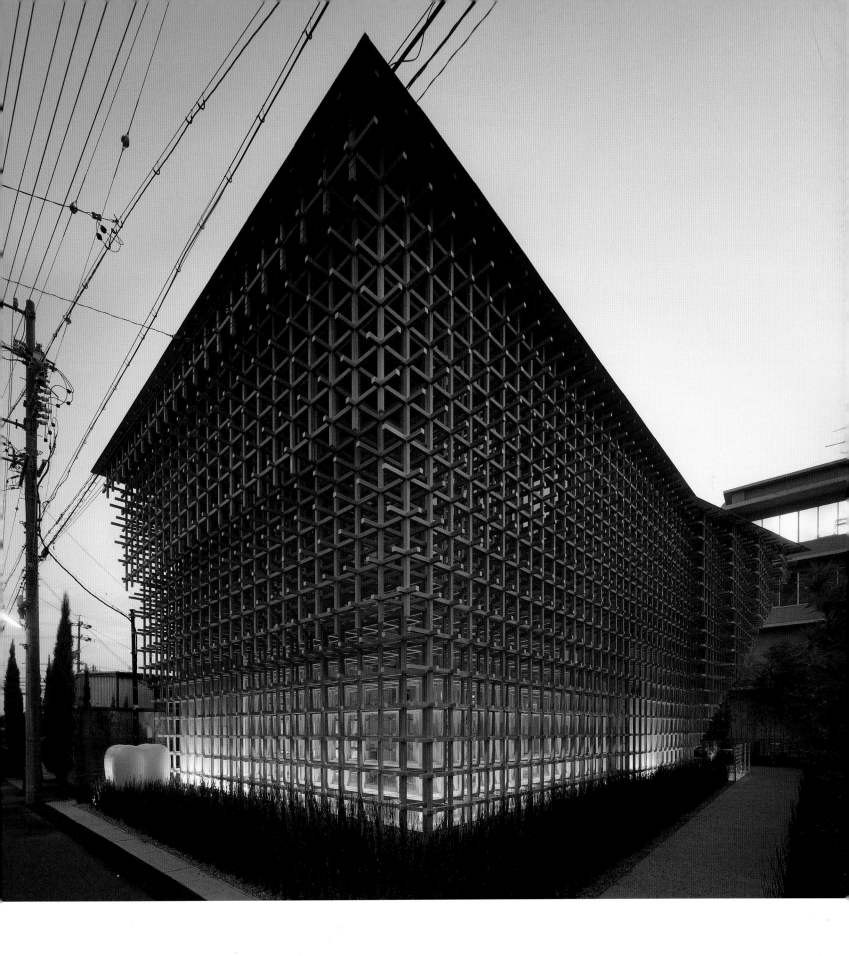

Kengo Kuma speaks of "forgetting about ready-made details in order to carve and cook materials in new and different ways." He has certainly done that in this building for a dental care company located in central Japan.

Kengo Kuma spricht davon, „Fertigbauelemente zu vergessen, um Materialien auf neue, andere Weise zu erfinden und zu erarbeiten". Bei diesem Gebäude für eine Zahnpflegefirma in Zentraljapan ist ihm das zweifellos gelungen.

Kengo Kuma parle « d'oublier le préfabriqué pour travailler les matériaux de façon nouvelle et différente ».
C'est ce qu'il a fait pour ce bâtiment d'une entreprise de matériel dentaire située dans le centre du Japon.

The architect used an old Japanese toy, the Cidori, a flexible assembly of wooden sticks with very particular joints, to inspire the design of this museum research center. The extendable nature of the original toy was tested by the structural engineer Jun Sato at the larger scale required for a building. He confirmed that the mechanism of the toy could indeed be used for architecture. The 10-meter-high structure has three stories above grade and one below. Kengo Kuma states: "We worked on the project in the hope that the era of machine-made architecture would be over, and that human beings would build again by themselves." The concept is certainly original.

Beim Entwurf dieses Forschungszentrums eines Museums ließ sich der Architekt von einem alten japanischen Spielzeug, dem Cidori inspirieren, einem Baukasten mit Holzstäben, die sich durch spezielle Gelenkverbindungen auszeichnen. Dass sich das Spielzeug in der Tat auf einen soviel größeren Maßstab übertragen ließ, der für den Bau eines Gebäudes erforderlich war, wurde eigens vom Statiker Jun Sato geprüft. Er bestätigte, dass sich das Prinzip des Baukasten tatsächlich architektonisch nutzen ließ. Der 10 m hohe Bau hat drei oberirdische Ebenen sowie ein Untergeschoss. Kengo Kuma erklärt: „Wir arbeiteten an diesem Projekt in der Hoffnung, dass die Ära der maschinengefertigten Architektur beendet ist und Menschen wieder selbst bauen." Zweifellos ein unverwechselbares Konzept.

Le cidori, ancien jeu de construction japonais fait de bâtonnets de bois reliés par des joints d'un type très particulier, a inspiré la conception de ce centre de recherche d'un musée. Extensible par sa nature même, ce principe de construction a été testé par l'ingénieur structurel Jun Sato à l'échelle du bâtiment, qui a confirmé sa validité en architecture. La construction de 10 m de haut s'étage sur quatre niveaux dont un en sous-sol. Pour Kengo Kuma : « Nous avons travaillé sur ce projet dans l'espoir que la fin de l'ère de l'architecture mécaniste approche et que les êtres humains recommencent à construire par eux-mêmes. » Ce concept ne manque pas d'originalité.

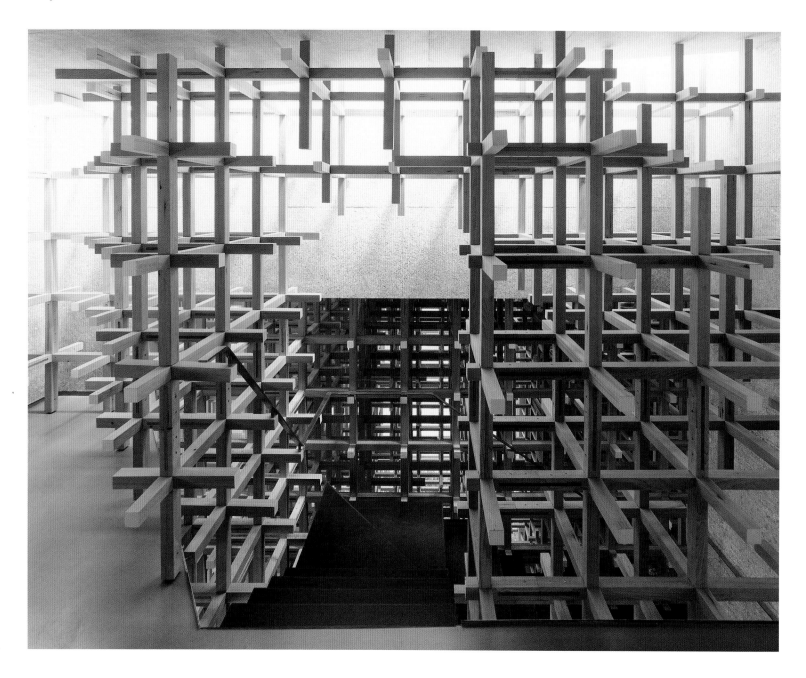

Using a children's wooden stick assembly toy as his source of inspiration, the architect develops a gridded web of wood that attains an unusual and haunting presence.

Inspiriert von einem Holzsteckkasten für Kinder entwickelte der Architekt ein Gitterwerk aus Holz, das von ungewöhnlicher und faszinierender Präsenz ist.

S'inspirant d'un jeu d'assemblage de pièces de bois pour enfants, l'architecte a mis au point une structure de tasseaux de bois d'une fascinante présence.

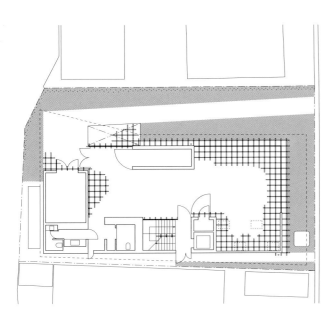

As the drawing to the left and the photos show, the wooden grid has a varying presence and density, but, in the case of the image above, there is a distinct impression that temple architecture has influenced Kuma.

Wie Zeichnung und Aufnahmen belegen, ist das Gitterwerk von unterschiedlich starker Präsenz und Dichte. Besonders oben im Bild scheint es, als wäre Kuma von Tempelarchitektur beeinflusst worden.

Comme le montre le plan à gauche et les photographies, la densité et la force de la présence de la trame de bois varient. Dans l'image ci-dessus, il semble que Kuma se soit inspiré de l'architecture des temples japonais.

JUGETSUDO
Paris, France, 2008

Address: 95 Rue de Seine, 75006 Paris, France,
+33 1 46 33 94 90, www.jugetsudo.fr. Floor area: 75 m². Client: Maruyama Nori Co. Ltd.
Cost: not disclosed. Collaboration: MCH (Local Architects)

Below, the store seen from the street. A plan is seen on the opposite page, as well as an interior view looking toward the Rue de Seine.

Unten das Geschäft von der Straße aus gesehen; gegenüberliegende Seite: ein Grundriss und ein Blick aus dem Laden auf die Rue de Seine.

Ci-dessous, la boutique vue depuis la rue. Sur la page opposée, un plan et une vue intérieure donnant sur la rue de Seine.

The Hinoki wood counter was designed by Kengo Kuma and manufactured by Nomura kougei, as were the shelves and suspended bamboo feature.

Die Theke aus Hinoki-Holz wurde ebenfalls von Kengo Kuma entworfen und von Nomura kougei hergestellt wie auch die Regale und die hängenden Bambuselemente.

Le comptoir en bois d'hinoki également dessiné par Kuma, a été fabriqué par Nomura kougei, de même que les étagères et les éléments décoratifs en bambou suspendus.

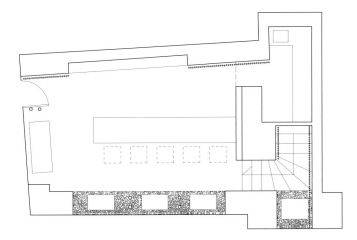

This is a tearoom located at the corner of the Rue de Seine and the Rue des Quatre Vents in Paris. The main space is on the ground level, with an old stone basement below. The Japanese elements in the design, and in particular the hanging bamboo, with stone arrangements along the bottom of the storefront windows, immediately set this space apart from other, more obviously French décors in neighboring boutiques. "I wanted to create a space like a bamboo thicket," says the architect Kengo Kuma. "In the thicket floats a different kind of air and light from those of our daily lives. At the center of this unique space, we placed a solid, jointless board of Japanese cypress. Cypress was a special tree in that it was believed to smoothen the things put on it. Our idea was that people could feel the nature of Japan on that board. In the underground lies a stone tearoom. In the stone cave that rests in Paris underground the teas might show another quality." The client's motto, blending a sense of tradition with one of "renewal," seems to fit well with this small but very attractive space.

Dies ist eine Teestube an der Ecke der Rue de Seine und der Rue de Quatre Vents in Paris. Der Hauptraum liegt im Erdgeschoss über einem alten Natursteinfundament. Die japanischen Elemente des Entwurfs, besonders der hängende Bambus und das Natursteinarrangement unter den Schaufenstern des Lokals, heben diesen Raum deutlich von anderen, französisch inspirierten Dekors in den benachbarten Läden ab. „Ich wollte einen Raum schaffen, der einem Bambusdickicht gleicht", sagt der Architekt Kengo Kuma. „Darin herrschen eine andere Luft und ein anderes Licht als in unserem Alltag. In den Mittelpunkt dieses einzigartigen Raums setzten wir ein massives, fugenloses Brett aus japanischem Zypressenholz. Die Zypresse war ein besonderer Baum, weil man glaubte, sie würde die Dinge glätten, die man darauf stellte. Unsere Idee war, dass die Menschen die Natur Japans an diesem Brett spüren können. Im Untergeschoss befindet sich ein steinerner Teeraum. In diesem Steingewölbe im Pariser Untergrund kann der Tee eine andere Qualität annehmen." Der Vorstellung des Bauherrn von einer Verbindung aus Tradition und „Erneuerung" scheint dieser kleine, aber sehr attraktive Raum durchaus zu entsprechen.

Ce salon de thé a ouvert à l'angle de la rue de Seine et de celle des Quatre-Vents à Paris. Le volume principal du rez-de-chaussée se prolonge en sous-sol par une cave voûtée en pierre. Les éléments japonais du projet et, en particulier, les bambous suspendus ou la présence de galets dans les vitrines distinguent immédiatement ce lieu de la décoration manifestement plus française des boutiques avoisinantes. « Je voulais créer un espace qui évoque un bosquet de bambous », a expliqué Kengo Kuma. « Dans un bosquet flotte toujours un air et une lumière différents de ce que nous vivons au quotidien. Au centre de cet espace très particulier, nous avons placé des planches de cyprès japonais massif, sans joint. Le cyprès jouissait jadis d'un statut spécial, car on croyait qu'il donnait de la douceur à tout ce qui était posé sur lui. Notre idée a été que les visiteurs pourraient ressentir la nature même du Japon en marchant sur ces planches. En sous-sol, se trouve un salon de thé aux murs en pierre apparente. Dans cette cave minérale nichée dans le sous-sol parisien, les thés peuvent faire montre d'autres qualités. » Le propos du client – fusionner le sens de la tradition avec celui du « renouveau » – semble avoir bien été traduit dans cet espace certes petit, mais très séduisant.

At the counter, the Sen Chairs were designed by Kengo Kuma and manufactured by Knoll. Left page, the level below grade.

Die Sen-Stühle an der Theke stammen von Kengo Kuma und wurden von Knoll produziert. Auf der gegenüberliegenden Seite das Untergeschoss.

Les chaises Sen du comptoir ont été dessinées par Kengo Kuma et fabriquées par Knoll. Sur la page de gauche, le sous-sol.

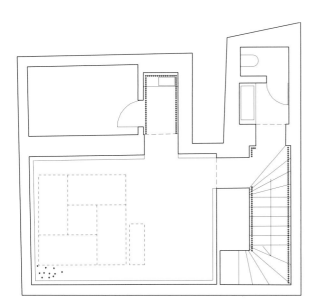

LASSILA HIRVILAMMI

OOPEAA Office For Peripheral Architecture
Hakalankatu 10 B
60100 Seinäjoki
Finland

Tel: +358 6 414 12 25
E-mail: info@oopeaa.com
Web: www.oopeaa.com

ANSSI LASSILA was born in Soini, Finland, in 1973, and **TEEMU HIRVILAMMI** was born in Seinäjoki, Finland, in 1974. They founded Lassila Hirvilammi Architects Ltd. in Oulu in 2001 (as Lassila Mannberg Architects Ltd.). In 2004, the office moved to Seinäjoki, a small town in west-central Finland known for its architecture by Alvar Aalto. Today the office works on churches, office buildings, housing, private houses, interior design, and renovations. Lassila Hirvilammi Architects has a construction-friendly approach to architecture. Their work includes the Kärsämäki Wooden Church (Kärsämäki, 2004); Klaukkala Church (Nurmijärvi, 2004); the Ulve House (Seinäjoki, 2009); Kuokkala Church (Jyväskylä, 2008–10, published here); and Tonttu Sauna (Soini, 2009–10). They are currently working on the Leppänen House (Soini, 2013); Puukuokka Wooden Housing (Jyväskylä, 2012–14); the Frasier House (Sydney, NSW, Australia, 2014); and Suvelan Chappel (Espoo, 2014), all in Finland unless stated otherwise. In 2014, Lassila Hirvilammi Architects changed its name to OOPEAA Office for Peripheral Architecture.

ANSSI LASSILA wurde 1973 in Soini, Finnland, geboren, **TEEMU HIRVILAMMI** wurde 1974 in Seinäjoki, ebenfalls Finnland, geboren. 2001 gründeten sie in Oula ihr Büro Lassila Hirvilammi Architects (zunächst als Lassila Mannberg Architects). 2004 zog das Büro nach Seinäjoki, eine Kleinstadt in Westfinnland, die für ihre Bauten von Alvar Aalto bekannt ist. Heute arbeitet das Team an Kirchen, Büro- und Wohnbauten, privaten Häusern, innenarchitektonischen Projekten und Sanierungen. Lassila Hirvilammi Architects verfolgen bei ihrer Architektur einen konstruktionsfreundlichen Ansatz. Zu ihren Projekten zählen eine Holzkirche in Kärsämäki (2004), die Klaukkala-Kirche (Nurmijärvi, 2004), das Haus Ulve (Seinäjoki, 2009), die Kirche in Kuokkala (Jyväskylä, 2008–10, hier vorgestellt) und die Tonttu-Sauna (Soini, 2009–10). Derzeit in Planung sind das Haus Leppänen (Soini, 2013), der Holzwohnkomplex Puukuokka (Jyväskylä, 2012–14), das Frasier House (Sydney, Australien, 2014) sowie die Suvelan-Kapelle (Espoo, 2014), alle in Finnland, sofern nicht anders angegeben. Im Jahr 2014 änderte Lassila Hirvilammi Architects seinen Namen zu OOPEAA Office for Peripheral Architecture.

ANSSI LASSILA est né à Soini, en Finlande, en 1973 et **TEEMU HIRVILAMMI** à Seinäjoki, en Finlande, en 1974. Ils ont fondé Lassila Hirvilammi Architects Ltd. à Oulu en 2001 (sous le nom de Lassila Mannberg Architects Ltd.). L'agence a déménagé en 2004 à Seinäjoki, une petite ville du Centre-Ouest de la Finlande connue pour son architecture par Alvar Aalto. Elle travaille aujourd'hui à des églises, immeubles de bureaux, logements, maisons individuelles, à des projets d'architecture intérieure et à des rénovations. Lassila Hirvilammi Architects a adopté une approche de l'architecture soucieuse de la construction. Leurs réalisations comprennent l'église en bois de Kärsämäki (2004) ; l'église de Klaukkala (Nurmijärvi, 2004) ; la maison Ulve (Seinäjoki, 2009) ; l'église de Kuokkala (Jyväskylä, 2008–10, publiée ici) et le sauna de Tonttu (Soini, 2009–10). Ils travaillent actuellement à la maison Leppänen (Soini, 2013) ; aux logements en bois de Puukuokka (Jyväskylä, 2012–14) ; à la Frasier House (Sydney, 2014) et à la chapelle de Suvelan (Espoo, 2014), tous en Finlande, sauf mention contraire. En 2014, Lassila Hirvilammi Architects a changé son nom en OOPEAA Office for Peripheral Architecture.

KUOKKALA CHURCH

Jyväskylä, Finland, 2008–10

Address: Syöttäjänkatu 4, Jyväskylä, Finland
Area: 1311 m². Client: Parish of Jyväskylä
Cost: not disclosed

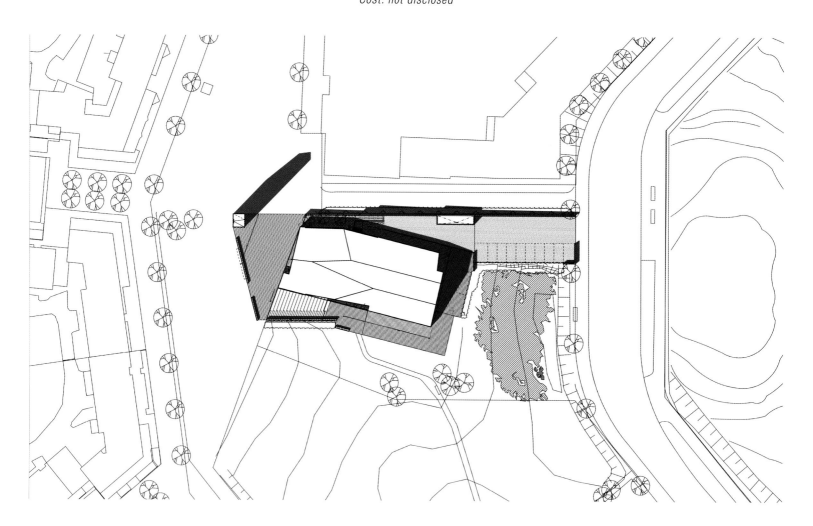

The architects were the winners of a 2006 invitational competition to design this church. One condition of the program was "to have a church that looks like one." Located in the Kuokkala market square, the church tower is in proximity to the actual center of the market. Overlapping dark Spanish slate tiles were used for the roof and exterior walls of the church. Finnish granite was used for stairways and entrance-area walls. The structure is arrayed on three levels, with offices that open directly into the market. The church hall itself and the parish meeting area can be combined for special functions. The entire design was based on the idea of a 100- to 200-year lifespan for the structure. The main structure of the church is in wood—with a ceiling made of glulam framework and a wooden grid-shell design. Spruce from central Finland was employed and whitened with wax. European ash was used for the specially designed furniture. The altar was made with limewood, "a wood species traditionally used for carving icons in wooden churches built by craftsmen."

Die Architekten gewannen 2006 mit ihrem Entwurf für den Kirchenbau einen eingeladenen Wettbewerb. Eine der Wettbewerbsvorgaben lautete „eine Kirche zu planen, die auch wie eine Kirche aussieht". Der am Marktplatz von Kuokkala gelegene Kirchturm liegt annähernd im Zentrum des Platzes. Dach und Fassaden des Baus wurden mit Schindeln aus spanischem Schiefer gestaltet, Treppen sowie Wände im Foyer mit finnischem Granit. Das Programm ist über drei Ebenen verteilt, die Büros gehen direkt auf den Marktplatz hinaus. Kirchenraum und Gemeindesaal lassen sich bei besonderen Anlässen zusammenlegen. Bei der Planung wurde von einer 100- bis 200-jährigen Lebensspanne des Baus ausgegangen. Das Tragwerk der Kirche besteht aus Holz, die Decke wurde als Schichtholzfachwerk und Holzgitterschale realisiert. Das Fichtenholz aus Mittelfinnland wurde weiß gewachst, das eigens entworfene Gestühl aus europäischer Esche gebaut. Der Altar wurde aus Linde gefertigt, „einer Holzart, die traditionell für geschnitzte Ikonen in Holzkirchen zum Einsatz kommt".

Les architectes ont remporté un concours organisé en 2006 pour la construction de cette église. L'une des conditions spécifiées était de créer « une église qui ressemble à une église ». Située sur la place du marché de Kuokkala, le clocher est à proximité du centre du marché. Des carreaux d'ardoise d'Espagne sombre se chevauchent pour recouvrir le toit et les murs extérieurs. Les escaliers et les murs de l'entrée sont en granite finlandais. La structure se déploie sur trois niveaux, avec notamment des bureaux qui donnent directement sur le marché. La nef et la salle paroissiale destinée aux réunions peuvent être réunis pour des occasions spécifiques. L'ensemble est basé sur une espérance de vie de 100 à 200 ans pour le bâtiment. La structure principale de l'église est en bois – avec un plafond à charpente en lamellé-collé et un motif gridshell en bois. L'épicéa du Centre de la Finlande qui a été utilisé a été blanchi à la cire. Le mobilier spécialement créé est en frêne européen. L'autel est en bois de tilleul, « une essence de bois traditionnellement choisie pour les icônes sculptées dans les églises en bois construites par les artisans finlandais ».

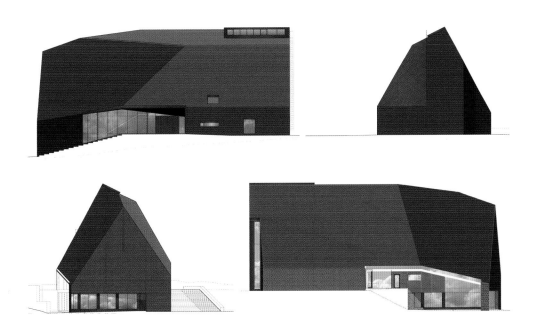

On the left page, a site plan reveals the placement of the church within its marketplace site. Left, the four elevations of the building. The very large roof is seen in the pictures above as well.

Eine Lageplan auf der linken Seite veranschaulicht die räumliche Situation der Kirche am Marktplatz. Links Aufrisse der vier Seiten des Baus. Oben ist das ungewöhnlich große Dach zu sehen.

Page de gauche, un plan de situation avec l'emplacement de l'église sur la place du marché. À gauche, les quatre élévations du bâtiment. On peut aussi voir le toit très large sur les photos ci-dessus.

A light, arcing wood pattern curves above the pews, recalling the inverted nave of a ship, a frequent Christian metaphor. A section drawing (below) demonstrates how the space rises up from the entrance area.

Ein filigranes Holzraster wölbt sich über dem Gestühl und erinnert an ein umgedrehtes Schiff, ein häufiges Motiv in christlichen Sakralbauten. Der Querschnitt (unten) illustriert, wie der Kirchenraum vom Eingang her ansteigt.

Une structure légère en bois courbe décrit un arc de cercle au-dessus des bancs et rappelle la nef inversée d'un navire, une métaphore chrétienne courante. La coupe ci-dessous montre comment l'espace se déploie vers le haut à partir de l'entrée.

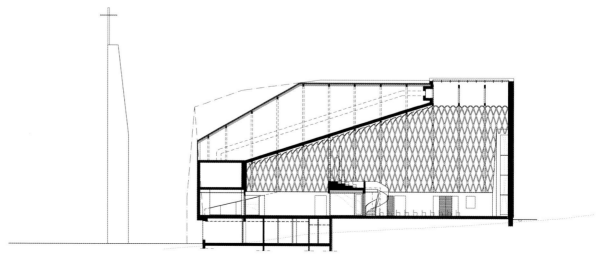

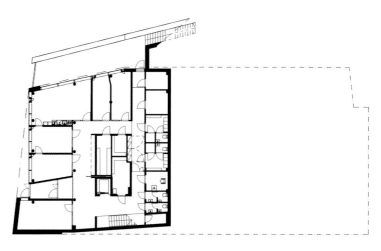

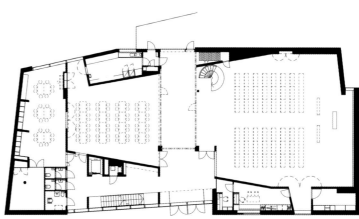

The church ceiling is a combination of a glulam framework and a wooden grid shell. The wood used here is spruce, while the seating is in ash wood, and the altar is made of limewood.

Das Kirchengewölbe wurde als Kombination aus Schichtholzfachwerk und Holzgitterschale realisiert. Gearbeitet wurde hierbei mit Fichte, während das Gestühl aus Esche und der Altar aus Linde gefertigt wurde.

Le plafond de l'église associe une charpente en lamellé-collé et un motif gridshell en bois. Le bois est de l'épicéa, tandis que le mobilier est en frêne, à l'exception de l'autel en tilleul.

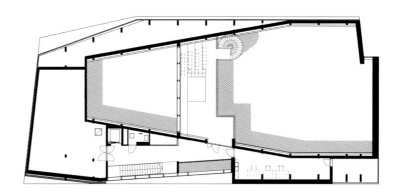

A curving stairway leads up from the main floor. Above, drawings show the relation of the dark, sloping exterior to this luminous church interior.

Eine Wendeltreppe führt vom Hauptraum nach oben. Die Zeichnungen oben veranschaulichen das Zusammenspiel des dunklen, schrägen Außenbaus mit dem hellen Innenraum der Kirche.

Un escalier en colimaçon monte depuis le niveau principal. Ci-dessus, les schémas mettent en évidence le contraste entre l'extérieur sombre en pente et la luminosité de l'intérieur.

CREDITS